UNITY AND DESIGN IN HORACE'S ODES

UNITY AND DESIGN
IN HORACE'S ODES

MATTHEW S. SANTIROCCO

The University of North Carolina Press

Chapel Hill and London

© 1986 The University of North Carolina Press
All rights reserved
Manufactured in the United States of America

Library of Congress Cataloging-in-Publication Data

Santirocco, Matthew S., 1950–
Unity and design in Horace's Odes.
Bibliography: p.
Includes index.
1. Horace. Carmina.   2. Horace—Technique.
3. Poetics.   I. Title.
PA6436.S26   1986   874'.01   85-20964
ISBN 0-8078-1691-4

The publication of this work was made possible in part through a grant from the National Endowment for the Humanities, a federal agency whose mission is to award grants to support education, scholarship, media programming, libraries, and museums, in order to bring the results of cultural activities to a broad, general public.

For my mother and my father

CONTENTS

Preface / ix

CHAPTER ONE
Horace's *Odes* and the Ancient Poetry Book / 3

CHAPTER TWO
The Parade Odes: The Poetics of Initiation / 14

CHAPTER THREE
The First Book Continued / 42

CHAPTER FOUR
The Second Book / 83

CHAPTER FIVE
The Third Book: Public and Private Voices / 110

CHAPTER SIX
The Third Book: The Poetics of Closure / 132

CHAPTER SEVEN
The Ensemble / 150

CHAPTER EIGHT
Conclusions / 169

Notes / 177

Bibliography / 215

INDEXES

I Index of Works Cited from Horace / 235

II Index of Other Ancient Authors and Works / 239

III General Index / 243

PREFACE

Horace's first three books of *Odes*, published together in 23 B.C., are the culmination of classical lyric and have done much to define our own idea and practice of personal poetry. Drawing on recent work on poetry books ancient and modern, as well as on several contemporary critical methodologies, I have tried to offer a new approach to the *Odes* both as individual poems and as components in a larger poetic design. This is not just another study of arrangement, but rather a new critical reading which attempts to show that the ensemble is itself one important context for understanding and appreciating the poetry.

The secondary literature that has grown up around the *Odes* in the last twenty years is enormous. Although it is not possible for any writer on Horace to control the entire bibliography, I have tried, wherever possible, to place my own opinions in the context of earlier and current views of the poet. To enhance the usefulness of this book, I have also provided translations for the Latin that I quote; the reader will soon discover that these versions have no literary pretensions. In all but a few cases I have followed Klingner's Teubner text (third edition, 1959).[1]

I am very grateful to Columbia University's Council for Research in the Humanities, which awarded me summer grants; to Columbia College, which provided a term off on a Chamberlain Fellowship; to the American Council of Learned Societies, which awarded the fellowship that enabled me to complete this book; and to the Stanwood Cockey Lodge Foundation, which aided publication.

Some of the material contained in these pages is based on ideas first explored in my Ph.D. dissertation on Books 2 and 3 of the *Odes*. Other material has appeared in different form in *Archaeologia Transatlantica*, *Arethusa*, *Ramus*, and *Transactions of the American Philological Asso-*

ciation; I am grateful to the editors of these journals for permission to reprint.

For helpful suggestions on individual chapters or points of interpretation I wish to thank Mervin Dilts, the late W. T. H. Jackson, G. N. Knauer, Andrew Miller, William Race, and John Van Sickle. The entire manuscript has profited greatly from the scrutiny of Helen H. Bacon, Alan Cameron, M. Owen Lee, and Kenneth Reckford. I am particularly grateful to Michael Putnam for discussion of several versions and for advice and encouragement throughout the project. I also wish to thank Lewis Bateman, Gwen Duffey, and Iris Tillman Hill, of the University of North Carolina Press, for their painstaking and gentle editing and Madeline Aria for her careful preparation of the indexes.

My greatest debt, finally, is to my teacher, colleague, and friend of sixteen years, the late Steele Commager. His own book on Horace gave new impetus to the study of this difficult author, and much of the work now being done on the *Odes* depends on his sensitive and sympathetic reading of the text. It saddens me that he is not here to see the publication of this work, *quidquid hoc libelli qualecumque*, which even in his last and most difficult illness he managed to read and improve. His advice, encouragement, and unfailing kindness will be sorely missed.

Matthew S. Santirocco
May 1985

UNITY AND DESIGN
IN HORACE'S ODES

HORACE'S ODES AND THE ANCIENT POETRY BOOK

ONE

One of the most important achievements of recent Horatian criticism has been the rediscovery of structure—not the mechanical dissection of poems into component parts, but an awareness of how form is inseparable from content and how unity proceeds from design.[1] Although the individual ode has by now received sufficient critical attention, the structure of the first lyric collection, the three books of *Odes* published together in 23 B.C., remains problematic. This is not to say that it has been neglected. The initial observations of von Christ and Kiessling a century ago inspired continental scholars to search for the one principle according to which all the odes were arranged.[2] Suggestions were usually numerological and spatial: applying the criteria of metrical, thematic, and verbal reminiscence, they described triads, pentads, enneads, and decads, with the poems in each group and the groups themselves disposed in an abstract pattern such as concentric framing or chiasmus.[3] By the turn of the century an investigator could justly complain that not a single possibility had been left untried.[4]

Detailed refutation is unnecessary as such grand schemes have ceased to convince most people, if they ever did so. They were possible only because their adherents isolated meter from content and were very selective in their handling of evidence, ignoring more obvious, not to say ostentatious, signs of order. Methodology aside, very elaborate patterns also raise the question of probability. One is reminded of the reviewer who discovered that the sections of Duckworth's book on the *Aeneid* were inadvertently related to each other in the same Golden Ratio that Duckworth detected in the *Aeneid*.[5] Finally, there is a further and more fundamental problem with any approach that sacrifices texture for architecture and that reads poetry only in terms of visual effects and not also in terms of music. As Charles Segal reminds us: "The danger is that such schemes, in their abstractional purity, lead us farther and farther away from the primary experience of the work as poetry.... These analytic patterns and numerologies, if developed beyond a certain point, lack any connection with either our fictions or our lives."[6]

It is not surprising that a reaction has set in. Though interest in structural study is running high, most current applications of the approach to Horace are less ambitious,[7] offering only an overview of the problem or focusing on isolated phenomena.[8] One scholar, for instance, speaks of "any stray principle" and another of "a little window dressing."[9] Recently there has been a further retreat from the large-scale schematizations of the past. In their commentary on the *Odes* Nisbet and Hubbard characterize studies of order as "such trivialities,"[10] and Gordon Williams, who omits the entire subject from his *Tradition and Originality*, mentions it elsewhere only to dismiss it: "While some plausible reasons for particular collocations may be guessed at, it is a waste of time to speculate on a matter of which the poet himself probably had no clear idea and which, in any case, has minimal literary relevance."[11]

Although understandable as a reaction to past excesses, this degree of skepticism is itself excessive for several reasons. First, several considerations suggest that Horace had at least some concern for design. These include the well-documented interest in poetry books among Hellenistic and Roman writers (discussed in sections two to four below); the aesthetic implications of the book roll, the physical format of which necessitates sequential reading; the existence of certain undisputed signs of arrangement in *Odes* 1–3, such as the frame of C. 1.1 and 3.30 or the grouping of Parade Odes (C. 1.1–9) and Roman Odes (C. 3.1–6); and, finally, the relatively restricted thematic repertoire that facilitates the discovery of connections among odes by poet and reader alike. It is not a priori unlikely, then, that the *Odes* should reveal signs of larger order.[12] In addition, the extremely skeptical position is based on two unwarranted preconceptions: first, that the whole inquiry is by nature too subjective, and second, that external arrangement has no real bearing on literary appreciation. But controls on subjectivity can be applied to this as to all other literary study (see section five below), and the critical relevance of the subject, if not yet apparent, is nonetheless precisely what remains to be tested. Ultimately, though, the skeptical position is unsatisfactory for the same reason that earlier imaginative schemes failed: both misrepresent the special nature of the collection, its heterogeneity. That this is unique to the Odes becomes apparent from consideration of the parallels and precedents available to Horace.

TWO

Most discussions of the order of the Odes cite as parallels the earlier Augustan poetry books, the works of the young Vergil, Tibullus, and Propertius,[13] and even of the young Horace himself.[14] For all these publications it is possible to demonstrate some sort of elaborate design even though scholars disagree on what the precise design is, or what bearing it has on interpretation.[15] And yet, to consider the Odes in light of these earlier poetry books is to set up false and misleading expectations. Although they are certainly precedents, these earlier collections, including Horace's own first book of Sermones, are not truly parallel to the Odes, for they enjoy what the Odes lack, namely a built-in coherence, both formal and thematic, apart from any coherence that conscious artistic arrangement might later impose. The Bucolics are all hexameters, so too are the Sermones, and elegies are composed in the couplet that gives its name to the genre. Similarly, a general affinity of subject matter unifies each collection: the Bucolics are largely pastoral, the Sermones satiric (in Horace's sense of the word, not ours), and the elegies erotic.

The first three books of Odes, on the other hand, are a very heterogeneous collection. Formally, they comprise eighty-eight poems in twelve different meters, an achievement that Horace repeatedly vaunted. In tone and topic, too, they range equally widely. Thus, whereas a unified plan may lie behind the other Augustan poetry books, the Odes are less likely to be structured in so coherent a fashion. For them, true parallels are to be found not in the homogeneous collections of the other Augustans but rather in the heterogeneous collections of earlier writers. The common misinterpretation that the ordered poetry book originated in the Augustan Age[16] and the fragmentary nature of literary survivals from other periods have obscured the relevance of Hellenistic and Roman republican practice.

THREE

The poetry book seems to be a Hellenistic phenomenon. Before that time (and even to some extent afterward) literature arose out of a specific social context, either ritual, agonistic, or sympotic, and was intended for performance within that social setting rather than for individual reading. It was in the fifth century that books began to be circulated, owing perhaps to the popularity of tragedy and the teaching methods of the sophists. However, we are totally ignorant about the principles of arrangement, if any, operative in these books, and, in any case, it was not until the Hellenistic Age that a truly "bookish" society emerged.[17]

The standard reconstruction of the origin and development of the poetry book during and after this period was offered by Kroll over fifty years ago.[18] Since then, however, impressive papyrus discoveries and literary analyses have made a new account necessary. Kroll, for example, maintained that the editions of the older poets which the Hellenistic scholars produced were used by the Hellenistic poets as models for the creation of new poetry books. Though the interaction between literature and scholarship was very great at Alexandria, this genealogy is nonetheless dubious because the Hellenistic editions of the classical authors and the books in which the Hellenistic poets published their own works were structured along very different lines. Basically, they arose out of two very different impulses which, for convenience, may be termed the editorial and the aesthetic.

The former is represented by the standard Alexandrian edition of the lyric poets in which Horace surely read his models.[19] For several of the authors contained therein, very general features of arrangement can be discerned. An epigram (A.P. 7.17) by Cicero's freedman, Tullius Laurea, alludes to a division of Sappho's works into nine books,[20] and the assignable fragments suggest that the first books were metrically homogeneous, with a shift to arrangement by subject matter in the last book, the Epithalamians.[21] Within the individual books no principle of ordering can be safely adduced despite Lobel's suggestion of alphabetization.[22] In the arrangement of Pindar, Bacchylides, and Simonides, on the other hand, meter played no discernible role as poems were grouped by *eidē* or types into hymns, paeans, epinicians, and the like. Again, there is no evidence as to how poems were arranged within these large categories, except for alleged alphabetization in the British Museum papyrus of Bacchylides's *Dithyrambs*[23] and for the fact that Pindar's epinicians are classed by festival[24] whereas those of Simonides were named after the type of event commemorated.[25]

From this brief and necessarily tentative reconstruction, it is nonetheless clear that the Hellenistic scholar's interest in the arrangement of earlier poets was a corollary of his larger scholarly activity, the classification and editing of texts. An arrangement based on meter, *eidē*, and perhaps alphabetization is editorial rather than aesthetic; that is, it exists for convenience of classification rather than to enhance meaning or create effect.[26] For this reason, the Hellenistic editions of the classical poets are far less significant than the collections the Hellenistic writers made of their own works. Here, for the first time, aesthetic design rather than editorial decision plays the major role in arrangement.

Basic to this type of collection is *variatio* as the Latins call it, or *poikilia* in Greek, the exact opposite of the editors' method of grouping poems by categories.[27] Diversification is now the key as meter, theme, and even dialect vary, with poems disposed to make the most of this variation. And yet, *variatio* has been overemphasized by Kroll and others. Ultimately it is a negative approach to arrangement, the avoidance of certain obvious groupings and collocations. But there are also more positive types of design.

In this, as in many other literary innovations, Callimachus seems to have led the way. His *Iambs*, for example, display most of the techniques available to the Hellenistic poet. There is, first of all, the framing of the collection by a programmatic prologue (1) and epilogue (13). Within this frame there is some grouping on the basis of affinity or contrast. Thus, on metrical grounds, two groups of stichic poems (1–4, 8–13) surround a group of epodes (5–7). On thematic grounds, 7 to 11 are placed together since all offer aetiologies, whereas 11 and 12 are set side by side to juxtapose their forms, an epitaph and a *genethliacon*. There is even greater formalization in the pairing of alternate poems and the creation of a midpoint break in the collection (i.e. *Iamb* 6 balances 12 in that both are personal poems at the end of varied half dozens).[28] The *Aetia* shares the same techniques. After the polemical apology (fr. 1 Pf.),[29] the second fragment and the last (fr. 112 Pf.) frame the work with references to the Muses and their initiation of Hesiod on Mount Helicon (cf. *Theog.* 22 ff.). There is also a break in the middle as the fiction of a conversation with the Muses, which provides the narrative structure of Books 1 and 2, seems to have been dropped in Books 3 and 4.[30] Finally, a new technique is now added to the poet's repertoire, a sort of cross-reference or connecting of works within a larger oeuvre. Thus, when Callimachus in the last fragment of the *Aetia* bids farewell to the Muses and announces that he will pass on to those goddesses' more prosaic pasture, Μουσέων πεζὸν . . . νομόν (fr. 112.9 Pf.), he seems to be looking ahead to the *Iambs*.[31]

Not all the Hellenistic poets display Callimachus's interest in design. For example, Lawall's suggestion that the first seven *Idylls* of Theocritus and the eight *Mimiamboi* of Herodas were arranged as poetry books[32] not only lacks any testimonial evidence but also seems contradicted by the manuscripts, the dissension among the three Theocritean families regarding the sequence of *Idylls*,[33] and the fragments of a ninth mime contained in the British Museum papyrus of Herodas.[34] One last category of Hellenistic poetry, however, is relevant to arrangement: the epigram. A revival of interest in this old genre led to the creation of new epigrams, either fictitious dedications and epitaphs or else new noninscriptional forms of erotic and sympotic content.[35]

The first book of such epigrams may be the *Soros* mentioned in the scholia to the *Iliad* (Schol. Ven. A to Il. 11.101). Because the *Soros* is there said to contain poems by Posidippus, and because Asclepiades, Posidippus, and Hedylus not only occur in a single couplet in Meleager's preface (*AP* 4.1.45–46 = 3970–71 G.-P.) but also share joint attributions in the *Anthology*, Reitzenstein concluded that the *Soros* contained works by all three poets.[36] The Homeric scholiast, however, does not indicate anyone other than Posidippus, and such literary collaboration is otherwise unknown from antiquity. Moreover, if the poem identified by Lloyd-Jones as the *sphragis* of Posidippus was originally attached to the *Soros*, it is too personal a signature for a joint collection.[37] Reitzenstein's hypothesis, then, remains unsubstantiated and the *Soros* may well have contained just poems by Posidippus. In any case, the title, which means a heap of grain, is very suggestive. First, it may suggest winnowing, i.e. the removal of chaff, and thus affirm Alexandrian standards of polish and labor.[38] And second, a heap or pile implies perhaps some degree of diversity or *poikilia*.[39] Thus, it is at least likely that this publication of epigrams shared with the other Hellenistic poetry books a commitment to Alexandrian aesthetic refinement in all areas, including its arrangement.

More relevant to Horace on account of its variety, size, and date is the *Garland* of Meleager. Although no longer extant, its principles of arrangement can be reconstructed from uncontaminated Meleagrian stretches in the *Anthology*. Alan Cameron has suggested that the *Garland* was divided into four books on the basis of subject matter.[40] This is an editorial mode of arrangement resulting from the special nature of the *Garland* as an anthology of many works on many subjects by many hands. But the framing by prologue (AP 4.1 = 3926 ff. G.-P.) and epilogue (AP 12.257 = 4722 G.-P.) and the variation worked out in topic, expression, and even author sequence (the rhythmical alternation of poems by the four major *Hauptdichter*)[41] are aesthetic devices. Meleager signals this when, in his opening poem, he calls his work a πάγκαρπον ἀοιδάν, "a many-blossomed song" (AP 4.1.1 = 3926 G.-P.). Gow and Page object that "ἀοιδάν is a little odd of a book the miscellaneous contents of which are emphasized by the adjective."[42] But the singular noun indicates that the *Garland* was conceived not as a mere anthology editorially arranged, but rather as an aesthetic whole, a poetry book.

FOUR

From republican Rome, as from Alexandria, much relevant literature is again either mutilated or missing. In the absence of much of Lucilius[43] and almost all of Laevius, Horace's unacknowledged predecessor in lyric, it is the Catullan corpus that most closely resembles Horace's *Odes* in being a miscellany of meters and subjects.[44] Although the verbal and thematic influence of Catullus on Horace has been amply documented,[45] no one has seriously explored the possibility that the two collections might be structured along similar lines, much as Horace in his first book of *Sermones* and Tibullus in his first book of elegies might have looked to Vergil's *Bucolics* as a model of arrangement.[46] The investigation, however, is complicated by the difficulty of determining the principles of arrangement employed by Catullus himself. Some sort of authorial organization is indicated by the mention of a *libellus* in the first poem and by references in Pliny (*Epist.* 1.16.5)[47] and Martial (4.14.4, 11.6.16) to a body of poems, the latter suggesting the title *Passer*. But despite the magisterial authority of Wilamowitz—"Catullus devoted the most careful thought to the arrangement of his book of poems. If there's anyone who can't see that, so much the worse for him"[48]—there is no real agreement concerning the extent of the original *libellus* and its relation to the present corpus.

Thus, the most obvious principle of arrangement, the tripartite division into *polymetra* (1–60), long *neoterica* (61–68, with 65 marking a permanent shift to the elegiac meter), and short, non-neoteric epigrams (69–116),[49] can afford a parallel to Horace's distribution of his *Odes* over three books only if several recent scholars are correct in maintaining that the entire Catullan corpus as it stands was arranged by the poet.[50] But this thesis is rendered problematic by the sad state of the text and by the fact that the total number of lines, over 2,300, far exceeds the known capacity of ancient books[51] and also violates Callimachean strictures against length. Thus, it is easier to follow Clausen in locating the original *libellus* among the *polymetra*,[52] and it is here, and not in the overall disposition of the corpus, that parallels to the order of the *Odes* can be found.

First of all, the *variatio* familiar from Hellenistic poetry books is here carried to such an extreme that interlocking and interrupting poems complicate whatever cycles or patterns have been discerned.[53] Hellenistic framing is perhaps also operative in that the *polymetra* nearly open (2–3) and nearly close (58) with poems on Lesbia, initially positive but at the end bitterly invective. Then there are certain recurrent techniques of grouping such as the separation of two related poems by a third to form an A-B-A pattern,[54] or the use of transitions either on the surface or at some deeper level,[55] to move the reader from one poem to the next. Although examples of all these techniques can be found in Horace's *Odes*, the most striking parallelism, perhaps, is the way in which both collections open. Building on Barwick's study of the first Lesbia poems, Charles Segal has shown that Catullus 2–11 are a cycle, tracing the progression of the love affair from its beginning (2–3), through its fruition (5, 7) to its bitter end (8, 11), and integrating it with other central themes.[56] If these poems stood at the head of the original corpus, they may have influenced Horace to open his book too with a cycle, the Parade Odes, which, as we shall see, introduce most of the meters and many of the themes and personalities prominent in his poetry.

FIVE

To sum up thus far: the origin and development of the pre-Augustan poetry book can only be reconstructed. Not only are we missing potentially relevant works such as the lyrics of Callimachus and Laevius, but also of those works that do survive, some, like the Iambs of Callimachus, are fragmentary, and others, such as the poems of Theocritus, Herodas, and to a lesser degree Catullus, do not reveal with any certainty the extent to which they were arranged by their authors. Nonetheless, a survey of the extant literature indicates that certain common assumptions about the poetry book are inaccurate. It did not, for example, arise in Augustan Rome but in Alexandria. Similarly, to locate its source in the scholarly edition ignores the very great distinction between an editorial response to a classic text and the more aesthetic designs a poet can work out in the publication of his own verse. Of these, *variatio*, though important, has been overemphasized. There were other, more positive, principles of arrangement, and, though the pre-Augustan poetry book was not coherently structured around any one of them, all were operative.

It has been necessary to dwell at some length on this background, for it has important critical implications for the study of Horace's *Odes*. First, the extensive prior history of the poetry book renders it very likely that Horace too had some concern for the larger unity and design of his lyric collection. Second, this concern appears to be yet another of his unacknowledged debts to Alexandria,[57] for a true parallel to *Odes* 1–3 is to be found not in the other Augustan poetry books which are relatively homogeneous, but in the Hellenistic collections which were formally and thematically varied. Finally, appreciation of this special characteristic of the *Odes* enables us to avoid the excesses of much previous scholarship, which has either ignored their heterogeneity by searching for a single principle of arrangement or made too much of their heterogeneity by denying any extensive ordering. As befits Horace, the champion of *aurea mediocritas*, the truth lies somewhere in between.

What we expect, and what we shall actually find, is that Horace shares the Hellenistic poet's familiarity with many methods of arrangement and that he relies on no one of them exclusively. Thus, the reader must be constantly alert to a wide variety of possibilities—to relationships based on contrast as well as similarity, to dynamic movements as well as static patterns, to groupings of contiguous poems and linkages among poems widely separated in the collection. Most importantly, the reader must be attuned to the various and ever-shifting criteria on which these larger designs are founded—not just meter, theme, and addressee, but internal structure, imagery, and that vague but crucial quality, tone.

Although it must be admitted that such an investigation might seem rather subjective, there are controls that can be applied to this as to all other literary study. Obviously, when a number of criteria converge—as, for example, in the Roman Odes—we can be sure of the poet's intent. We must not insist on such certainties, however, for many of the most interesting and suggestive relationships among poems exist at only one of these many levels. But that does not mean that they are fortuitous. Faced with the formidable task of arranging so many and varied poems, Horace would have had to exploit connections, random or planned, at whatever level they appeared.[58] Fortunately, a second control is provided by sequential reading. As a methodology, the consideration of the poems in their published order not only reproduces their effect on the ancient audience, for whom the physical format of the papyrus roll necessitated such a sequential reading, but it also respects the intention of their author, who is reasonably assumed (in the absence of evidence to the contrary) to have put them in this order in the first place. Finally, and most importantly, we can control subjectivity by pursuing arrangement not as an end in itself but as part of the larger interpretative enterprise. In other words, a perception of design, in order to be plausible and meaningful, must accord with an interpretation of the individual odes that is self-consistent. Recent studies of other lyric traditions—of the modern poetic sequence by M. L. Rosenthal and Sally Gall, or of Keats's odes by Helen Vendler—suggest the fruitfulness of such an approach, which places the individual poem within the larger context provided by the other poems.[59] Something similar is needed for Horace's Odes—not another study of arrangement but a new critical reading of the poetry which recognizes that the ensemble is itself one important context for understanding and appreciation.

THE PARADE ODES
THE POETICS OF INITIATION

ONE

In 23 B.C., when *Odes* 1–3 were published, Horace was forty-two years old, a successful satirist in the tradition of Lucilius and the adapter into Latin of the iambic spirit of Archilochus and Hipponax. Though distinguished, this literary output hardly presaged the dazzling precocity of his new achievement, which purported to revive and rival the Greek lyric poets. The nine canonical lyricists had flourished roughly between 650 and 400 B.C., with Horace's acknowledged models, Alcaeus and Sappho, composing rather early in the period. Afterward, the function and spirit of lyric were gradually subsumed by other genres such as tragedy and epigram. In the Hellenistic Age there was some experimentation with monody by Callimachus, Theocritus, and Cercidas, and, at Rome, by Laevius and Catullus.[1] For all intents and purposes, however, lyric had been dormant for hundreds of years when Horace decided to transfer it to an intractable language and an alien culture.

Something of his ambition and of the novelty and sheer daring of his enterprise is conveyed by a series of poems that open the collection, the so-called "Parade Odes."[2] The first nine in the book, they are defined by a striking diversity of meters, addressees, and themes. This is not a simple program, however, merely dedicating the collection and anticipating some of its forms and contents. Rather, these poems are an elaborate attempt to place the *Odes* both within Horace's oeuvre and within a larger poetic tradition. While they are programmatic in establishing new generic expectations, they are also retrospective, for they define the Horatian achievement by setting it against the genres that had gone before it, specifically satire, Greek lyric, and epic.

TWO

The first ode, addressed to the patron Maecenas, enumerates a variety of occupations only to end by rejecting them in favor of Horace's own vocation, poetry. "The worst in the book, excepting the second," is Landor's savage judgment.[3] But what appears on the surface to be a mere catalog also contains within it an implicit and thoroughgoing poetic:

> Maecenas atavis edite regibus,
> o et praesidium et dulce decus meum:
> sunt quos curriculo pulverem Olympicum
> collegisse iuvat metaque fervidis
> evitata rotis palmaque nobilis
> terrarum dominos evehit ad deos;
> hunc, si mobilium turba Quiritium
> certat tergeminis tollere honoribus;
> illum, si proprio condidit horreo
> quidquid de Libycis verritur areis.
> gaudentem patrios findere sarculo
> agros Attalicis condicionibus
> numquam demoveas, ut trabe Cypria
> Myrtoum pavidus nauta secet mare;
> luctantem Icariis fluctibus Africum
> mercator metuens otium et oppidi
> laudat rura sui: mox reficit rates
> quassas indocilis pauperiem pati.
> est qui nec veteris pocula Massici
> nec partem solido demere de die
> spernit, nunc viridi membra sub arbuto
> stratus, nunc ad aquae lene caput sacrae;
> multos castra iuvant et lituo tubae
> permixtus sonitus bellaque matribus
> detestata; manet sub Iove frigido
> venator tenerae coniugis inmemor,

> seu visa est catulis cerva fidelibus,
> seu rupit teretes Marsus aper plagas.
> me doctarum hederae praemia frontium
> dis miscent superis, me gelidum nemus
> Nympharumque leves cum Satyris chori
> secernunt populo, si neque tibias
> Euterpe cohibet nec Polyhymnia
> Lesboum refugit tendere barbiton.
> quodsi me lyricis vatibus inseres,
> sublimi feriam sidera vertice. [C. 1.1.1–36]

Maecenas, sprung from royal ancestors, O my protection and sweet glory, there are some whom it pleases to collect Olympic dust in a little chariot and whom the goalpost cleared with fiery wheels and the noble palm raise to the gods as lords of the earth. This man [is pleased] if the mob of fickle Quirites strives to raise him to triple honors; that man, if he hides in his own granary whatever is swept from Libyan threshing floors. The man who rejoices to cut his paternal fields with a hoe you would never persuade to plough the Myrtoan Sea as a fearful sailor on a Cyprian ship. The sailor who is afraid of the southwester struggling with Icarian waves praises leisure and the country around his town; [but] soon he repairs his shattered boat, untaught to endure poverty. There is one who spurns neither cups of old Massic nor to steal away part of the day, now stretching his limbs under the verdant arbutus, now at the gentle source of a sacred spring. The camp pleases many and the sound of the tuba mixed with the trumpet and wars hated by mothers. The hunter, forgetful of his tender wife, stays out under a cold sky if a doe has been sighted by his faithful hounds or a Marsian boar has burst through the flimsy nets. As for me: ivy, the reward of learned brows, mingles me with the gods above, and the chill grove and delicate choruses of Nymphs and Satyrs separate me from the people, if Euterpe does not hold back the flutes nor Polyhymnia refuse to tune the Lesbian lyre. But if you enroll me among the lyric bards, I shall strike the stars with my uplifted head.

Here, at the very beginning of the collection, Horace looks back to his previous writings, particularly the *Satires*.[4] In addition to specific verbal echoes, the very form of the ode recalls the first satire which also contained an occupational catalog. Of course, there are rhetorical differences. The list in the satire is technically a *mempsimoiria*, that is, an illustration of the dissatisfaction men feel with their lots in life. The ode, on the other hand, is a *priamel* in which occupations that satisfy their practitioners are shown to be inferior to Horace's own. But even this difference in strategy is not allowed to obscure the fundamental formal relationship between the two poems, for Horace has managed to work a brief *mempsimoiria* into the ode (11–18), thereby pointedly alluding to his earlier work.

This formal allusion is reinforced by the generally satiric treatment to which most of the occupations are subjected in the ode. The Olympic charioteer, for instance, rides a diminutive *curriculo* (3) in a race that is itself reduced to dust-collecting (*pulverem . . . / collegisse*, 3–4). The worth of the politician's achievement is similarly demeaned by the fickleness of the electorate (*mobilium turba Quiritium*, 7). The careers of the large landholder (9–10) and the merchant-sailor (15–18) are called into question by their own inconsistency and greed. Finally, warfare and hunting are undercut by the perspectives from which they are viewed, that of mothers to whom militarism is hateful (*bellaque matribus / detestata*, 24–25), and of the wife neglected by a sportsman husband (*tenerae coniugis inmemor*, 26).

The first ode, then, subtly alludes to the *Satires*, both in the generally satiric treatment accorded most occupations and in specific formal echoes such as the occupational catalog and the *mempsimoiria*. In this way, Horace establishes generic continuity, assuring us that the *Odes* will share the moral aims and interests of his earlier work. Such retrospection also characterizes other first poems of Horace. Thus, when Epistle 1.1 purports to abandon *versus et cetera ludicra*, "verses and other playthings" (10), it is looking back to the body of lyric that preceded it. And when lyric is later resumed, C. 4.1 refers to the first collection of *Odes* by the ambiguity of its opening word, *Intermissa*, and by its open quotation in the phrase *mater saeva Cupidinum* (5 = C. 1.19.1).

It is typical, then, of Horatian practice that C. 1.1 should look backward. But, as befits an opening poem, it also looks ahead by placing before our eyes a vision of the poet which ultimately sets the lyricist apart from the satirist. This is first glimpsed in the description of the hedonist at lines 19 to 22.[5] Attention is drawn to the passage in several ways. It begins at the exact center of the poem (line 19 out of

36); the introductory formula, *est qui*, picks up the *sunt quos* (3) which opened the catalog and thus suggests a new beginning; the way of life represented here is one of *otium*, whereas all the others are types of *negotium*; finally, and most importantly, this way of life is exempted from satiric treatment. It is tempting, therefore, to identify the hedonist with Horace himself. Though a strict identification violates the *priamel* structure which reserves the climactic element for last,[6] there is a sense in which the hedonist at least prefigures or anticipates the poet's most congenial and familiar role in the *Odes*, that of the country dweller who dispels care by drinking and who invites his friends to do likewise.

Such is Horace's philosophy of life. What is missing from these lines is any direct mention of art. There are, however, overtones of it, for later in the *Odes* a *locus amoenus* setting, the Bacchic associations of wine, and even the simple life itself are fully worked out as analogues for Horace's style of poetry.[7] Thus, the description of the hedonist prepares the way for the more explicit and complete revelation of Horace as poet at the end of the poem (29–36). In many important details, this picture corrects the deficiencies of the alternative vocations enumerated and rejected in the preceding lines.[8] The Olympic victor's *palma* (5) and apotheosis (*evehit ad deos*, 6) are now transformed into the ivy (*hederae*, 29) which makes Horace one with the gods (*dis miscent superis*, 30). The politician's dependence on the mob (*turba*, 7) is contrasted with the poet's elitist isolation (*secernunt populo*, 32). The avarice of the landowner and the sailor "untaught (*indocilis*, 18) to endure poverty" is repudiated by the wisdom of the artist (*doctarum . . . frontium*, 29) which confers more lasting gain (*praemia*, 29). The soldier's alarms (*lituo tubae / permixtus sonitus*, 23–24) yield to the gentler strains of *tibias* (32) and *barbiton* (34). Finally, the cool grove (*gelidum nemus*, 30) which the poet inhabits is an improvement not only on the chill sky (*Iove frigido*, 25) of the hunter but also on the pleasance of the hedonist, for it is an explicitly poetic landscape. The Nymphs, Satyrs, Muses, and other traditional elements of the scene point to the Greek sources of Horace's inspiration. The Lesbian lyre, *Lesboum . . . barbiton* (34), further specifies these as Sappho and Alcaeus. But the mention of flutes (*tibias*, 32) also hints at Pindar, for those instruments normally accompanied choral lyric, and the poet's separation from the crowd (*secernunt populo*, 32) is a Callimachean gesture.[9]

Set apart from other men, enjoying a life of peace and sufficiency, protected and inspired by gods, and destined for eternity—this picture of the poet will recur in many odes, but here, at the very outset of the collection, it functions as an accurate gauge of the distance Horace has traveled from satire to lyric.

THREE

What precisely this journey entails is clarified by some of the following poems which, together with the first, constitute a more ambitious overture to the collection. As noted earlier, these nine "Parade Odes" display nine different meters, and this diversity is reinforced by variation of theme and addressee. There is general consensus that the meters demonstrate the poet's technical virtuosity, that the choice of addressees is largely honorific, and that the topical coverage is comprehensive, embracing poetry, politics, philosophy, and love. The traditional view, then, is that the Parade Odes are programmatic in a literal sense, that their diversity in these several respects anticipates what the reader will encounter in the collection as a whole.

But does it? With respect to Horace's meters, for instance, the variety of the Parade is far greater than that of the collection, in which the vast majority of poems (63%) are composed in just two meters, the Alcaic (33) and Sapphic (22). Furthermore, of the nine meters heading Book 1, two never recur (C. 1.4, 8), and two others recur only once (C. 1.1 = 3.30, 1.7 = 1.28). Finally, three meters are missing from the Parade, though they will appear later, distributed over the three books (C. 1.11 = 1.18, 2.18, 3.12).

In no literal sense, then, do the Parade Odes provide a metrical conspectus for the ensemble.[10] Nor are their addressees strictly representative as they include more prominent persons than any other comparable run of odes. In addition to Maecenas, Augustus, and Vergil, there is Sestius, the consul in the year of publication, Agrippa, the military man who was for a time second in command under Augustus, and Plancus, the consular who had proposed the name Augustus for the emperor. Also, for some of them praise may be balanced by admonition,[11] and, in any case, honorific intent is irrelevant to fictitious addressees such as the coquette Pyrrha (C. 1.5), whose occurrence between the consul Sestius (C. 1.4) and the general Agrippa (C. 1.6) requires some other explanation.[12] Finally, though the Parade does to some extent reflect the major concerns of the collection, there runs through its subject matter, as we shall see (in section four below), a specific unifying thread.

These poems at the beginning of Book 1, then, are not really an accurate foretaste of *Odes* 1–3. They are, however, programmatic at a much deeper level, for the features that bind them together as a group also serve two other purposes. The first is to establish Horace's affiliation with Greek lyric. Recent critics of post-Enlightenment poetry have called attention to "the anxiety of influence" or "the burden of the past."[13] While particularly apt to Hellenistic literature and to certain "Silver" Latin authors,[14] such notions can also describe the predicament of the Augustan poet. Horace's own earlier career bears this out very well. Though satire was the one genre that the Romans could, and did, acknowledge with pride as their own creation,[15] when Horace embarked on the form he felt the need not only to acknowledge a Roman predecessor, Lucilius, but also to invent a wholly specious Greek pedigree from Old Comedy.[16] The Augustan poet's first task, then, was somehow to place himself within a literary tradition, for in most cases he was not in fact born into one. His next task, though, was to distinguish himself from his predecessors. Thus, Horace is at pains in his *Satires* to dissociate himself both from the parrhesia of Old Comedy and the invective and slovenly style of Lucilius.

The same process of association and dissociation is also operative in the Parade Odes. Indeed, the very features that establish literary affiliation with Greek lyric also serve to set Horace apart from that tradition. Horace's intellect resembles that of Milton as described by Hazlitt: the nearer it approaches to others, the more distinct from them it becomes.[17] The meters of the Parade best exemplify the process. They were used by, and in some cases even named after, Horace's Greek predecessors. Even their number, nine, perhaps conjures up the size of the Greek lyric canon.[18] This association, moreover, is conveyed as much by the meters Horace suppresses as by those that he includes. The most conspicuous omission (from the Parade and from the entire collection) is Catullus's favorite, the Phalaecian hendecasyllable. When placing himself in the tradition of Aeolic song, therefore, Horace disqualifies any outside competition.[19]

For all these associations with a tradition, however, there is something fundamentally alien about a book that opens with so many and varied meters, for the Alexandrian editions in which Horace surely read his models organized poems into homogeneous groups by meter and other categories.[20] Horace's exuberance here is only the first of many innovations, as he regularized metrical tendencies inherent in the Greek, restored the strophe, and at least on occasion brilliantly suited meter to sense.[21]

It may seem odd that metrical forms, especially when they are viewed apart from their content, should be a vehicle for an implicit poetic program. The ancient attitude toward genres, however, differed from our own, defining them by form not content, and regarding them as liberating rather than inhibiting creativity.[22] Thus, a lyric poem was a poem composed in one of the meters traditionally associated with the lyre (even after actual singing and instrumental accompaniment were discontinued).[23] Ovid characterized Horace as *numerosus*, literally "full of rhythms," and Horace himself, in the last ode of this collection and in a later epistle, retrospectively defined his own poetic achievement in largely metrical terms.[24]

Though it is important, however, meter does not bear the programmatic burden alone. Thus, the addressees of the Parade Odes, the fictitious as well as the real ones, are essentially an attempt to re-create the wonderful immediacy of Greek lyric in which a true "I-You" lyrical discourse could take place.[25] But the actual conditions of performance had so changed by Horace's time that the addressee often functions as a metaphor for the reader. Furthermore, the real persons in the group have not only a rhetorical function but also a political role that would have been alien to Greek lyric: a virtual roll call of prominent citizens, they attest to the program of the new regime, namely the securing of peace, the co-option of the opposition, and the restoration of republican forms.

This sort of complex relationship to a literary tradition is also evident in the themes of the Parade. On the one hand, they are generally of the sort familiar from Greek lyric, and they are developed with constant reference to Greek models.[26] So thoroughgoing is the allusive technique that it extends even to the most minute details of placement; thus, Mercury's presence in the second ode covertly recalls the position he occupied (as Hermes) in the Alexandrian edition of Alcaeus.[27] On the other hand, this material from Aeolic lyric is handled according to a very different aesthetic, for it is blended with Hellenistic and Roman material, or used as a "motto" to open an ode which then veers off in an original direction. Horace's second ode, for example, may follow the placement of Alcaeus's Hermes hymn, but it is otherwise independent of it (drawing instead on Vergil's first *Georgic*),[28] and the ode that more closely resembles Alcaeus's is C. 1.10. In his handling of themes and sources, Horace's attitude toward the literary past may best be characterized as "postmodern" or even "revisionist," for it is classical on the surface but radically different in its fundamental structure.

Every beginning, as Edward Said reminds us, represents a discontinuity from what has gone before.[29] At the beginning of Horace's collection, the Parade Odes establish this discontinuity, not so much by what they actually say (for we have still to consider them from that point of view), as by what their meters, addressees, and general themes imply, the very features that established the affiliation with Greek lyric in the first place.

Discontinuity had already been implied in the explicit statement of affiliation with which the first ode concluded:

> quodsi me lyricis vatibus inseres,
> sublimi feriam sidera vertice.   [C. 1.1.35–36]

But if you enroll me among the lyric bards, I shall strike the stars with my uplifted head.

Although Horace is deferential to Maecenas, representing the achievement of his goal as contingent upon his patron's approval, the goal is itself a bold one. Amidst all the Greek accoutrements of inspiration—ivy, Nymphs, Satyrs, Muses, and Lesbian lyre—the definitive phrase, *lyricis vatibus*, strikes a somewhat discordant note. It is not an exact equivalent for "lyric poets," as *vates* does not quite equate to the Greek *poeta*. Greek adjective and Latin noun, the phrase is a *callida iunctura*, one of those clever conjunctions for which Horace is justly famed.[30] It makes the same point as his choice of title, not the Greek word "Odes" but the Latin "Songs," *Carmina*. In both cases, the choice of a specifically Latin word over an available but not quite identical Greek one has social and aesthetic implications. Characterizing the poet not as a craftsman or maker but as a priest and prophet, it points to the distinctly Roman side of the *Odes*.[31]

This has implications not just for Horace but for the larger tradition. The image of insertion (*inseres*, 35) into a fixed canon, after all, can mean only one of two things: either one of the original nine lyric poets must be replaced, or else the canon must be enlarged to accommodate another poet (as had happened before to make room for Corinna).[32] In either case, Horace's achievement is such that it not only differentiates him from his predecessors but also actually alters the tradition itself. As T. S. Eliot observed in a different context: "What happens when a new work of art is created is something that happens simultaneously to all the works of art that preceded it. The existing monuments form an ideal order among themselves, which is modified by the introduction of the new (the really new) work among them. The existing order is complete before the new work arrives; for order to persist after the supervention of novelty, the *whole* existing order must be, if ever so slightly, altered."[33]

FOUR

When we turn from the gross inspection of the features that unify the Parade to a closer reading of the poems themselves, a number of schematic arrangements are possible to account for their distribution. Salat, for example, extends the group to include C. 1.10, the hymn to Mercury, which repeats both the god and the Sapphic meter of C. 1.2.[34]

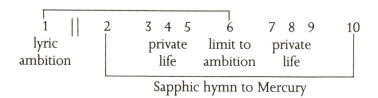

Sapphic hymn to Mercury

Salat is certainly correct in demonstrating that the concerns of the Parade extend beyond the ninth ode, and also in relating the first and the sixth to each other as poetic testaments. He misrepresents the great diversity of the other poems, however, by grouping them together into two triads as treatments of the private life. Because of this he also misses the way in which C. 1.7 grows out of C. 1.6 as a further development of its ideas about poetry. Finally, by setting the first ode apart as a prelude, Salat ignores the close interconnection of the first three odes.

More successful is Seidensticker's arrangement.³⁵

```
1  2  3  —  4       5     6       7       8     9
            spring  love  poetry  poetry  love  winter
            death                 life-         death
            carpe                 style         carpe
            diem                                diem
```

Here the first three odes are correctly grouped together (as we shall see), and the remainder are no longer just lumped together under the rubric "private life." Their diversity is now accurately assessed and shown, in fact, to be the basis for the poems' pairing into concentric rings.³⁶

Though convincing as far as it goes (and we shall return to it later), this way of conceiving of the Parade Odes' unity approaches them only in terms of their topical affinities. Also, and more importantly, it is based on a static rather than dynamic reading of the poems. C. 1.5, for example, resembles C. 1.8, just as C. 1.4 resembles C. 1.9. But to represent their complex interrelationship only as a matter of balance or correspondence is to ignore the crucial role played by the intervening poetic program, C. 1.6, and also to underrate the extent to which C. 1.9 provides not only a balance to C. 1.4 but also a sense of climax and closure for the group as a whole. The Parade's unity, in other words, ultimately depends not on the patterned disposition of its poems by general topic, but on the progressive development of an underlying theme. Having set the *Odes* apart from his own earlier *Satires* and from his Greek predecessors in lyric, Horace now explores their status with reference to one other important genre, epic.

The first three poems introduce this theme. They stand together not only by virtue of their central characters—the patron Maecenas, the *princeps* Augustus, and the poet Vergil—but also by their sheer weight, as their total number of lines is equivalent to that of the remaining six odes in the Parade (128 lines).³⁷ Furthermore, the three odes are also carefully interlocked. The first word of C. 1.1 is *Maecenas* and the last word of C. 1.2 is *Caesar*. Within this frame, the end of the first poem with its covert allusion to Pindar is also linked to the beginning of the second, a political ode and one of Horace's most

Pindaric. That poem and the Vergil *propempticon* that follows are interconnected in a similar fashion. The notion of sin informs both odes (C. 1.2.23, *vitio*; 29, *scelus*; 47, *vitiis*; C. 1.3.26, *nefas*; 39, *scelus*), and they are bound together in the same sort of chiastic structure: C. 1.2 opens and C. 1.3 closes with the image of Jupiter Tonans punishing sinners, just as C. 1.2 closes and C. 1.3 opens with a prayer.

In addition to these static symmetries, however, there is also a dynamic progression among the three odes, for they refer to Vergil's works in a sequence representing both the chronological development of Vergil's poetry and its generic ascent from pastoral to didactic to heroic epic.[38] In the first ode, for instance, the two passages that dispense with satire and implicate the poet are very suggestive. The first is the central vignette of the hedonist (19–22) which, as we have seen, represents one aspect of Horace's lyric persona. The other is the final picture of Horace in the fullness of his role as inspired poet (29–36). Although neither passage is a specific echo of the *Bucolics*, the *locus amoenus* inhabited by the hedonist and the sacred wood inhabited by the poet at least conjure up a pastoral tone, with their cool shade, holy stream, and rustic gods. And the poem does end, after all, with what is perhaps a Vergilian echo, for the phrasing of the poet's hope for immortality, *sublimi feriam sidera vertice* (36), recalls the ninth *Bucolic* in which swans will bear Varus's name to the stars, *sublime ferent ad sidera cycni* (29).[39]

This allusion in the last line of the poem leads to C. 1.2, the first line of which adapts another Vergilian text. The ode opens with a description of the storm sent by Jove to punish the Romans for the recent civil war, and then goes on to consider possible divine saviors, settling at last on Mercury who is incarnate in the person of the young Caesar. Although the descriptive elements owe something to the storm scene in the first book of the *Aeneid* (81 ff.),[40] the opening words of the ode, *Iam satis*, establish the definitive link with the end of the first *Georgic* (*satis iam pridem*, G. 1.501). The parallelism extends to elements of thought as well as of expression. Thus, both works catalog disasters that beset Rome (although Vergil's are of a more supernatural sort);[41] both attribute these not only to the civil war but also to a mythical original sin (Laomedon's perjury at Troy, G. 1.501–2; Ilia's drowning in the Tiber, C. 1.2.17–18);[42] and in both a sense of war-weariness inspires a prayer for a youthful savior (*iuvenem*, G. 1.500; C. 1.2.41) who is eventually identified as Augustus.

Despite these resemblances, there is one crucial difference: Horace seems more acutely aware than Vergil of the problematic nature of the savior.[43] This becomes clear from the deities he considers for the part: Apollo was Augustus's special patron after the battle of Actium, Venus is the ancestor of the Julian house, and Mars is the god of war to whose avenging spirit, *Mars Ultor*, Augustus vowed a temple before the battle of Philippi. All three, in other words, are implicated in those civil wars by which Octavian came to power and for which the Romans are now suffering. It is interesting, however, that Horace hints at the rehabilitation of these gods: Apollo is invoked in his prophetic capacity as *augur* (32), Venus is the "smiling" (*ridens*, 33) goddess of love whom Mirth and Cupid accompany (34), and Mars, at last "sated with the game [of war]" (*heu nimis longo satiate ludo*, 37), is called upon as *auctor* of the race (36). The search for a savior ends on an even more positive note, for Horace's ultimate choice, Mercury, is significantly referred to as the son of a "gentle" mother (*almae / . . . Maiae*, 42–43), and as one who only "endures" to be called the avenger of Caesar (*patiens vocari / Caesaris ultor*, 43–44).

The gods of Horace's catalog, then, suggest the danger of renewed civil war but also the challenge of peace that confronts Octavian in the future. Encomium, in other words, is mixed with admonition. Vergil's encomium had been less complicated, the only disquieting element in it being heaven's worry that Augustus desires (*curare*, G. 1.504) human triumphs.[44] When Horace ends his ode with the prayer that Mercury-Augustus may love (*ames*, 50) triumphs, he is not so much controverting Vergil's point as pursuing its implications, because the triumphs Horace has in mind are not those won over other Romans but those exacted from foreign foes (51–52), whose defeat had earlier been held up as an alternative to civil war (21–24).[45]

Vengeance is the theme that runs through this ode which opens, after all, with the punishments visited upon Rome by Jupiter. Horace's imagination ranges widely, from the Tiber whose "boast" (*iactat*, 18) that he avenged Ilia earned Jove's disapproval (*Iove non probante*, 19), to Mercury-Augustus who only "endures" his role as Caesar's avenger and who is urged to seek future vengeance from the Parthians. Prominently placed as the second ode of the collection, this is a celebration of the *princeps*. But in its departures from the Vergilian encomium on which it depends, it also constitutes a strong plea that the civil wars not be renewed.

After a poem that so dramatically alludes to him, Vergil is at last named openly in C. 1.3, the *propempticon* or bon voyage on the occasion of his trip from Italy to Greece. But whereas the previous ode made reference to the *Georgics*, the third is now informed by the *Aeneid*, not only in specific allusions to that work, but also in the larger poetic implications of Vergil's journey.[46]

Journeys had often been used figuratively by ancient poets who were familiar not only with ships of state, love, and life, but also with the ship of poetry motif.[47] Horace used the conceit in his very last ode, C. 4.15, which disclaims any ability to write heroic epic:

> Phoebus volentem proelia me loqui
> victas et urbis increpuit lyra,
>   ne parva Tyrrhenum per aequor
>   vela darem.   [C. 4.15.1–4]

When I wished to sing of wars and conquered cities, Phoebus struck his lyre to warn me not to spread my tiny sails on the Tyrrhenean Sea.

Even more to the point is Vergil's use of the image for his own poetry at least three times in the *Georgics*: when he asks the godlike Caesar to grant him an easy course (*da facilem cursum atque audacibus adnue coeptis*, G. 1.40), when Maecenas is asked to facilitate the continuation of his poem (*pelagoque volans da vela patenti*, G. 2.41), and when he anticipates the completion of his journey (*vela tradam et terris festinam advertere proram*, G. 4.117).[48] In C. 1.3 Vergil's itinerary fits this symbolism, itself Vergilian, with remarkable ease. A trip from Italy to Greece is an apt, almost irresistible, metaphor for the *Aeneid* itself, in the composition of which Vergil did indeed travel from Italy to Greece, i.e. to Homer, for his inspiration. This impression is confirmed by linguistic ambiguities. There are, for example, echoes of Callimachus's *Aetia* prologue, the Hellenistic poetic program which championed personal, small-scale, refined poetry over its outmoded opposite, and which Horace and other Roman poets endorsed as their own stylistic standard. Thus, the phrase *fragilem truci . . . pelago ratem*, "a fragile bark on a savage sea" (10–11), virtually enacts the Callimachean contrast between the two sorts of poetry, for *fragilem* translates the *Aetia* prologue's programmatic catchword, λεπταλέη ("slender," "slight"), and the vocabulary and sea imagery is familiar not only from the *Aetia* but also from other Callimachean works (e.g. H. 2.105–12, Epigr. 28 = AP 12.43 = 1041–46 G.-P.) and from Roman *recusationes* or refusal poems.[49]

As these intimations of epic are appreciated, specific echoes of the *Aeneid* can be recognized, not so much as sources for the ode, but rather as functional elements in its overall design and strategy. (That the *Aeneid* postdates the *Odes* presents no real problem since the Augustan poets all show familiarity with parts of it from prepublication readings or recitals.) It is no accident, for example, that a bon voyage for the creator of *pius Aeneas* should excoriate seafaring under the image of *inpiae / . . . rates*, "impious ships" (23–24). In addition, most of the characters in the ode have Vergilian associations.[50] Venus (1) is the mother of Aeneas; Aeolus who checks the winds in the ode (3–4) unleashes them in the storm scene in the epic (*Aen.* 1.50–82); Daedalus's flight appears not only in Horace (34–35) but also in the *ekphrasis* on Apollo's temple in *Aeneid* 6 (14–41); and Hercules who visited hell in the ode (36) is celebrated as the conqueror of the monster Cacus in *Aeneid* 8 (184–279). It may be objected that these characters, when they appear in Horace, have less to do with the *Aeneid* than with their new context. In aggregate, however, and in a poem about Vergil, their Vergilian resonance becomes more forceful and unmistakable.

There are, finally, even verbal echoes of the epic, the most dramatic of which is the phrase *aes triplex*, "triple bronze" (9), applied by Horace to the harshness of the man who first ventured forth on the sea. The image is clarified by a parallel passage in the tenth book of the *Aeneid* in which Aeneas's spear pierces Mezentius's triple shield, *aere . . . triplici* (784). It is significant that these are the only two occurrences of the phrase in Latin literature.[51] It is, of course, impossible to determine with certainty the direction of influence but, if Horace remembered the phrase from some prepublication experience of the *Aeneid*, this would be yet another, and in fact the closest, Vergilian reminiscence in the ode.

For all these reasons, Horace's bon voyage for Vergil can now be understood as a reflection on the composition of the *Aeneid*. As such, it reveals Horace's attitude to the epic to be very complicated. The ode opens with affectionate prayers for Vergil's safety, but then abruptly shifts to deprecation of the inventor of sailing and, finally, to an attack on human daring in general. Some of the structural and tonal inconsistency, of course, is mitigated by the recognition that generic constraints are operative here. In other words, the cursing or *schetliasmos* was a conventional element in *propemptica*, and is exemplified in other extant examples and in the Greek rhetorician Menander's prescriptions for the form.[52] But the curses here don't quite fit the generic bill. They are still unusually vehement and go far beyond their proper target, the inventor of sailing, to bear on Vergil's own audacity in setting sail and then on all human achievement.

That the curses on seafaring have a bearing on Vergil is not tactless but deliberate, for Horace means to suggest that the literary enterprise on which Vergil has embarked is both daring and dangerous. The insight is important and accurate, as the composition of the *Aeneid* was not only politically but also artistically risky. The ancient *obtrectatores Vergili* carped at oddities of expression, but these are less crucial than the work's larger novelty of conception. To resurrect Homeric epic was already highly artificial in the Hellenistic Greek literary world. In Augustan Rome the enterprise was even more difficult because of the contemporary political message which the heroic myth was expected indirectly to convey.

Yet the reader senses a tension here, especially at the end of the poem. Prometheus, Daedalus, and Hercules were not just archetypal sinners but also, and more commonly, symbols for human achievement.[53] Horace's avowed disapproval of "sin," *nefas* (26) and *scelus* (39), seems balanced by a latent admiration for the courage and daring that man displays in its commission: *nil mortalibus ardui est*, "Nothing is too difficult for mortals!" (37). The poet's attitude here resembles the tension that animates the *Aeneid* itself where an awareness of man's tragic heroism complements the theme of Roman destiny.[54] In the ode, however, it also constitutes an implicit literary judgment, an accurate assessment of Vergil's poetic achievement by another poet who was in a position to appreciate its implications.

None of the Augustan poets remained unaffected by the greatest literary event of their day. Even the placid Tibullus rouses himself to Vergilian themes on at least one occasion (2.5).[55] Propertius too concludes his second book of elegies by contrasting himself, wounded by Cupid, with Vergil hard at work on the *Aeneid*:

> cedite Romani scriptores, cedite Grai:
> nescioquid maius nascitur Iliade.
>
> [Prop. 2.34.65–66]

> Make way Roman writers, make way you Greeks: a work of some sort or other greater than the *Iliad* is being born.

Of course, the compliment is not without some irony: *nescioquid* undercuts *maius*, and Propertius goes on pointedly to observe that Vergil wrote bucolic as well as epic verse.[56] Indeed, in the elegists' frequent attempts to dissociate themselves from epic ambitions, we often sense the presence of the *Aeneid* hovering over the polemic.

Horace's attitude toward Vergil, here as elsewhere, is far more complex.[57] The possible bucolic overtones of the first ode, followed by allusions to the *Georgics* and *Aeneid* in the next two odes, constitute a dynamic tribute to the poet whose own ascent up the stylistic register is reproduced here. On another level, however, these poems explore the problematics of the Vergilian achievement, the second ode pursuing the ambiguities of its political stance and the third reflecting on the dangers inherent in its poetic stance. All of this has implications for lyric. The third ode, for instance, is very inclusive when it announces that we seek heaven itself in our folly: *caelum ipsum petimus stultitia* (38). The plural verb may implicate Horace, and the imagery even recalls his poetic ambition to strike the stars with his head: *sublimi feriam sidera vertice* (C. 1.1.36).[58] The epithet Horace applies to Vergil in the third ode, "the half of my soul" (*animae dimidium meae*, 8), attests not only to a personal but also to a literary affiliation.[59] In a very real sense, what Horace set out to do in lyric was analogous to what Vergil was doing in epic: to resurrect an archaic literary past, to transfer it to an alien culture and language, and to make from it something of his very own.

Although these first poems are set apart structurally, their Vergilian resonance may be said to generate the rest of the Parade Odes which pursue the implications for lyric that are latent in Horace's treatment of epic. Indeed, C. 1.3 launches—the word is used advisedly—the spring ode, C. 1.4. Spring, after all, is the season for sea journeys such as that undertaken by Vergil (cf. the use of a west wind as a seasonal indicator in both poems: *Iapyga*, C. 1.3.4; *Favoni*, C. 1.4.1), and C. 1.4 even opens with nautical imagery, characterizing spring as the time when ships are dragged out of dry dock and into the sea (2). So smooth is the transition that Horace would later join Vergil and spring together in a single ode, C. 4.12.[60]

There may, however, be a further connection if C. 1.4 also has a poetic subtext. Crucial to this interpretation is the symbolic significance attached to spring. In the thematic structure of the poem, spring is equivalent to youth. This analogy between the seasons of nature and those of human life carries through to the very end of the poem, which portrays youths and maidens "warming up" (*calet*, 19; *tepebunt*, 20) like the weather itself. It is fitting that this analogy should be established so early in the collection, for the use of nature as a moral metaphor is one of the most characteristic features of Horace's lyric imagination.[61]

On another level, though, a political significance is suggested for spring by the choice of addressee. Implicit in the second ode, we recall, was the injunction to forget the civil wars. Augustus seems eventually to have followed this advice, for one aspect of his policy was to co-opt old republicans to the service of his new regime. Sestius was a dramatic example of this policy, as he was appointed consul suffect to replace Augustus himself. Because he probably did not assume office until June at the earliest, the spring setting of this ode (February, to be precise, since the mention of Faunus in lines 11–12 points to the Lupercalia)[62] is not a literal reference to the timing of the event, but is rather a more general allusion to the milder political climate that made such an event possible.

The addressee's biography is perhaps relevant to the interpretation of spring in one other way. Sestius was consul suffect in the year Horace published his *Odes*, 23 B.C., a fact to which the poem probably owes its prominent placement in the book. As noted earlier, C. 1.4 follows quite smoothly from C. 1.3 in which a sea journey is symbolic of poetry. When C. 1.4, then, opens with ships putting out to sea, the reader perhaps recalls not only the nautical imagery of the previous poem but also its literary relevance. Certainly, in that other great celebration of spring, the opening of Lucretius's didactic epic to which Horace here ostentatiously alludes (Lucr. 1.1 ff.; cf. also 5.737–40), the season was explicitly associated with poetic creativity.[63] And so, the coming of spring in C. 1.4 may be an inceptive allusion, a reference to the commencement of the *Odes* themselves, just as the winter setting of certain poems toward the end of Book 3 may be an allusion to closure.[64] In addition, not just the beginning of the collection but its very novelty may be hinted at, for this poem, unlike the later spring ode, C. 4.7, focuses not on the season's fullness but on its newness, the very first moment of its arrival.[65]

In any case, whether or not one perceives a poetic subtext in its setting, as the first ode after the Vergilian triad C. 1.4 seems quintessentially lyric. It is fitting that Horace should bypass the *Georgics* and the *Aeneid* of the two preceding poems to return instead to the nonepic world of pastoral which C. 1.1 had earlier evoked. It is not just the poem's setting, the countryside in spring, that conveys the association, but also the name of the young man at the end of the ode, Lycidas, which is borne by characters in the seventh and ninth *Bucolics*.[66] Now, Horace says, is the time to deck one's head with garlands and to sacrifice to Faunus. Death will come to rich and poor alike, and the shortness of life forbids Sestius from entertaining long-range hopes. The observation that once he has descended to the underworld he will no longer be able to feast and to love contains an implicit injunction to Sestius, to enjoy both of these pleasures in the here and now:

> quo simul mearis,
>   nec regna vini sortiere talis
>   nec tenerum Lycidan mirabere, quo calet iuventus
>   nunc omnis et mox virgines tepebunt.   [C. 1.4.17–20]

When once you have traveled there, you will neither win by lot the lordship of the feast nor marvel at the tender Lycidas, for whom all the young men are now burning and the girls will soon grow warm too.

The lyrical eroticism of this concluding vignette is then developed further in the next poem, the Pyrrha ode (C. 1.5), which is devoted entirely to love. Even specific details facilitate the transition. Thus, the attraction that Lycidas will soon hold for women marks his passage from the homosexual affairs of youth to the heterosexuality of adulthood,[67] and so leads smoothly into C. 1.5 where the *gracilis puer* who is infatuated with Pyrrha is an example of just such an inexperienced lover (*flebit*, 6; *insolens*, 8; *credulus*, 9; *sperat*, 11; *nescius*, 11).

As the first love ode in the collection, C. 1.5 is programmatic in a number of ways. It is, of course, typical of the many poems in which Horace plays the role of a detached observer of the love lives of others, and both Pyrrha and her hapless suitor are types that will recur. By virtue of its conclusion, however, in which the poet confesses a past involvement with Pyrrha (13–16), this ode also anticipates that larger group of poems in which Horace's own emotions are at issue. In all of his love odes, Horace focuses not on consummation or mutuality, but on the impediments to true affection—the rival suitor (C. 3.20), the interfering uncle (C. 3.12), problems of age (C. 1.23, 25; 2.5; 3.11, 15), class differences (C. 2.4), and the most common of all difficulties, unrequited love. It is always the irony of the situation that attracts the poet's attention: two rivals compete fiercely to win a youth who is indifferent to them both (C. 3.20); Asterie is reassured of her husband's fidelity, only to have her own called into question (C. 3.7); girls who are ripe for love fear it (C. 1.23, 2.5, 3.11), whereas those whose charms have fled remain haughty or in hot pursuit (C. 1.25, 3.15). Nor is the poet immune from his own sense of irony. Even in the midst of a jealous rage, he achieves sufficient distance (as did his model, Sappho) to catalog dispassionately the physiological symptoms of his emotional distress (C. 1.13). Elsewhere he quarrels with Lydia, but puts into her mouth a critique of his own temperamental behavior (C. 3.9); he falls in love with Glycera, but just when he thought that his infatuation was over (C. 1.19); he abandons Chloe, but then asks Venus to flick her just once with her lash (C. 3.26).

In all of his love odes, then, whether he is the observer or the participant, Horace's stance is basically the same as in the first love ode: never obsessive like Catullus and the elegists, he is mildly bemused, even detached, and appreciative of the ironies inherent in the situation.[68]

C. 1.5 has implications, however, not just for the love poems but for Horatian lyric in general. According to an accepted literary convention, love can stand for love poetry. Hence the ambiguities that run through Latin elegy: *amores* are "love affairs" but also "love poems" (as in Ovid's title and Propertius 2.1.1., *scribantur amores*); *querel(l)a*, the lover's complaint, becomes also a technical term for the genre; and *modus* can signify either the lover's way of life or his poetic measures.[69] Horace exploits the convention openly in C. 4.1, where he signals his return to lyric by announcing a return to love. Similarly, when he wished to signal that *Odes* 1–3 were coming to an end, Horace represented himself as giving up love affairs. In fact, that poem, C. 3.26, ostentatiously looks back to C. 1.5, the first love ode, both in its placement (fifth from the end of the collection) and in specific details.[70] The love interest in C. 1.5, then, is like the spring of C. 1.4: both allude to the commencement of the *Odes*. Furthermore, coming directly after the Vergilian triad, C. 1.4 and 5 embody those concerns, convivial and erotic, that most clearly set Horatian lyric apart from epic.

After two such odes with an implicit program, C. 1.6 follows almost as a literary apologia, making explicit for the first time Horace's rejection of epic. The poetic pretext is that the general Agrippa has asked for a heroic poem celebrating his exploits. Horace politely declines the commission and volunteers instead the poetic services of the epic writer, Varius.

As a literary apology, this and other *recusationes* ultimately go back to Callimachus's expression of literary preferences in the prologue to his *Aetia*.[71] In that work Callimachus contrasted the thundering Zeus whom he could not imitate with the restrained and restraining Apollo, the fat sheep with the thin (λεπταλέην) Muse Apollo recommended, the wide road with the narrow path, the braying ass with the delicate cicada, and, at the end of the *Hymn to Apollo* (H. 2.105–12), the pure stream of Demeter with the muddy Assyrian river. In Rome, Catullus signified the neoterics' allegiance to this Alexandrian standard by reiterating the contrasts (Cat. 95), and in the Augustan Age rejections of public poetry in favor of pastoral, amatory, or other personal verse either varied Callimachean motifs such as the god's prohibition, or else retained the contrasts implicit therein by means of a highly specialized vocabulary. The key word, λεπταλέη, strictly translated by the Latin *tenuis*, gives rise to a whole series of adjectives—*gracilis, deductus, angustus, mollis, parvus, exiguus, humilis, lepidus*—which epitomize the refined style and which contrast with those subjects and treatments characterized as *pinguis, tumidus, grandis, durus, magnus, inflatus*, and *turgidus*.

The Agrippa ode works in these terms:[72]

> nos, Agrippa, neque haec dicere nec gravem
> Pelidae stomachum cedere nescii
> nec cursus duplicis per mare Ulixei
>   nec saevam Pelopis domum

> conamur, tenues grandia, dum pudor
> inbellisque lyrae Musa potens vetat
> laudes egregii Caesaris et tuas
>   culpa deterere ingeni. [C. 1.6.5–12]

I, Agrippa, do not try to sing these things nor the heavy anger of Peleus's son who did not know how to yield, nor the journey through the sea of tricky Ulysses, nor the ruthless house of Pelops, since I am too slender for grand themes, while shame and the Muse who has power over the unwarlike lyre forbid me to wear out your praises and Caesar's with my lack of talent.

Horace rejects heroic subjects and modes on the grounds of inability, *culpa . . . ingeni* (12). Underlying this disclaimer, however, are Callimachean aesthetic principles. These had earlier been implied in the Vergil *propempticon*'s image of a fragile ship on a savage sea (10–11), and they are now even more succinctly formulated in the oxymoron, *tenues grandia* (9), and the use of the motif of the god's prohibition (*Musa . . . vetat*, 10). In true mimetic fashion, Horace proves his point by deliberately botching epic in his catalog of rejected topics, where the divine wrath of Achilles, the μῆνιν of the Iliad, is cut down to cholic, *stomachum* (6), and Odysseus's richly associative Greek epithet πολύτροπος ("much-traveled," "much-experienced," "much-suffering," "much-plotting") is mistranslated by the one-sided and slightly pejorative *duplicis*, "tricky" (7). Even in the fourth strophe (13–16), where Horace seems more successful in the heroic style, it is significant that his list of epic topics is posed as a question—"Who can sing of these?"—to which the expected answer is "Not me." And so, the final strophe announces convivial and erotic poetry as an alternative to these impossible heroics:

> nos convivia, nos proelia virginum
> sectis in iuvenes unguibus acrium
> cantamus vacui, sive quid urimur,
>   non praeter solitum leves. [C. 1.6.17–20]

We sing of banquets, we sing of battles carried on by maidens attacking youths with their cut nails, whether we are free from love or are aflame, trifling as is our custom.

It is interesting that love is cast here in military terms as *proelia virginum*, "battles carried on by maidens." Thus, heroics, when achieved at the end, are redefined in purely personal and private terms.

In a sense, the themes of *convivia* and *proelia virginum* had already been exemplified in the poems immediately following the Vergilian triad, C. 1.4 and 5. But the Agrippa ode now explicitly identifies them as the proper subjects of lyric as opposed to epic, and thus generates two more poems that prove the point, C. 1.7 which is convivial and 1.8 which is erotic.

The connection between C. 1.7 and the Agrippa ode is particularly close, since the first half of the poem recapitulates elements of the *recusatio*. The poem opens with a catalog of famous Greek cities, the undeniable excellences of which are surpassed by the Italian countryside around Tibur. Horace's interest, however, is not primarily geographic but literary,[73] for the Greek cities mentioned are all sites of heroic myths. Also, that the ode is a *priamel* inevitably calls to mind the use of that form only a few poems earlier, in the first ode, as the vehicle for a poetic program. Finally, the very language is loaded. Horace does not say "Some will like Rhodes . . . others Athens . . . still others Argos . . . but I prefer Tibur." What he says is: "Some will praise (*Laudabunt*, 1) Rhodes . . . others have as their work (*opus*, 5) to celebrate (*celebrare*, 6) Athens in perpetual song (*carmine perpetuo*, 6) . . . and still others will sing (*dicet*, 9) of Argos . . . but Tibur inspires (*percussit*, 11) me." In other words, the language is suggestive of literary activity. This activity is defined even more precisely, as the phrase *carmine perpetuo* is a translation of Callimachus's ἄεισμα διηνεκὲς, a technical expression for long, continuous poetry.[74] Horace, then, is distancing himself from such poetry, and so the first part of the ode is consistent with the preceding *recusatio* to Agrippa.

At this point the poet urges Plancus to drink, whether he finds himself off at war or resting home at Tibur. Tibur is the ostensible link between the two parts of the poem, but there is also a logical connection: just as the rejection of epic in C. 1.6 was followed by the endorsement of *convivia* and *proelia virginum*, so in C. 1.7 the *recusatio* element is followed by a convivial injunction. To support this, Horace ends with Teucer's speech to his companions, urging them to drink even in the face of adversity:

> Teucer Salamina patremque
> cum fugeret, tamen uda Lyaeo
> tempora populea fertur vinxisse corona
> sic tristis adfatus amicos:
>
> "quo nos cumque feret melior fortuna parente,
> ibimus, o socii comitesque,
> nil desperandum Teucro duce et auspice Teucro.
> certus enim promisit Apollo
>
> ambiguam tellure nova Salamina futuram.
> o fortes peioraque passi
> mecum saepe viri, nunc vino pellite curas:
> cras ingens iterabimus aequor." [C. 1.7.21–32]

When fleeing Salamis and his father, Teucer is nonetheless said to have bound a poplar garland around his temples wet with wine, speaking sadly to his friends as follows: "O comrades and companions, wherever fate, kinder than my parent, brings us, we shall go. There should be no despair under the leadership of Teucer and his auspices. For Apollo promised me with certainty that there would be a second Salamis in a new land. O brave men who have often endured worse with me, now dispel your cares with wine. Tomorrow we shall sail again on the huge sea."

With these ringing words, the poem that began as a rejection of epic ends on what appears to be a strong epic note. The style is lofty, the speaker an authentic hero, and his words modeled on those of an even more famous hero, Odysseus.[75] Closer observation, however, reveals Horace's characteristic withdrawal from the heroic implications of his subject and style, for Teucer's speech is given a radically private meaning. Teucer had been exiled by his father for not having prevented the suicide of his brother, Telamonian Ajax, at Troy. Plancus too had lost a brother in the proscriptions of the civil wars, and some at least attacked him for complicity in the event.[76] By incorporating this speech into his ode, Horace sets up an analogy between Plancus and Teucer; that analogy both exculpates and consoles, for it implies that Plancus was not unwilling but simply unable to come to the aid of his brother.[77]

In C. 1.7, then, Horace initially denies that he will compose epic, but then he exploits that genre for his own purposes. There is no inconsistency for he retreats from its heroic implications and recasts the myth in more personal and private terms.[78] That is precisely what happens in the next poem as well. C. 1.8 returns to the theme of love, describing the effect (predictably negative) that affection for Lydia is having on Sybaris. As in C. 1.5, Horace is the detached observer addressing himself to a woman who is destroying a young and inexperienced lover. But his pose of complete detachment is belied by the vehemence of his attack on Lydia which opens with a strong oath (per omnis / te deos oro, 1–2) and which continues as a relentless cross-examination (cur, 2; cur, 3; cur, 5; cur . . . cur, 8; quid, 13). This impression of involvement is confirmed only five poems later when Horace openly admits to being jealous of another of Lydia's young admirers (C. 1.13).[79]

Motivated by personal interest, then, Horace spends the greater part of C. 1.8 cataloging what Sybaris has given up for Lydia: the Campus Martius, horseback riding, swimming in the Tiber, the athlete's olive oil, weapon practice, the discus and the javelin.[80] The list is unified by several contrasts that run through it: youth is set against experience, male values against female ones, the past (in which Sybaris used to endure, 4, and excel, 12) against the present, and Roman toughness against eastern decadence (suggested even by the very names the characters bear). Common to all these athletic pursuits, however, is their implicit militarism, for they call to mind such Augustan institutions as the *militia equestris* and the *lusus Troiae*. And so, they lead to the final strophe which alludes to that greatest of all military heroes, Achilles:

> quid latet, ut marinae
>   filium dicunt Thetidis sub lacrimosa Troiae
> funera, ne virilis
>   cultus in caedem et Lycias proriperet catervas?
>
> [C. 1.8.13–16]

Why does he hide, as they say the son of the sea goddess Thetis did before the tearful destruction of Troy, [fearing] that manly clothing would hasten him into the slaughter and the Lycian bands?

This concluding image, which is the point of the poem, comes as a bit of a surprise, since it is not Achilles's prowess in war that is evoked, but his earlier attempt to avoid military service by hiding out in women's clothing on the island of Scyros.

The relevance of the myth to Sybaris extends beyond the mere fact that Achilles shuns what the poet describes in a neat pun as *viriles cultus*, "manly clothing," but also "manly customs." Achilles, we recall, is also young (a fact to which his mother's presence in line 14 may call attention), and he also, like Sybaris, has an amatory involvement (with Deidamia on Scyros). Most importantly, because every reader would certainly know that Achilles did eventually fight at Troy, Horace may be implying that Sybaris will grow out of his disastrous infatuation for Lydia.[81]

It is always difficult to know just how far to pursue a mythological allusion beyond the details to which the poet explicitly draws our attention. But if these implications underlie the comparison with Achilles, this allusion resembles the myth in C. 1.7 which, as we have seen, also served to exculpate the addressee. A more significant connection, however, is that both C. 1.7 and 8 enact the literary program announced in C. 1.6, not only by exemplifying the *convivia* and *erotica* which are there set forth as the proper themes for lyric, but also by developing these with relation to epic. In fact, the announcement (and demonstration) in C. 1.6 that Horatian lyric could not accommodate an epic treatment of Odysseus or Achilles (5–8) is then followed by C. 1.7 which reworks a speech of Odysseus, and by C. 1.8 which makes a comparison to Achilles. However, the speech is given a radically private meaning, and the comparison is to Achilles's preheroic days. Both poems, in other words, rework epic material to make it conform to lyric expectations.

This brings us to the last poem in the group, C. 1.9. We have passed from the Campus where Sybaris shuns manly exercises to the vision of chill Soracte (1–4). But we eventually end up again in the Campus, where young lovers play at nightfall (18–24).[82] Though this is a neat link with the preceding poem, it does not obscure the more striking parallelism that exists between C. 1.4 and 9.[83] Both derive some of their descriptive material from Alcaeus; both turn on seasonal imagery (though they move in different directions, for C. 1.4 is set in the spring, whereas C. 1.9 starts out in the winter); and in both this imagery is made to convey a moral message, that we should enjoy the present while we can.[84]

On one level, these echoes provide a sense of closure for the

Parade, although (as we shall see in Chapter Three below) this is a false closure, as the effect of the Parade is felt for several poems beyond the ninth. On another level, though, the correspondence between C. 1.4 and 9 is not exact, and the discrepancies between the two poems are a measure of just how far the poet has come in his attempt to define his version of lyric. In C. 1.4, *convivia* and *erotica* were joined, but only in the last strophe where their hortatory force was merely implicit. In C. 1.9, on the other hand, virtually the entire ode is taken up with explicit injunctions to drink (5–8) and to love (15–24), the two being linked by the underlying advice to leave everything else to the gods and to cease worrying about what the future has in store (9–15):

> dissolve frigus ligna super foco
> large reponens atque benignius
>   deprome quadrimum Sabina,
>   o Thaliarche, merum diota.
>
> permitte divis cetera, qui simul
> stravere ventos aequore fervido
>   deproeliantis, nec cupressi
>   nec veteres agitantur orni.
>
> quid sit futurum cras, fuge quaerere, et
> quem Fors dierum cumque dabit, lucro
>   adpone, nec dulcis amores
>   sperne puer neque tu choreas,
>
> donec virenti canities abest
> morosa. nunc et campus et areae
>   lenesque sub noctem susurri
>   conposita repetantur hora,
>
> nunc et latentis proditor intumo
> gratus puellae risus ab angulo
>   pignusque dereptum lacertis
>   aut digito male pertinaci.   [C. 1.9.5–24]

Dissolve the chill by piling the wood high upon the hearth and produce rather generously a four-year-old wine in a Sabine jug, O Thaliarchus. Leave the rest to the gods, for as soon as they have calmed the winds that war with the raging sea, neither cypresses nor old elms are shaken. What will be tomorrow, cease to inquire, and whatever sum of days Fate will grant, credit it to your account, and do not scorn sweet loves and dances while deadly gray hair is far away from your youthful bloom. Now let the Campus and the squares be sought, and quiet nighttime whispers at the appointed hour, and the pleasant laughter of a girl which betrays her hiding in an intimate corner, and the token snatched from her arm or finger that resists unconvincingly.

This is much more emphatic and explicit than anything in C. 1.4. All the qualities that set C. 1.9 apart from its corresponding poem can be fully understood only with reference to the intervening odes, namely C. 1.6 which announced a program for lyric as opposed to epic, and C. 1.7 and 8 which enacted that program by domesticating epic material in the service of *convivia* and *erotica* respectively. C. 1.9, then, comes as the climax or culmination of this sequence—first, because it reunites both lyric themes in a single poem, and second, because it is written in the Alcaic meter. The postponement of the Alcaic to the final emphatic position in the Parade is surely honorific. But it is also programmatic, for the Alcaic is statistically the most common meter, and the poet after whom it is named serves not only as a model for Horace but is also, in several odes, reinvented by Horace as a cover for his own achievement.[85] In the Soracte ode, then, lyrical matter and meter coalesce in a particularly dramatic way. It is interesting that C. 1.9, unlike so many of the odes that precede it, makes no obvious epic allusions and reworks no epic themes, for there is no longer any need to do so. The dialectic between lyric and epic that was carried out in the Parade Odes has finally been resolved.[86]

THE FIRST BOOK CONTINUED

ONE

When C. 1.10 repeats the Sapphic meter of C. 1.2, *variatio* is at last broken and the Parade is officially over. Yet, because the very next poem, C. 1.11, introduces another new meter, Kiessling argued that the Parade Odes were the first twelve in the book.[1] This view, however, entails a good deal of special pleading. Although the repetition of the Sapphic in C. 1.12 can be explained away as an attempt to balance C. 1.2 and thus provide a frame of sorts for the cycle, the presence of the Sapphic at C. 1.10 poses more serious difficulties. It has been suggested that technical anomalies in that poem's handling of the Sapphic mean that, for all intents and purposes, C. 1.10 can be regarded as composed in a different meter. But breaks after the sixth syllable are not unexampled in the Sapphic,[2] and C. 1.10 most certainly violates the metrical *variatio* which is the basic unity of the Parade.

Though it is incorrect, Kiessling's view does call attention to an important, if neglected, feature of Horace's organizational technique. Horace has deliberately blurred the boundaries of the Parade, demarcating at C. 1.10 only to resume metrical *variatio* in C. 1.11 and then, perhaps, to supply a new sense of closure with C. 1.12. It is significant that the collection should open in this fashion, for imprecision of this sort frequently recurs. Just as a mechanical division into component parts cannot fully describe the sophistication of an individual ode, so the collection as a whole and the groupings within it resist the imposition of rigid patterns and communicate also, or instead, a more fluid and dynamic movement. This quality characterizes not only the metrical but also the thematic disposition of the poems. Just as the metrical *variatio* of the Parade is informally prolonged, so its thematic influence extends to several of the odes that follow it. Although the diagram illustrates the most basic connections, a closer study of C. 1.10 through 13 will demonstrate that they not only look back to the Parade but also improve on or augment their counterparts in that group.

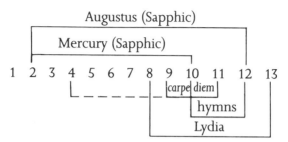

C. 1.10 clearly recalls C. 1.2 not only in its meter but also in its topic, Mercury. In addition, both owe something to Alcaeus's hymn to Hermes (308 L.–P.), C. 1.2 its second position in the book and C. 1.10 certain details of the god's treatment.[3] One major difference between the two odes, though, is in the prominence and functions each ascribes to the god. In C. 1.2 Mercury is the culmination of a catalog of deities and is invested with a contemporary political relevance. In C. 1.10, on the other hand, where he shares the limelight with no one else, Mercury is celebrated for his other, more traditional roles, as inventor of speech, athletic competition, and the lyre, and as herald, thief, guide, and psychopomp. It is interesting that in so varied a list one particular aspect of the god should stand out: his cultural role. Though his invention of the lyre is mentioned only in the second strophe (*curvaeque lyrae parentem*, 6), the first strophe represents him as the civilizing agent of mankind, emphasizing his eloquence (*facunde*, 1), the *palaestra* which is conceived of as the Greek gymnasium (4), and his family connection with Atlas, the great teacher (2).[4] Similarly, in the last strophe the *virga* or magic wand with which he shepherds the dead covertly alludes to his poetic role since he procured the wand from Apollo in exchange for the lyre.[5] The first poem after the Parade, then, continues the celebration of Mercury that was begun in C. 1.2. But now, appropriately enough, the god's patronage of poetry and culture underlies a number of his more traditional aspects.

The final image of Mercury among the dead makes an elegant

transition to C. 1.11, which opens by chiding Leuconoe for inquiring of astrologers what end the gods have ordained for Horace and herself. The poem has clear affinities with two odes in the Parade, C. 1.4 and particularly C. 1.9 from which it is separated by only one poem. Commager has aptly characterized C. 1.11 as "a more explicit redaction of the Soracte ode," and has suggested that "The similarity in theme of the two poems, as well as their proximity, makes it easy to read them together."[6]

Both poems turn on nature imagery. The wintry seascape of C. 1.11 with its striking picture of the sea wearing itself out on the rocks (4–6) recalls the seasonal setting of C. 1.9, particularly the ice in the river (3–4) and the winds whipping up the sea (9–11). In both the winter is suggestive of death and is set against an alternative that is aptly imaged in agricultural terms. Thus, in C. 1.9 youth is "blooming" (*virenti*, 17), and in C. 1.11 hope is to be "pruned" (*spem longam reseces*, 7) and the day "harvested" (*carpe diem*, 8). Finally, this message is reinforced in each poem by the same sort of explicit injunctions, to stop inquiring into the future (*fuge quaerere*, C. 1.9.13; *Tu ne quaesieris*, C. 1.11.1) and to drink wine in the here and now (*benignius / deprome . . . / merum*, C. 1.9.6–8; *vina liques*, C. 1.11.6).

Despite these close similarities, there is one crucial difference between the two poems. In C. 1.9 Horace advises his addressee to love. Such an injunction is missing from C. 1.11 since Leuconoe's inquiry reveals that she is in love—with the poet. By virtue of this latent and personalized eroticism, C. 1.11 not only repeats the theme of C. 1.9 but also takes it one step further by bringing its message to bear more directly on Horace himself.

The next poem, C. 1.12, stands in sharp contrast to this. Searching for a suitable subject to celebrate, Horace works his way through gods, heroes, and men, finishing with Augustus whose rule on earth is second to that of Jupiter in heaven. The poem looks back to C. 1.2, not only in its meter but also in its Pindaric style,[7] catalog structure, and political stance. Although both odes culminate with Augustus who is accorded nearly divine honors and whose foreign exploits are the object of the poet's prayer, C. 1.12 represents an advance over the earlier poem in several respects. First, Augustus is now set in a larger context, the grand panorama of Roman history.[8] Then, the gods who are celebrated are not so ambiguous as those in C. 1.2, and the encomium is less guarded. Furthermore, that poem identified Augustus with Mercury, whereas in C. 1.12 he enjoys a special relationship with Jupiter himself. Finally, C. 1.12 introduces a more orthodox method of encomium that will recur in the collection, not direct deification as in C. 1.2, but association with a god.[9] The treatment of Augustus, though, is hardly less honorific, for he now occupies the position next to Jupiter (*tu secundo / Caesare regnes*, 51–52) that had earlier been denied even to Pallas Athena (*nec viget quidquam simile aut secundum. / proximos illi tamen occupavit / Pallas honores*, 18–20).[10]

C. 1.12 ends as the god shakes his chariot on Olympus and hurls thunderbolts upon polluted groves. This image of anger leads amusingly into the next poem where Horace has been wronged by Lydia's infidelity and vents a more splenetic wrath. Adapting Sappho's famous catalog of symptoms (31 L.–P.) to which Catullus also had recourse (51), Horace deliberately lowers the stylistic and tonal level by unifying his symptoms around a kitchen metaphor: his liver boils, swells, changes color, and shifts position (4–8)—as if it were being cooked in a pot![11] This incommensurability between Jove's anger and the poet's, and between Sappho's symptoms and Horace's, is an important source of the poem's humor and success. It is also one of several features that set it apart from its obvious counterpart in the Parade, C. 1.8, where Horace again complains about Lydia's involvement with a younger man and again turns to a Catullan model (Cat. 55).[12] But whereas Horace's involvement with Lydia had to be inferred from the tone and setting of that earlier poem, in C. 1.13 it is explicit. Also, whereas the poet's attention had been turned to the rival suitor in the former ode, he now focuses exclusively on Lydia, on her constant boasting about Telephus (mimicked in the repetition of his name at lines 1–2) and on the marks of passion the young man has left on her shoulders and lips (9–12). Finally, C. 1.8 remained relentlessly angry throughout, but C. 1.13 closes with a touching evocation of a happy and enduring love (*copula*, 18).

To sum up: the effect of the Parade is felt beyond the ninth ode, because C. 1.10 through 13 not only repeat certain themes from the earlier group but also take them one step further. The celebration of Mercury, which was restricted to his novel political function in C. 1.2, is expanded in C. 1.10 to include his more traditional roles, particularly as a patron of poetry and culture. The *carpe diem* theme of C. 1.4 and 9 is more concisely expressed in C. 1.11 where it is also brought to bear directly on the poet himself by the erotic context. The divine qualities of Augustus which were introduced in C. 1.2 are developed further in C. 1.12 by means of a new strategy that associates the princeps with Jupiter himself. Finally, C. 1.13, while continuing the assault made upon Lydia in C. 1.8, also reveals explicitly the true nature of Horace's feelings for the woman.

Such connections with the Parade Odes could be pursued indefinitely, since that initial group introduced most of the themes that would recur in the collection. Thus, the very next poem, C. 1.14, addresses an allegorical ship damaged in a storm and so has affinities both with C. 1.3, also an address to a ship, and C. 1.5, which turns on the metaphor of shipwreck and is even composed in the same meter. And yet, as we get farther away from the opening of the book, the literary critical importance of such linkages diminishes, and the most obvious and significant relationships poems enjoy are with their own immediate neighbors. C. 1.14, for example, emerges by gentle linguistic and tonal transitions from C. 1.13;[13] more importantly, it displays a striking thematic connection with the poem that follows it, C. 1.15.

TWO

C. 1.14 addresses a ship that has been damaged in a storm, advising it to hasten to the safety of a nearby port because new waves threaten to carry it out to sea again. C. 1.15 follows with a description of Paris and Helen sailing away together and being intercepted by the sea god, Nereus, who prophesies war and the eventual destruction of Troy. A twofold relationship is usually acknowledged between the odes. At the most basic level, they share nautical imagery. More importantly, this underscores a possible thematic link. According to the traditional interpretation which goes back to Quintilian (8.6.44), the ship in C. 1.14 stands for the Roman state, the waves for civil war, and the port for peace. Similarly, C. 1.15 can also be read as a political allegory, for not only did the Romans claim descent from the Trojans, but Antony and Cleopatra could also be assimilated in propaganda to Paris and Helen.

This appealing thematic connection is not certain, however, as the individual interpretations upon which it depends can be called into question. There is nothing in C. 1.15, for example, that necessitates reading into the poem a contemporary political significance. That interpretation seems to have originated only in the fifteenth century under the inspiration of Quintilian's reading of the preceding poem.[14] Because Porphyrion claims that Horace was imitating Bacchylides whose *Dithyrambs* seem to have reworked epic themes and to have included speeches such as that of Nereus here, C. 1.15 can be read not as a political allegory but as a purely literary experiment, an attempt to incorporate epic narrative into lyric poetry.

The traditional interpretation of C. 1.14 is also problematic, for, although allegory is guaranteed by the passionate language of the final strophe which would hardly suit a real ship, the specific direction of the allegory is remarkably indeterminate. The authorities and alleged Alcaean parallels for the ship of state are not definitive.[15] More importantly, the poem lacks two features prominent in other examples of the *topos*. First, the ship of state metaphor is most commonly used to point to the need for a good helmsman, i.e. governor. But such a figure is missing from the ode. And second, a speaker who manifests anxiety for the state usually places himself on board the ship. But Horace seems to remain on the shore since he refers to the ship as a *desiderium* (18), literally an object of desire that one does not actually possess.[16]

These difficulties, however, are probably less serious than they seem because they result from an excessively rigid application of strict logic to poetry. Thus, although the ship of state metaphor does usually focus on the helmsman, Horace was quite capable of adapting it to a different point, not the need for good rulers but rather the peril of renewed civil war. Similarly, though an impassioned citizen might be expected to sail on the vessel, Horace may not have been so literal-minded and, in any case, *desiderium* is not conclusive evidence for his position on the shore.[17]

The traditional interpretation, then, is not impossible, but the lack of the usual clear signals for such a metaphor might have troubled an ancient reader. It has certainly troubled modern ones who have suggested three other plausible interpretations. According to one view, the sea journey can be read as a philosophical metaphor for Horace's, or man's, passage from the vicissitudes of life to spiritual or political tranquillity. This view is supported by the emphasis that is placed on the harbor, *portum* (3), which is a very common metaphor for a refuge or retreat.[18] Or the battered ship may represent an aging mistress (like Lydia in C. 1.25) whom Horace tries to dissuade from embarking on another love affair. This has the advantage of making sense of the elaborate personification of the ship and of the erotic language of the final strophe, and it also suits the meter, the Third Asclepiadean, which is most often used for amatory subjects.[19] Finally, it has even been suggested that the ship represents Horatian lyric about to embark on the dangerous seas of grand poetry. This would neatly account for the Catullan echoes in the poem as reminders of Horace's usual preference for lighter verse rather than the heroics that are under apparent consideration.[20]

Ships of life, love, and poetry are all familiar metaphors (in Horace himself as well as other authors), and each fits not only the general situation of the poem but also certain specific details. In addition, they all obviate at least some of the difficulties encountered with the ship of state (e.g. the lack of a helmsman), although, as we have seen, these difficulties are not sufficient to invalidate even that interpretation. Finally, these various allegories are not even mutually exclusive, since the harbor sought by the ship of life can stand for political as well as spiritual tranquillity, and since the seas on which the ship of poetry ventures to sail represent epic which, at Rome, was most often political.[21]

That C. 1.14 is hospitable to so many different readings requires some explanation. In part, this results from the very nature of allegory. As Steele Commager very acutely observes: "Nothing in the poem tells us what the ship represents, for allegory, unlike the simile and many metaphors, customarily leaves one term tacit. To say 'my love is like a red, red, rose' involves no difficulty, and the statement 'my love is a red, red, rose' is hardly more abstruse. But were we to write simply a description of a red, red, rose, readers might justly be excused for failing to grasp its significance, unless they received sufficient hints."[22] What is remarkable about C. 1.14, however, and what sets it apart from many other allegories, is that it contains no such hints. This must represent a deliberate decision by the poet, a decision not to be imprecise so much as to offer multiple precisions. The ship is certainly to be taken allegorically as the final strophe indicates. But by refusing to be more specific, Horace invites the reader to make his own choice and thereby participate in the act of creation.

To return to the thematic relationship between C. 1.14 and 15, this revaluation of C. 1.14 as an open allegory, and of C. 1.15 as not necessarily an allegory at all, in no way affects the fact of a link between the two poems. Thus, nothing prevents us from reading both as political allegories; as a matter of fact, if that is the interpretation one chooses to place on C. 1.14, it will almost inevitably suggest itself for the following poem as well. If, on the other hand, C. 1.14 is read as an erotic allegory, then interpretation of C. 1.15 can comfortably stop at the most literal level, according to which the poem is an account of two lovers, Paris and Helen. Similarly, if C. 1.14 is taken to represent the ship of Horatian poetry about to set sail on deeper and more dangerous poetic waters, it would be an excellent preface to C. 1.15 which does, in fact, incorporate epic material and style into a lyric poem.[23] Finally, if C. 1.14 is a philosophical allegory for man's journey through life, the metaphor is so vague as to accommodate virtually any connection with C. 1.15. The relationship between these two poems is so close, then, that any reasonable allegorical interpretation of the first will harmonize with the second.

THREE

When we move on to the next poem, we see that the nautical connection is now dropped. But the mention of Helen in C. 1.15 establishes a new link as her presence is at least hinted at in C. 1.16. That poem's opening address to a "daughter more beautiful than a beautiful mother" (*O matre pulcra filia pulcrior*, 1) would be a singularly apt description of Leda's child by Tyndareus. Furthermore, the very form of the poem, a palinode, calls to mind Stesichorus who had penned an attack on Helen and then, to atone, a recantation. Perhaps Horace is even quoting from Stesichorus's lost work, because the opening address looks like a Greek motto and because *recantatis* (27) is a Horatian coinage exactly reproducing the Greek παλινῳδεῖν.[24] In addition to this continuing association with Helen, C. 1.16 is also related thematically to the poem that precedes it. An amatory interest underlies each poem, for C. 1.15 opens with the abduction of Helen by Paris, and C. 1.16 represents Horace's attempt to become reconciled with a woman who had once been his mistress (*fias . . . amica / . . . animumque reddas*, 27–28). Also, both poems expand beyond these immediate love affairs, C. 1.15 to encompass the Trojan War as a disastrous consequence of the love between Paris and Helen, and C. 1.16 to explore even further the disastrous consequences of anger, among which the poet numbers the destruction of cities (18–21).

An even closer relationship exists between C. 1.16 and 17. Again, Helen provides a link as the latter ode is addressed to a girl who bears her patronymic, Tyndaris.[25] More crucial, however, is the metrical link which guarantees a deeper connection. This has often eluded readers, however, because the two odes are superficially very different.

C. 1.16 opens with a straightforward premise: Horace has written invective poems (*criminosis . . . / . . . iambis*, 2–3) which he now hands over to a woman to destroy with fire or water (2–4). The body of the poem is then devoted to an exploration of anger—its violence (5–8), tenacity (9–12), cause (13–16), and destructiveness (17–21). At line 22 the poem returns, in ring composition, to its basic premise:

> conpesce mentem: me quoque pectoris
>   temptavit in dulci iuventa
>   fervor et in celeres iambos
>
> misit furentem: nunc ego mitibus
>   mutare quaero tristia, dum mihi
>   fias recantatis amica
>   opprobriis animumque reddas.   [C. 1.16.22–28]

Restrain your anger. In my sweet youth passion tempted me too and sent me raging into impetuous iambics. Now I seek to change those sad verses for gentle ones, provided that you become my friend now that I have recanted my insults, and that you give back your heart to me.

The abrupt injunction to the girl to give up *her* anger and the poet's citation of himself as one whom youthful anger once drove to verse (*me quoque*, 22) come as a bit of a surprise. We had been assuming all along that the lengthy excursus on anger was relevant to Horace. We now learn, however, that the observations apply equally well to the girl. Thus, in what is both a witty and a charming close, the girl is asked to put aside her anger at the poet's *iambi* just as the poet has put aside his anger that prompted the *iambi* in the first place.[26]

At the most basic level of narrative, it is hard to see a connection with what follows. C. 1.17 opens with a picture of Faunus exchanging his Greek haunt, Mount Lycaeus, for a hill in Horace's neighborhood, Lucretilis. The effect of the god's arrival is described in great detail as bringing peace and prosperity to the countryside. Horace then invites Tyndaris to visit him there, to drink, and to sing, protected by the same immunity that Faunus provides for the poet and his flocks.

Attempts to relate these two very different odes have usually been grounded in the hypothetical biography of their addressees. The process started very early with Porphyrion's allegation that the nameless girl of C. 1.16 is none other than the Tyndaris of C. 1.17. The subsequent search for the identity of this person who took offense at Horace's iambi led inevitably to Canidia who had been attacked in Iamb 5 (and Satire 1.8) and had been the recipient of a mock recantation in Iamb 17. But because Tyndaris did not fit the description of Canidia, she was identified instead with that woman's daughter who, it was assumed, would share her mother's outrage.[27]

That both poems address the same woman cannot be proved, but is at least a plausible inference based on the hint of Helen in each and on their common meter. However, there is nothing in the text to warrant the further identification of Tyndaris with either Canidia or her hypothetical daughter. C. 1.16 does not, in fact, refer to any specific invective poems but is, rather, a more general allusion to Horace's Iambi. Just as the Parade Odes had earlier defined Horatian lyric by setting it against satire, Greek lyric, and epic, so C. 1.16 now defines it with reference to invective poetry. Such a program for lyric is implicit in the form of the ode, a renunciation, but it is also confirmed in the final lines where Horace explicitly states that he is changing (mutare) angry poetry, tristia, to gentler verse, mitia (25–26).[28]

It is an example of just such lyric mitia that C. 1.17 provides. Such continuity is perhaps signaled by the repetition of the motif of exchange at the beginning of C. 1.17 where Faunus changes (mutat, 2) Mount Lycaeus, his Greek haunt, for the Italian Lucretilis. To the picture of anger that forms the centerpiece of C. 1.16 the poet now juxtaposes an idyllic landscape whose inhabitants enjoy divine protection. Just as C. 1.16 makes explicit reference to the Iambi, so C. 1.17 everywhere hints at the lyric poetry that replaces them.[29] Faunus, for instance, is assimilated to the musical Greek god, Pan, and his very transference of locale from Greece to Italy may suggest the dual nationality of Horatian lyric (much as Vergil's itinerary from Italy to Greece in C. 1.3 alluded to the *Aeneid*). The protection Faunus provides also has poetic implications. Not only was such divine care traditionally a mark of one's status as a poet, but also here, in the first of its many occurrences in the *Odes*, it is explicitly presented as such: *di me tuentur, dis pietas mea / et musa cordi est* (13–14). Finally, even Tyndaris carries poetic associations. The wine she will drink, for instance, is a Lesbian vintage (21) and thus may conjure up Horace's models, Sappho and Alcaeus.[30] More definite, however, is the fact that Tyndaris is herself a poet:

> hic in reducta valle caniculae
> vitabis aestus et fide Teia
> dices laborantis in uno
>   Penelopen vitreamque Circen.   [C. 1.17.17–20]

Here in a secluded valley you will avoid the heat of the Dog Star and you will sing on a Teian lyre of Penelope and radiant Circe laboring for one man.

It is interesting that both the musical instrument and the subject of the song are lyric: the Teian provenance of Tyndaris's lyre conjures up Anacreon, and, though the persons of whom she sings are epic characters, their action here is not heroic but lyric, the struggle of two women for the affections of one man.

FOUR

The change from *tristia* to *mitia*, which is announced in C. 1.16 and exemplified in C. 1.17, clearly implies a poetic program that defines lyric as a pastoral-convivial-erotic alternative to the violence of iambic. This program is then pursued in the next two odes which continue to negate violence, treating instead those two concerns that characterize Horatian lyric, *convivia* and *erotica* respectively.[31]

C. 1.18, in praise of wine and its god Bacchus, is set, like the preceding ode, in the Italian countryside where the addressee, a certain Varus, presumably owns property.[32] In addition, the gods who preside over both poems are closely related, for Faunus was associated in myth with the Satyrs, Sileni, and other woodland attendants of Bacchus. Most important, though, is the thematic connection. In C. 1.17 Horace invites Tyndaris to his party, reassuring her that the wine served will be harmless (*innocentis*, 21), that Bacchus will not fight with Mars, i.e. that there will be no drunken brawling (22–24) and that she will be safe from the violent advances of a certain Cyrus (24–28). C. 1.18 continues to banish drunken violence, for its encomium of Bacchus soon modulates into a stern injunction that the god's gift not be misused:

> ac ne quis modici transiliat munera Liberi,
> Centaurea monet cum Lapithis rixa super mero
> debellata, monet Sithoniis non levis Euhius,
> cum fas atque nefas exiguo fine libidinum
> discernunt avidi.   [C. 1.18.7–11]

And lest anyone should transgress the moderate enjoyment of Bacchus's gift, a warning is provided by the battle of the Centaurs with the Lapiths over wine, and by Euhius [Bacchus] who is stern with the Sithonians when they greedily distinguish right and wrong by the narrow limit of their passions.

Not only is the recommendation of decorous festivity consistent with the terms of Horace's previous invitation to Tyndaris, but also the two negative examples he cites here recall that invitation's sexual overtones, since the Centaurs and Lapiths fought over a bride on her wedding day and the unspecified crime of the Sithonians is elsewhere identified as incest.[33] The poem then ends in hymnic fashion as Horace dissociates himself not only from drunkenness and lust but also from ritual sins against the god who is transformed now from the patron of wine into the object of orgiastic cult (11–16). In its emphasis on moderation and restraint rather than ecstasy and release, C. 1.18 differs from the other odes primarily devoted to Bacchus, C. 2.19 and 3.25. But it is precisely because of this special, if unexpected, emphasis that it can be read as a sequel to C. 1.17.[34]

The transition to the next poem is equally smooth, for we move from *convivia* to *erotica*, from praise of Bacchus who is coupled with Venus in C. 1.18.6, to a prayer to Venus who is attended by Bacchus in C. 1.19.2. There is also the same distaste for violence. C. 1.19 parodies the style of the kletic hymn in which a deity is asked to leave his or her cult sites and assist the votary. Horace complains, however, that Venus has left her cult site at Cyprus, not to aid him but to rekindle old feelings for Glycera that were best forgotten (*finitis . . . amoribus*, 4).

In C. 1.18 Venus was graced with the epithet *decens* (6), which assimilated her to the peaceful Bacchus whose praises Horace was singing. In C. 1.19, on the other hand, she is called *saeva*, "cruel" (1), the word used in the previous poem to describe the savage beat of Cybele's drums (13). Indeed, her intervention is characterized not as the kindly epiphany prayed for in a kletic hymn, but as a military onslaught (*ruens*, 9). Yet Horace's posture here is the same as in the previous ode, for he attempts to negate this violence by offering a sacrifice to encourage the goddess to come more gently, *lenior* (13–16). Finally, this gentleness even has the same programmatic implications as the *mitia* of C. 1.17, as Horace makes explicit reference to his poetry:

> nec patitur Scythas
> et versis animosum equis
> Parthum dicere nec quae nihil attinent.
>
> [C. 1.19.10–12]

Nor does [Venus] allow me to sing of Scythians and of the Parthian, courageous with retreating cavalry, and of other irrelevant things.

The entire ode is a *recusatio* of sorts, for Horace claims that his renewed love for Glycera has rendered him incapable of writing political verse on Parthians, Scythians, and (in a prosaic phrase that neatly proves his point) "other irrelevant things."

FIVE

This literary content of C. 1.19, as well as the presence of Bacchus here and in the preceding ode, provide a transition to the next poem, a drinking song which, as we shall see, has an implicit literary content. In C. 1.20 Maecenas is invited to drink wine that Horace bottled on the day when his patron's recovery from illness was applauded in the theater. With this poem the midpoint of Book 1 has been reached. The practice of dedicating this position to Maecenas is one of the very few structural features that all three books of *Odes* have in common. Of course, there are differences among them. The center of Book 2, for instance, is determined roughly by line totals

(C. 2.1–11 = 288, 12–20 = 284), whereas Books 1 and 3 find their centers by dividing the total number of poems they contain (C. 1.20 and 3.16 being the first poems in such halves). Also, in Books 1 and 3 the midpoint simply renews an earlier dedication to Maecenas (C. 1.1, 3.8), whereas in Book 2 it reorients the volume that had been previously dedicated to Pollio (C. 2.1).[35]

While C. 1.20 is an important poem, marking Horace's first step away from his patron, discussion of it is best postponed until Chapter Seven when all the Maecenas odes can be considered together.[36] For now, it is sufficient to note only its relationship to its neighbors. As an invitation to drink, it certainly is consistent in tone and spirit with the two preceding poems, as we have seen. It is less closely related to the hymn to Apollo and Diana that follows it, although the oblique reminder of Maecenas's illness (3–4) perhaps establishes a slight link, as C. 1.21 prays to the gods for (among other things) protection from famine and plague (13–14). That poem's religious form and serious tone then lead smoothly into C. 1.22, which opens with what appears to be a bit of moralizing, the observation that the upright man has nothing to fear. Although this has often been taken at face value, the ode's erotic close makes clear that Horace's *integritas vitae* has nothing to do with traditionally ethical behavior, but is humorously equated with his love for Lalage and his poetry about her. Thus, the final vignette of the girl's sweet laughter and prattle (23–24) effects an elegant transition to the next poem, C. 1.23, which addresses another of the poet's girlfriends, the youthful Chloe.[37]

These smooth, albeit superficial, transitions are not the only way in which the poems relate to one another. Standing at the beginning of the second half of Book 1, they correspond as a group to the poems that open the first half of the book, not only in specific details but also in the sequence of their presentation.

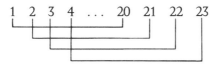

C. 1.20 looks back to C. 1.1 not only because it addresses Maecenas but also because its encomium is similar, since the reference to the Etruscan Tiber as the patron's "paternal river" (5–6) is an indirect allusion to his Etruscan lineage which was celebrated in C. 1.1. Furthermore, Horace's role as host inviting Maecenas for a drink calls to mind the first ode's portrayal of the hedonist which, as we have seen, suggests the poet's persona. Finally, C. 1.1 is explicitly about poetry, and, though C. 1.20 does not address artistic concerns openly, we shall see in Chapter Seven that they are latent in the poem's vocabulary and imagery (e.g. Latin wine in Greek jars!).[38]

The correspondence between the two halves of Book 1 then extends to the second poems in each. C. 1.2 is the lofty Pindaric ode which lists potential divine saviors and finally settles on Mercury who is incarnate in the person of Caesar. C. 1.21 is a short hymn to Apollo and Diana, but its choral pretensions (dicite virgines / ... pueri dicite, 1–2) convey Pindaric associations to balance those of C. 1.2.[39] In addition, both prayers involve Caesar and resemble each other very closely. Thus, in C. 1.2 Horace prays that Caesar may survive for a long time (45–49) and earn the title pater et princeps by punishing the Medes (49–52), and in C. 1.21 he prays that disasters may be averted from the Roman people and their leader, a populo et principe, and sent instead against the Persians and Britons (13–16). In both odes Horace urges foreign exploits against the Parthians (who are styled Medes and Persians) as an alternative to renewed civil war; in both the nation's safety is closely linked with that of Caesar; and in both Caesar assumes a paternal role, for he is called pater in C. 1.2.50, and, in the striking phrase of C. 1.21.14, a populo et principe, "the princeps replaces the patres who are frequently linked with the populus."[40]

When we pass to the third position in the book, the correspondence is not so exact. And yet, there are certain points of resemblance. Both C. 1.3 and 22 involve travel: Vergil's trip from Rome to Greece, and the righteous man's fantastic itinerary through the Syrtes, Caucasus, and Punjab. More importantly, both poems are about the safety of the poet, for Vergil's journey (as we have seen) is symbolic of his composition of the Aeneid, and Horace's immunity from the wolf in C. 1.22 results from his singing (dum meam canto Lalagen, 10). Finally, although the Lalage ode is admittedly very different in other respects from the Vergil propempticon, the appearance of Vergil only two poems later, at C. 1.24, encourages the reader's perception of a rough balance between the two halves of the book.

Neat alignment returns, in any case, with the fourth poems. C. 1.4 and 23 are both spring odes in which nature imagery evokes the seasons of human life and so gives rise to the same injunction, that we should enjoy the springtime of our days. Both poems convey this in erotic terms: Sestius is enticed with the image of the youthful Lycidas, and Chloe is admonished to take a lover now that she is ripe for one. Only one important element of the former spring ode is missing from the latter, namely the argument from death which is incarnated by *Pallida Mors* in C. 1.4. But in a very real sense that argument is supplied by the very next poem, C. 1.24, the consolation to Vergil on the death of Quintilius. The book's progress from C. 1.23 to 24, then, reproduces the internal movement of the individual ode, C. 1.4.

To sum up: the first and second halves of Book 1 open in parallel fashion. The individual correspondences, however, have no inherent meaning but are important for their larger effect, which is not so much to divide the book as to signal a new beginning. In a book that contains almost half (43%) of all the poems in the collection and that is thematically and metrically the most varied, this reinitiation or renewal imparts a sense of shape or larger structure. Once this has been accomplished, the parallelism between the two halves of the book breaks down. But the rest of the poems continue to relate to one another.

SIX

It has been noted that C. 1.23, 24, and 25 constitute a distinctive triad concerned with the passage of time and man's proper response to it.[41] The two end poems are clearly meant to be read together, for they explore the theme in erotic terms and are structured as mirror images of each other. Both are addressed to women, Chloe and Lydia, respectively, and both are concerned with their addressees' attitude toward men in general and Horace in particular. In C. 1.23 the poet reveals his involvement by reassuring Chloe that his intentions are not predatory (9–10), and in C. 1.25, though his interest in Lydia is not directly expressed, it is to be inferred from the komastic setting and agitated tone.[42]

Once the basic erotic component in both poems is recognized, their antithetical relationship can be appreciated. Chloe lives in the country, Lydia in the city.[43] Chloe is young, Lydia past her prime. Chloe fears a lover, Lydia will seek out men in back alleyways. Basic to this antithesis is nature imagery. In a simile drawn from Anacreon, Chloe is compared to a fawn fearful of losing its mother; Lydia is compared to a mare in heat. Or again, C. 1.23 is set in the springtime (*veris*, 5) as gentle zephyrs cause the leaves to rustle (5–6); C. 1.25 is set in the winter (*hiemis*, 19) as the north wind unleashes its fury (11–12). In both poems, furthermore, a connection is made between these seasons of nature and those of human life. Thus, in C. 1.23 Chloe's very name means in Greek a green sprig or shoot, and she is characterized as *tempestiva . . . viro*, literally "ripe for a man" (12). In C. 1.25 a similar correspondence between nature and man is established by the closing image which associates youth with green ivy, maturity with dark myrtle, and old age with sere leaves.[44] Finally, this correspondence between the seasons and human life imposes a standard of decorum upon us, a moral necessity to conform to the passage of time. Thus, the shy Chloe is urged to take a lover, and, though it is not spelled out, the message is the same for the haughty Lydia who is warned that her charms are fast fading.

In the midst of all this comes C. 1.24, the poem to Vergil on the death of Quintilius. The opening question—"What sense of modesty or measure (*pudor aut modus*) can be set to grief over the loss of one so dear?" (1–2)—and the subsequent invocation of Melpomene to teach a song of mourning (*praecipe lugubris / cantus*, 2–3) may appear to set the scene for an unrestrained lyrical dirge. It soon becomes clear, however, that Horace's point is precisely the need for *pudor* and *modus*.

Indeed, the traditional elements of the *consolatio* form are adapted specifically to impart this lesson to the addressee. Vergil's mourning is characterized as excessive:

> multis ille bonis flebilis occidit,
> nulli flebilior quam tibi, Vergili.
> tu frustra pius, heu, non ita creditum
>   poscis Quintilium deos.   [C. 1.24.9–12]

> That fine man perished mourned by many good men, but by none more than by you, Vergil. You, alas, pious in vain demand from the gods Quintilius who was not entrusted to you on those terms.

The financial connotations of *creditum* (11) recall the imagery of the first Vergil ode (C. 1.3.5–8, especially *creditum*, 5). More important, however, are the echoes of Vergil's own poetry.[45] In demanding Quintilius back from the gods (12), Vergil is in effect reenacting the experience of Orpheus who was a character in his own fourth *Georgic* (G. 453–527) and who follows immediately in this ode as an example of the poet's inability to bring the dead back from the grave:

> quid? si Threicio blandius Orpheo
> auditam moderere arboribus fidem,
> num vanae redeat sanguis imagini,
>   quam virga semel horrida
>
> non lenis precibus fata recludere
> nigro conpulerit Mercurius gregi?   [C. 1.24.13–18]

What if you should tune more charmingly than Thracian Orpheus the string [that was] heeded by trees? The blood would not return, would it, to the empty shade which Mercury, not receptive to opening the fates to our prayers, has once compelled to the dark crowd [in the underworld] with his horrid wand?

The *Aeneid* is also pointedly recalled, particularly in the abstract terms of the discussion. Thus, the *pudor* and *fides* of Quintilius (6–7) are qualities upon which the Dido episode turns. But Vergil's excessive grief for Quintilius is an expression of *fides* without *pudor*. Similarly, the hero of the *Aeneid* was conspicuous for his piety and endurance. However, Vergil's own piety is futile—*tu frustra pius* (11)—and the ode must end by enjoining patience upon him:

> durum: sed levius fit patientia
>   quidquid corrigere est nefas.   [C. 1.24.19–20]

It is hard. But by endurance that becomes lighter which it is sinful to change.

Taken on its own, then, this poem is a lesson to Vergil on proper measure in mourning. As such, it is the concrete realization of the didactic role assigned to the Muse in its opening invocation. When read in conjunction with the two poems that surround it, however, C. 1.24 takes on added meaning and intensity. The coyness of Chloe, the excessive mourning of Vergil, and the haughtiness of Lydia are now all revealed as attempts to cling to the past, to deny the passage of time. And in all three odes Horace's message is the same, to meet the demands that time makes upon us. Placed in the middle of the triad, the poem to Vergil aptly reflects the centrality of death as the most dramatic example of time's flight and the ultimate test of our ability to conform to the decorum of nature.

SEVEN

C. 1.25 ends with the image of young men throwing withered leaves to the wind. C. 1.26 opens as Horace throws cares to the wind. The linkage, however, goes deeper than this surface connection which Collinge characterizes as a "cinematographic continuity."[46] As we have seen, the foliage at the end of C. 1.25 stands metaphorically for the ages of women, with the withered leaves, of course, corresponding to Lydia. But the green ivy, which the young men understandably prefer, and the dark myrtle suggest also the symposiastic garland of Bacchic revelry. It is interesting that the next ode, C. 1.26, asks the Muse to weave a "bright garland" for Lamia (*apricos necte flores, / necte meo Lamiae coronam*, 7–8). Furthermore, as a metaphor for poetry, this garland can be plausibly identified with C. 1.27, a cheerful song about just such Bacchic revelry.

C. 1.26 opens with a picture of Horace dispelling cares:

> Musis amicus tristitiam et metus
> tradam protervis in mare Creticum
> portare ventis, quis sub Arcto
> rex gelidae metuatur orae,
>
> quid Tiridaten terreat, unice
> securus. [C. 1.26.1–6]

Dear to the Muses, I shall hand over sadness and fear to the violent winds to be carried to the Cretan Sea, singularly unconcerned about which king of the frozen edge of the Arctic is feared, [or] what frightens Tiridates.

The connection between *Musis amicus* and *unice securus* is a causal one, and recalls other passages in which the motif of divine protection conveys Horace's special status as a poet. Just a few poems earlier, Faunus watched over Horace's flocks because of his piety and his Muse (C. 1.17.13–14), and a wolf fled him while he was singing

(C. 1.22.9–12). The next lines follow naturally as a poet's prayer to the Muses:

> o quae fontibus integris
> gaudes, apricos necte flores,
>   necte meo Lamiae coronam,
>
> Piplei dulcis. nil sine te mei
> prosunt honores: hunc fidibus novis,
>   hunc Lesbio sacrare plectro
>   teque tuasque decet sorores.   [C. 1.26.6–12]

O you who rejoice in untouched springs, weave sunny flowers, weave a garland for my Lamia, sweet Piplean Muse. Without you my tributes are to no avail. It is fitting for you and your sisters to celebrate him with new strings and with the Lesbian lyre.

The pure springs go back to Callimachus and the garland of poetry to older classical writers.[47] But Horace's immediate source is Lucretius:

> iuvat integros accedere fontis
> atque haurire, iuvatque novos decerpere flores
> insignemque meo capiti petere inde coronam
> unde prius nulli velarint tempora musae.
>   [Lucr. 1.927–30]

It is pleasing to approach untouched springs and to drink, it is pleasing to pluck new flowers and to seek for my head an excellent garland with which the Muses have previously wreathed no man's brow.

In both passages, the issue is poetic novelty. For Lucretius this consists of transferring Epicurean philosophy to Latin verse. For Horace, the phrases *fidibus novis* (10) and *Lesbio . . . plectro* (11) signify the adaptation of Aeolic lyric. This is the first time since C. 1.1 that Horace has mentioned his literary pedigree, and the first time ever that he has openly asserted his originality, for C. 1.1 had only implied it.

However, C. 1.26 introduces two other elements missing from his Lucretian model into Horace's cumulative definition of lyric. The first is poetry's encomiastic role, for the crown Lucretius seeks for his own head is here placed on Lamia's instead. And if lyric is celebratory, it is consolatory as well. Only two poems earlier, in C. 1.24, Horace had comforted Vergil. That poem also raised the question of poetry's relationship to grief, by invoking the Muse to teach *lugubris / cantus* (2–3) and by conflating moral and literary vocabulary, so that *modus* meant both the "limit" imposed on mourning (1) and poetic "measure" (*moderere*, 14), and *fides* referred to both the fidelity of the deceased (7) and the string of the lyre (14).[48] This association of lyric with consolation, which C. 1.24 both puns on and puts into practice, is now announced in C. 1.26 where Horace offers Lamia not just praise but cheer. At the very opening of the ode, the poet characterizes himself as one who can dispel sadness and fear, and now he offers Lamia "sunny" (*apricos*, 7) blossoms which the Muse "rejoices" (*gaudes*, 7) to weave.[49] The poem Lamia is to receive, then, is not just an encomium but also a consolation, not just C. 1.26 itself but also the poem that immediately follows it.[50] Indeed, C. 1.27 is precisely the sort of cheerful ode Lamia requires, for it portrays a raucous drinking party at which the poet teases one of the revelers about his love life. It is not just the topic that relates C. 1.26 and 27, as if the former were the invitation and the latter the party itself. Both are written in the same meter, and both share the same moral and aesthetic perspectives, embodying not only the characteristically Horatian attitude toward life, cheerful and temperate, but also a certain view of poetry's function in communicating that attitude to others.

EIGHT

When we move from C. 1.27 to 28, the Archytas ode, no such connection is immediately apparent. Not only has the meter changed, but also subject and tone have undergone a radical shift, from the conviviality of C. 1.27 to the morbid preoccupations of C. 1.28. And yet, closer observation reveals possible connections at several other levels. There may perhaps be a surface glide whereby the end of the one poem is linked to the beginning of the next by means of a shared image or motif. At the end of C. 1.27, the characterization of the lover as "drowning" (*laborabas*, 19) in the whirlpool Charybdis and "entangled" (*inligatum*, 23) in the Chimaera's toils leads smoothly into C. 1.28, which opens by the sea (*prope litus . . . Matinum*, 3) and which represents the philosopher Archytas "confined" (*cohibent*, 2) in a tiny tomb.

This admittedly superficial linkage established by the sea imagery and the motif of enclosure perhaps alerts us to other, deeper connections. Thus, even on the topical level where the two odes seem farthest apart, there may be some connection, not of similarity, to be sure, but of dependence. Though the two poems do not explicitly relate their subjects, drinking and death respectively, elsewhere in Horace's work the two ideas are often brought into contact, as human mortality supplies the poet with one of his most compelling arguments for enjoying the present. In a sense, the movement of the book from C. 1.27 to 28 imitates the internal structure of many individual odes that move from sympotic to sepulchral concerns and leave it to the reader to supply the precise connection. Just as *Pallida Mors* follows naturally upon the invitation to Sestius in C. 1.4, so the preoccupation with death's inevitability in C. 1.28 can be read as a sequel to the preceding ode's revelry.

It is at the formal level, however, that C. 1.27 and 28 are most explicitly related: both are dramatic monologues. Although this has often been noted, the full extent and importance of the resemblance has not been appreciated. As a mimetic rather than narrative form, the category can hospitably accommodate most of Horace's sympotic and admonitory addresses. Strictly speaking, however, a dramatic monologue need not be delivered in the poet's own character; in addition, it usually has a more ostentatiously dramatic context, for the words enact or accompany progressive action which the reader is required to reconstruct from clues or implicit stage directions embedded in the text.

In C. 1.27 the poet speaks *in propria persona* and the clues are fairly straightforward. As a party in progress rapidly degenerates into a brawl, the poet urges moderation and restraint (1–8). A question at line 9 indicates that he too (*me quoque*) has been urged to join in the merriment. Perhaps to distract his comrades from their rioting, Horace agrees to participate, but only on condition that one of the revelers, the brother of a certain Megilla, reveal the name of his girlfriend (10–12). Another question at line 13 indicates that Horace's request has met with stony silence. And so, the address shifts from the group (7) to the unfortunate young man (*te*, 14; *puer*, 20) who is cajoled to speak of his love (14–18). As the poet's rare exclamation, *a miser!* (18), shows, Megilla's brother finally does confess, but only to find himself the object of mock commiseration (18–24).

The situation of C. 1.28 is very different. According to the most plausible reconstruction (about which more will be said shortly), the first section lectures Archytas on the inevitability of death (1–22). That proposition, tersely formulated at lines 15–16, is illustrated by cases specifically chosen for their relevance to him. At line 21, however, the speaker includes himself (*me quoque*) among the dead, thereby revealing that he is not Horace, as we had assumed, but rather the soul of a drowned man whose corpse has been washed ashore beside the philosopher's tomb. After this surprise, the speaker's attention shifts abruptly from Archytas to a passing sailor (*at tu, nauta,* 23) to whom the rest of the ode, an appeal for burial, is addressed.

Despite their very different situations, the two poems resemble each other not only in their overall form as dramatic monologues, but also in several very specific structural details. In both, the speaker introduces himself into the situation by means of the phrase, *me quoque* (C. 1.27.9, 28.21).[51] In both, this is followed closely by an abrupt shift in addressee (C. 1.27.14, 28.23). Both poems also chart a temporal progression: in C. 1.27 two questions and an exclamation signal pauses from which we are to infer action; similarly, the shift in addressee in C. 1.28 presupposes a gap in time during which the speaker has caught sight of the passing sailor. Finally, both odes display the same overall movement from general reflection (on the impropriety of brawling in C. 1.27, and on the inevitability of death in C. 1.28) to a highly personalized and carefully argued request (for information in C. 1.27, and for burial in C. 1.28).

This extremely close formal resemblance between the two poems is all the more remarkable in light of the very different demands each makes upon the reader. C. 1.27 is fairly simple to interpret, delivered in the poet's own voice and set at the familiar symposium. C. 1.28, on the other hand, has proved notoriously difficult and has been misread as a dialogue and even, at times, as two separate poems.[52] The reader's difficulty arises from the highly experimental nature of the ode which fuses two incompatible types of sepulchral epigram, one in which the deceased is spoken to or about, and the other in which the deceased speaks from the tomb to a passerby. This source of confusion accounts for the general unreality of the situation, the abrupt change of addressee, and, most importantly, the identification of the speaker which is not only postponed but also unexpected. In most odes, after all, the poet speaks in his own voice. It is true that he sometimes puts words into the mouth of a character.[53] But such speech is usually incorporated into a larger narrative or dramatic context and does not constitute an entire poem on its own. Thus, dramatic monologues in character are rare. The Archytas ode closely resembles Iamb 2; however, that is not a real monologue owing to its narrative coda. The only other possible example of the form is C. 3.12, Neobule's soliloquy, but it is very problematic.[54]

This unique status for C. 1.28 makes it difficult for the reader to recognize it for what it is. There is nothing with which to compare it—except, perhaps, C. 1.27. This is where placement helps. Insofar as C. 1.27 is simpler but nonetheless anticipates many of the formal features of C. 1.28, it actually prepares the reader for that more difficult ode, enabling him to reconstruct its setting and follow its movement. Thus, placement is neither accidental nor gratuitous, but serves what may be called a propaedeutic function. Though it does not reinforce the theme here, it does set up structural expectations that facilitate our understanding of one of Horace's most ambitious compositions.

NINE

Ending with an address to a passing sailor, the Archytas ode leads gently into the next poem, an address to a certain Iccius who is sailing away. This superficial linkage is apt, since C. 1.29 also explores one of the subsidiary themes of the Archytas ode, the inadequacy of philosophy. Just as the neo-Pythagoreanism of Archytas with its doctrine of transmigration is discredited, so the Stoicism of Iccius is now called into question. Of course, there is a difference: it is Archytas's very precepts that are false, whereas Iccius is false to his precepts, for he has put aside his study of philosophy to fight for material gain in Arabia. But the basic point remains the same: in each case philosophy yields to a stronger reality, death in C. 1.28 and greed in C. 1.29.

This basic similarity is reinforced in a number of ways. For instance, these two ideas, death and greed, are closely associated in individual odes elsewhere in Horace. In particular, many poems in the second half of Book 2 link the acquisitive life both literally and figuratively with death, and set it against the poet's own more philosophical existence.[55] Here in Book 1, of course, these ideas occur in two separate poems and are not explicitly related. Yet their association is perhaps implied, for the placement of C. 1.28 and 29 which juxtaposes death and greed resembles the placement of C. 1.27 and 28 which juxtaposed conviviality and death: in both instances the arrangement of odes within the collection imitates the collocation of ideas in individual odes.

Another and more direct connection between the Archytas and Iccius odes is that both treat their philosopher-addressees with the same combination of pathos and irony. C. 1.28 opens by evoking the vastness of the universe and of Archytas's intellectual achievement only to circumscribe the latter by the physical reality of his tiny tomb:

> Te maris et terrae numeroque carentis harenae
>   mensorem cohibent, Archyta,
> pulveris exigui prope litus parva Matinum
>   munera, nec quicquam tibi prodest
>
> aerias temptasse domos animoque rotundum
>   percurrisse polum morituro.   [C. 1.28.1–6]

You, Archytas, the measurer of sea and land and the countless sands, a tiny tomb of meager earth confines beside the Matine shore, nor is it any profit to you that you made trial of heavenly domains and ran through the round pole in your mind, about to die.

Even sound and metrical form reinforce the point, as "The open sonorities of *o* and *a* yield to narrow *i*'s and *u*'s,"[56] and as the expansiveness of the hexameters is contracted in the shorter lines with which they alternate. *Morituro* (6), like a death knell, cuts short the list of a life's accomplishments, and what follows is another list, of those who have died. This appears at first to be a consolatory *topos*, but soon betrays its specific relevance to the argument. To illustrate the proposition that all must die, the speaker has chosen precisely those whom popular tradition credits with immortality of one sort or another: Tantalus, Tithonus, Minos, and Euphorbus (7–15). The inclusion of the last among the dead is particularly ironic: it is a reference to Archytas's master, Pythagoras, who claimed to be the reincarnation of Euphorbus. But the deaths of master and disciple discredit their belief in reincarnation and the transmigration of souls. Such irony and pathos are then compounded at the end, as the speaker, glimpsing a passing sailor, abandons all certainty about death's finality, even to the extent of invoking superstitions and threats to ensure his own burial (30–36).

The same tonality informs C. 1.29, which also criticizes human ambition and pretensions. Iccius's anticipated military success is implicitly undercut by the sentimental description of the two young barbarians he will enslave, a boy who once learned to shoot arrows in his father's palace and a girl who had been engaged to be married before Iccius killed her fiancé:

> quae tibi virginum
> sponso necato barbara serviet,
>   puer quis ex aula capillis
>   ad cyathum statuetur unctis
>
>   doctus sagittas tendere Sericas
>   arcu paterno?   [C. 1.29.5–10]

Which barbarian virgin will be your slave after her fiancé has been killed? Which boy from a palace with perfumed hair will be your cupbearer, [though] taught to shoot Chinese arrows from his father's bow?

These pathetic details undercut the glory of Iccius's potential achievement. They are also heavy with irony. The boy destined to rule[57] and the girl destined to marry are both examples of frustrated promise. But so too is Iccius who had "promised better things," *pollicitus meliora* (16):

> tu coemptos undique nobilis
> libros Panaeti Socraticam et domum
>   mutare loricis Hiberis,
>   pollicitus meliora, tendis?   [C. 1.29.13–16]

Do you who promised better things aim at giving up the Socratic school and the famous books of Panaetius which you purchased from everywhere, in exchange for Spanish breastplates?

To the riches of Arabia with which the poem opened, and the kings of Sheba, Persian warriors, and Chinese arrows which it mentions, Horace has now added Spanish armor! The geographic absurdity further deflates the ambitions of Iccius and contrasts with his earlier "wide-ranging" (*undique*, 13) pursuit—of books, not loot. When he exchanges that library for armor, he not only abandons philosophy but also betrays it, revealing himself to be as much a victim of his new career as are his barbarian captives.[58]

If this mixture of pathos and irony, this deflation of futile ambition, is akin to that in the Archytas ode, there is one other, and final, connection between the two poems. The inadequacy of philosophy in the face of reality would seem to be explored with reference to two very different schools, the neo-Pythagoreans in C. 1.28 and the Stoics in C. 1.29. Such a sharp distinction, however, is anachronistic in view not only of the philosophical eclecticism prevailing at the time, but also of the addressees' intellectual predilections. The coupling of the Stoic Panaetius with the Socratics (14), for instance, probably reflects the degree to which contemporary Stoicism was influenced by Platonism.[59] One result of this was a widespread belief in the transmigration of souls, which had been taught by Pythagoras and discredited in the Archytas ode. But it is also attested in the fragments of Panaetius, and it is very interesting that in the only other poem Horace addresses to Iccius, *Epistle* 1.12, the jests concerning that doctrine clearly presuppose Iccius's adherence to it.[60] Thus, far from presenting two different philosophical schools, Horace is probably referring to the same core of belief in C. 1.28 and 29, and this consistency lends further strength to his critique of it as inherently flawed (in C. 1.28) and then as incompletely followed (in C. 1.29).

TEN

It is interesting that the attempt to dissuade Iccius from travel should be followed immediately by a travelogue of sorts, for C. 1.30 is a kletic hymn calling upon Venus to leave her favorite cult sites at Cnidos and Paphos and visit the shrine Glycera has set up for her. This superficial link perhaps serves to soften the otherwise sharp break that occurs here as a new poetic sequence is inaugurated, for C. 1.30, 31, and 32 are all hymns, and they are related to one another and also to C. 1.33 on a number of levels.

The structure of C. 1.30 is quite simple: the first strophe contains the address to Venus, the listing of cult sites, and the request for an epiphany; the second then enumerates the goddess' attendants. Cupid, the Graces, Nymphs, and Youth personified are all expected, but then Mercury occurs prominently as the last word (and line) of the poem. As the Greek Hermes, the god was, of course, associated with Aphrodite in a number of ways: as an incarnation of her persuasiveness, Peitho; as the recipient with her of several joint cults; and, in Orphic genealogy, as her son by Dionysus. These aspects of the god, however, are somewhat obscure and none is sufficient to account for his prominence in the ode. Thus, Nisbet and Hubbard may be correct when they endorse pseudo-Acro's suggestion that Mercury is invoked because he is the god of gain and Glycera is a courtesan![61] Another possibility, however, is that he functions here as a god of poetry. Even if we discount his special tutelary and symbolic significance for Horace, Mercury is traditionally the inventor of the lyre (C. 1.10.6; 21.12; 3.11.1–2). Thus, in addition to any other associations he may have in C. 1.30, his attendance on Venus probably also alludes to the function of song as an accompaniment to lovemaking.

These Mercurial associations of material gain and of poetry are then picked up in the next poem, C. 1.31, a prayer to that other god of poetry, Apollo, in which Horace rejects wealth for a life of simplicity and art. There is a further link, as C. 1.30 alludes to the dedication of a private shrine (*aedem*, 4) and C. 1.31 alludes to the dedication of a public one, the temple of Palatine Apollo (*dedicatum . . . Apollinem*, 1), which was consecrated on 9 October 28 B.C. It has even been suggested that the next ode was composed for the same event.[62] In any case, C. 1.31 and 32 are clearly meant to be read together. They are both hymns and are written in complementary meters, the Alcaic and Sapphic. Their addressees are also related: Apollo in C. 1.31, and the lyre which is characterized as "the glory of Apollo" in C. 1.32 (*decus Phoebi*, 13). Finally, there are numerous motival and verbal parallels, the most prominent of which is the use of a form of the prayer verb *poscere* in the first line of each poem.

C. 1.31 opens with a question: "For what does the poet beseech (*poscit*) the newly enshrined Apollo?" (1). Horace's answer is cast in the form of a *priamel*: to the traditional examples of material wealth which he rejects, Horace opposes his own modest existence, symbolized by his simple diet (15–16), and then goes on to pray for continued enjoyment of this way of life, for a sound mind and body, and for an old age neither physically destitute nor lacking the lyre:

> frui paratis et valido mihi,
> Latoe, dones et precor integra
>   cum mente nec turpem senectam
>   degere nec cithara carentem.   [C. 1.31.17–20]

I pray, Latoe, that you may grant that I enjoy what I have with sound body and mind, and that I pass an old age neither destitute nor lacking the lyre.

That the very next poem opens with *Poscimus*,[63] which is resumptive of the earlier *poscit* (as well as *precor*, C. 1.31.18), and that it addresses the lyre directly (*barbite*, 4; *testudo*, 14) signals that the prayer initiated in C. 1.31 is to be understood as continuing into C. 1.32. The difference is only that Horace's petition, like his addressee, is now more sharply focused: he prays no longer for general well-being, but specifically for his poetry, namely Latin lyric in the tradition of Alcaeus.

Taken together, these two odes constitute another installment in Horace's ongoing exploration of the nature of lyric which began in the Parade Odes and continued in C. 1.16–17 and in C. 1.26. The association of Horace's poetry with modest means in C. 1.31 and with Greek precedents in C. 1.32 is unexceptionable. In the latter ode, the very collocation of Greek and Latin words in the prayer itself—*age dic Latinum, / barbite, carmen* (3–4), "Come, lyre, sing a Latin song"—imitates the status of Horatian lyric as an original creation out of Greek elements.[64] This was perhaps suggested by the occasion of the ode. In his new temple on the Palatine, a statue represented the god as *Apollo Citharoedus*, "Apollo Playing the Lyre," and the architecture developed the theme since it incorporated two libraries, one of Greek and the other of Latin literature.

The temple, however, had not only a literary but also a political significance, for it was built to commemorate Octavian's victories, especially the battle of Actium which was fought near a shrine of Apollo to whose assistance Octavian later attributed his success. The god of poetry, then, also became the patron of the new regime. Thus, in C. 1.31 and 32 Horace explores one other literary issue: not the social function of literature but, rather, the place of the private poet in the public world. These two odes explore the possibility and status of love poems and drinking songs in the new Augustan scheme of things.

The issue is implicit in C. 1.31. Although Horace casts himself in a priestly role as *vates* (2), his prayer is essentially private, for his own lot in life. The apparent tension between the public nature of his assumed role and the personal quality of his petition is resolved by the poem's setting. There is, it is true, an allusion to the dedication of the temple of Palatine Apollo. But the libation of new (*novum*, 2) wine and the prayer for health (*valido mihi*, 17) that accompanies it actually point to the Meditrinalia, a holiday that occurred two days later and that was more suitable to private prayer than the politically charged temple dedication.[65]

This combination of public stance and private expression which is implicit in C. 1.31 is then made explicit in the characterization of Alcaeus in the very next ode, C. 1.32:

> age dic Latinum,
> barbite, carmen,
>
> Lesbio primum modulate civi,
> qui ferox bello tamen inter arma,
> sive iactatam religarat udo
>   litore navim,
>
> Liberum et Musas Veneremque et illi
> semper haerentem puerum canebat
> et Lycum nigris oculis nigroque
>   crine decorum.   [C. 1.32.3–12]

Come sing a Latin song, O lyre, first tuned by the citizen of Lesbos who, though fierce in war, nevertheless amidst the fighting or if he had moored his storm-tossed ship on the wet beach, used to sing of Bacchus and the Muses and Venus and the boy who always clings to her and Lycus, attractive for his dark eyes and dark hair.

Borges's observation that poets create their own precursors is particularly apt here. Emphasizing certain details while omitting others (such as Alcaeus's authorship of *stasiotika*),⁶⁶ Horace has created an image of the Greek poet that can also accommodate his own achievement. Represented as a citizen (*civi*, 5) actively engaged in public life, Alcaeus is also shown singing convivial and erotic themes (9–12). Bacchus, the Muses, Venus, Cupid, and the youthful Lycus—these subjects of Alcaeus's song are almost identical to those of Horace in the ode which opened this sequence, C. 1.30.⁶⁷ This striking similarity underscores that what Horace says about his predecessors in lyric also applies to himself. Thus, for Horace, as for Alcaeus, public and private roles are not incompatible.

Having opened with a prayer to the lyre for a *Latinum . . . carmen*, C. 1.32 now closes by characterizing that desired song more specifically:

> o decus Phoebi et dapibus supremi
> grata testudo Iovis, o laborum
> dulce lenimen mihi cumque salve
>   rite vocanti. [C. 1.32.13–16]

O lyre, glory of Phoebus and pleasing in the banquets of Jove on high, hail, O sweet relief from troubles, whenever I call upon you rightly.

Horace pointedly adheres to the definition of lyric as consolation that had just been announced in C. 1.26. This casts serious doubts on the traditional interpretation of C. 1.32 which reads it as self-referential, as itself the *Latinum . . . carmen* for which it prays. The characterization of lyric as *laborum / dulce lenimen*, "sweet relief from troubles," does not quite fit C. 1.32. It is, however, an apt description of the ode that follows, for C. 1.33 offers comfort to Albius who is grieving over his unrequited love for Glycera.⁶⁸

The echo of the girl's name from the poem that opened this sequence, C. 1.30, perhaps provides a sense of enclosure: having begun with an amatory ode, Horace moved on to larger poetic issues which such personal themes raised, but now returns to the subject of love. The larger poetic issues are not forgotten, however, because the addressee of C. 1.33 is probably the elegist, Albius Tibullus, and his complaints are described in specifically literary terms as *miserabilis / . . . elegos* (2–3). In comforting his friend by pointing out the universal incommensurability of lovers' affections, Horace is criticizing not only Tibullus's inadequate view of love but also his inadequate view of poetry.[69] However congenial Horace found the elegists' allegiance to Alexandrian aesthetics, he repeatedly deprecated their preoccupation with personal affairs to the neglect of everything else, their obsessive self-absorption, and their failure to integrate public and private values in their lives and art. The ode to Tibullus, then, is not just the consolatory poem anticipated in the prayer at the end of C. 1.32. It is also the exemplification of a lyric, as opposed to elegiac, treatment of love: ironic, sophisticated, and put in its proper perspective. In the Parade Odes lyric was defined in relation to satire and epic, and in C. 1.16 and 17 it was set apart from iambic. Having portrayed the lyricist in C. 1.32 as the politically engaged poet of private themes, in C. 1.33 Horace sets lyric apart from elegiac poetry as well, and thereby adds another important dimension to the cumulative definition of his art.

ELEVEN

The next ode, C. 1.34, purports to recount the poet's religious conversion or, more properly, reconversion. Having witnessed the proverbial bolt from the blue (an impossibility according to Epicurean physics),[70] Horace is compelled to return to an earlier belief in the power of god which, by the end of the ode, has become synonymous with the power of Fortuna. Although this differs dramatically in subject and tone from the preceding ode to Tibullus, there are certain continuities. The poet's own personal involvement links the end of the one poem to the beginning of the next. Thus, C. 1.33 closes as Horace consoles Tibullus by recalling his own unhappy love affair with Myrtale, and C. 1.34 opens by recalling the circumstances of his religious awakening. Both poems also describe these personal experiences in terms of sea imagery, for Myrtale is compared to the tempestuous Adriatic, and Horace's conversion is represented as his setting sail on a course he had abandoned. Finally, it is fitting that a poem demonstrating the impermanence of love affairs should be followed by a testimonial to divine power, particularly as it is demonstrated by the changeable goddess, Fortuna. Indeed, Venus's cruel joke in uniting incompatible lovers (*saevo . . . ioco*, C. 1.33.12) is akin to the pleasure Fortuna takes in overturning the high and the lowly (*gaudet*, C. 1.34.16).

These links move the reader from C. 1.33 to 34. A much more significant relationship, however, exists between C. 1.34 and 35, the lofty hymn to Fortuna which prays for Caesar and the Roman state. This is the third time so far in the collection that two poems in the same meter (here the Alcaic) are placed together. As on the two earlier occasions (C. 1.16–17, 26–27), the suspension of metrical *variatio* alerts us to other connections. The most obvious one is topical: the goddess who ends C. 1.34 is the subject of C. 1.35. But there are also formal and attitudinal affinities between the two odes. Thus, in C. 1.34 a hymnic feature such as the repetition of *quo* in lines 9–10 anticipates the hymnic form of C. 1.35. In addition, both odes conceive of Fortuna in basically the same way, as a destabilizing force. The most important connection between the two poems, however, is that in each of them Fortuna is the agent of specifically political change, and as such has a relevance to contemporary politics, which is implied in C. 1.34 and explicit in C. 1.35.

C. 1.34 moves from the thunderbolt of Diespiter which converted Horace, to the poet's confession of belief in a rather vague *deus* (13) and then in *Fortuna* (15):

> valet ima summis
> mutare et insignem attenuat deus
> obscura promens: hinc apicem rapax
>   Fortuna cum stridore acuto
>   sustulit, hic posuisse gaudet.   [C. 1.34.12–16]

The god has the power to exchange the lowly with the lofty and he humbles the noble while bringing forth the obscure. From this man grasping Fortuna with a sharp hissing [of her wings] snatches the crown, on this [other] man she rejoices to place it.

Because the word *apex* can signify an eastern king's diadem or tiara (as at C. 3.21.20, *regum apices*), this scene may glance at the internal dissension in Parthia between Phraates IV and Tiridates who challenged him for the crown.[71] But the *apex* is also the mitred cap worn by Roman priests, and the image of Fortuna here as a winged creature (*rapax*, 14; *cum stridore acuto*, 15) would immediately call to mind a famous incident from Rome's own political past. According to Cicero (*De Leg.* 1.4) and Livy (1.34.8), Tarquinius Priscus was on his way to the city when an eagle descended upon him, snatching his priestly hat (*pilleus*) and then replacing it on his head. Tanaquil, Tarquin's wife, interpreted this as an omen of her husband's future rule. The image, then, conveys a subtle mythological allusion which represents Fortuna as the maker and unmaker of kings.[72]

Although no contemporary application is specified, this concept of Fortuna is at least potentially relevant to Augustus who did, after all, win control from "eastern" monarchs, Cleopatra and Antony, and who, it is implied, might lose it, as they did, should Fortuna fail him. With this in mind, it is easy to read back into the poem a larger political significance.[73] In the *Odes* religious language often conveys political concerns, particularly when Horace assumes a vatic stance (as in, for example, the Roman Odes). Furthermore, the alleged cause of Horace's conversion here, Jove's thunderbolt, very frequently has Augustan associations. In two of its three previous occurrences in Book 1, for example, it has a clear political relevance, standing for the civil wars from which Mercury-Augustus will deliver Rome (C. 1.2.1–4), and symbolizing the power of Jove which validates that of Augustus (C. 1.12.57–60).[74] Thus, when Horace states in C. 1.34 that Jove's thunderbolt compelled him to set sail on a sea journey that he had previously abandoned, he is perhaps confessing not only a religious but also a political conversion. Like that other nautical poem, C. 1.14, C. 1.34 can be read as an expression of renewed interest in Augustus and the policies of his regime.

At this level, C. 1.34 also has a poetic relevance. As noted earlier with respect to C. 1.3 and 14, sea journeys often function as metaphors for poetry. That such a subtext underlies the image here is suggested by possible echoes of Callimachus's *Aetia* prologue.[75] These echoes also demonstrate that there is no inconsistency with Horace's previous literary stance (e.g. in C. 1.6 and elsewhere), for what he is contemplating is not epic but political lyric. The description of this as a course that had been previously abandoned is particularly apt, because there had been no ode about Caesar since C. 1.21, the hymn to Apollo and Diana which prayed for the *princeps* and his foreign expeditions. But now, after the longest interval between political poems in the book, Horace renews his earlier concern for politics and political poetry. The cause is not far to seek. Just two poems earlier, in C. 1.32, he had redefined lyric to accommodate public as well as private themes. In particular, he associated himself with Alcaeus, the citizen actively engaged in politics who also wrote about wine and love. As we have seen, C. 1.33 exemplified the last concern. C. 1.34 now introduces the first in the guise of a religious conversion. But it is only in the next poem, C. 1.35, that Horace's political interests are fully and openly developed.

The ode opens by picking up the preceding poem's characterization of Fortuna:

> O diva, gratum quae regis Antium,
> praesens vel imo tollere de gradu
>   mortale corpus vel superbos
>   vertere funeribus triumphos.   [C. 1.35.1–4]

O goddess, you who rule over pleasant Antium and are able either to raise mortal men from a lowly position or to change proud triumphs into funerals.

Even the phrasing resembles the close of C. 1.34: *praesens* here corresponds to *valet* there (C. 1.34.12), *vertere* corresponds to *mutare* (C. 1.34.13), *imo* recalls *ima* (C. 1.34.12), and *vel ... vel* balances *hinc ... hinc* (C. 1.34.14–16). But whereas the image of the eagle and the *apex* in C. 1.34 only obliquely alluded to Roman politics, the phrase *superbos / ... triumphos* here is more explicit and perhaps even suggests the most illustrious recent *triumphator*, Augustus, whose victory at Actium is characterized only two poems later by the same phrase (in the same meter and position in the strophe: *superbo / ... triumpho*, C. 1.37.31–32).

Political implications continue to underlie the treatment of Fortuna.[76] Thus, in the next two strophes, which enumerate her votaries, Horace quickly passes from the farmer and the sailor to concentrate instead on those nations and rulers whose prayer is primarily political, ending with tyrants who pray to Fortuna to avert civil wars that could topple them from the throne. Here too there are contemporary allusions, in the inclusion of Rome's current enemies, the Dacians and Scythians (9–10), and in the reference to the *imperium* which internal dissension can destroy.

From Fortuna's votaries Horace then turns to the goddess herself (17–24). Necessity, Hope, and Faith attend her like the lictors who accompany Roman magistrates. Similarly, the implements that Necessity carries are not, as is often alleged, tools of the building trade and thus symbols of permanence and inexorability; they are, rather, instruments of war and torture, and thus consistent with the other political overtones in the poem.[77] These continue in the following description of Fortuna abandoning the home of a great man, for the situation and language recall the patron-client relationship around which all Roman society was structured. Finally, the references to the *volgus infidum* (25), *meretrix . . . / periura* (25–26), and the *amici* who scatter once the wine runs out (26–28) call to mind Cleopatra and Antony, the prostitute and drunkard of Augustan propaganda, and the Egyptian troops who deserted them for Augustus in the civil wars.

Thus far, the ode has pursued the idea that was introduced in C. 1.34, portraying Fortuna in political terms, emphasizing her disturbing ability to unseat established power, and hinting at a specific contemporary relevance. This is finally confirmed in the prayer for Caesar with which the ode closes:

> serves iturum Caesarem in ultimos
> orbis Britannos et iuvenum recens
>   examen Eois timendum
>   partibus Oceanoque rubro.
>
> heu heu, cicatricum et sceleris pudet
> fratrumque. quid nos dura refugimus
>   aetas? quid intactum nefasti
>   liquimus? unde manum iuventus
>
> metu deorum continuit? quibus
> pepercit aris? o utinam nova
>   incude diffingas retusum in
>   Massagetas Arabasque ferrum.   [C. 1.35.29–40]

May you guard Caesar who is about to attack the Britons, the farthest people of the world, and his fresh band of youths to be feared in eastern lands and at the Red Sea. Alas, alas, the shame of our scars and the crime of fratricide. From what have we, a harsh age, shrunk? What crime have we left untouched? From what have the youth held back their hands fearing the gods? What altars have they spared? O would that you reforge on a new anvil our blunted sword for use against the Massagetae and the Arabs.

Though the poet's prayer is ostensibly for the safety and success of Caesar's expeditions to Britain and the Red Sea, the indictment of civil war that immediately follows raises other, more domestic, worries. In the other political poems of Book 1, encomium blends with admonition, and foreign exploits are pointedly recommended as an alternative to renewed civil war (C. 1.2.51–52, 12.53–56, 21.13–16). When Horace returns to political poetry here in C. 1.35, he utters the same prayer but with greater urgency, for it is now inspired by an appreciation of Fortuna's role in political life which can render even Caesar's power insecure should civil war be resumed.

To sum up: although Horace had defined lyric initially in terms of *erotica* and *convivia*, he nonetheless included several political poems in Book 1, notably C. 1.2, 12, and 21. In C. 1.32, he finally provided the theoretical basis for this practice by broadening the definition of lyric to accommodate a public dimension. This provides the background for his return to politics and political poetry which is announced in C. 1.34 and accomplished in C. 1.35. The two poems are related by much more than their common topic, Fortuna. In both it is the goddess' fickle nature in political matters that engages the poet's imagination. The relevance of this to contemporary politics is implied in C. 1.34 where the myth underlying the eagle-*apex* image calls to mind the early kings of Rome, and where Jove's thunderbolt perhaps suggests their contemporary successor, Augustus. This becomes explicit, however, only in C. 1.35 where every detail of Fortuna's description has political implications, and where an appreciation of the goddess' changeable nature leads Horace to pray for Augustus.

TWELVE

After these overtly political poems, Book 1 closes with three drinking songs.[78] They do not, however, represent a simple return to the older convivial-erotic definition of lyric, for the festivities in C. 1.36 and 37 arise out of a political context. Thus, C. 1.36 celebrates the return of a certain Numida from Spain. Although no further information is provided about the person or the occasion, the reader would most likely have associated Numida's trip with Augustus's recent expedition to Spain in 27–25 B.C., especially since Lamia figures prominently in this ode and a Lamia (his father?) succeeded Augustus in governing the province in 24 B.C.[79] Thus, the ostensible occasion of C. 1.36 is a foreign expedition of the sort recommended in the preceding hymn to Fortuna. It is interesting that this public occasion is made to accommodate both of the traditional themes of lyric, *erotica* as well as *convivia*, for the first half of the poem recalls the friendship of Lamia and Numida who grew up as boys together, and the second half then shifts to another guest at the party, the lovely Damalis, hinting at her love for Numida.

This is followed by C. 1.37, the great ode celebrating the defeat of Cleopatra. Horace has modeled the opening on a poem of Alcaeus (332 L.–P.), which employs the form of a drinking song to celebrate the overthrow of a tyrant. As in C. 1.36, then, *convivia* arise from a political event. The same three features also characterize the festivities: drink, dance, and thanksgiving offerings to the gods; and both poems even refer to the rites of the Salian priests: their dancing in C. 1.36.12 and their feasting in C. 1.37.2–4. Of course, there is a major difference between the two poems: the former, although occasioned by a public event, remains a private celebration, whereas the Cleopatra ode retains a political significance throughout. It is unnecessary to rehearse the considerable scholarly discussion this poem has attracted in recent years.[80] But it is worth noting its function in the larger context comprised by the other political odes in Book 1. All of these without exception blend encomium with admonition, hinting at the possibility of renewed civil wars and, in effect, advising Caesar to undertake foreign expeditions as a preferable alternative. This rationale received its most explicit statement in C. 1.35. Now, only two poems later, the ambiguity is finally resolved, for Caesar's defeat of Antony and Cleopatra is represented not as a victory in the civil war but as a victory over a foreign enemy. Furthermore, Fortuna rendered proud triumphs uncertain in C. 1.35. But Augustus's proud triumph in C. 1.37 is portrayed as definitive and final. This suits the placement of C. 1.37, which is the last political ode in Book 1 and the next-to-last poem in the volume.

After this impressive flourish, Book 1 ends with a much slighter drinking song in which Horace rejects Persian trappings (*Persicos ... adparatus*, C. 1.38.1) and luxurious garlands, choosing to wear instead a simple myrtle crown and to drink beneath a shady vine. By its apolitical stance, simple form, and rejection of eastern luxury, C. 1.38 does not represent a repudiation or palinode of what has gone before. Rather, it is the same sort of diminuendo ending familiar from many individual odes and serves to bring the book itself to a dying close.[81]

A sense of closure, however, is reinforced by all three drinking songs, for they look back to the very beginning of the book. Indeed, the last three poems link up in reverse order with the first three to constitute a frame for the volume.[82]

C. 1.3 is a *propempticon* for Vergil who is setting out on a journey, whereas C. 1.36 is a *prosphoneticon* which welcomes Numida back from a trip. Similarly, C. 1.2 and 37 are both political poems, the former celebrating Augustus as Rome's savior, the latter celebrating his triumph over Cleopatra. Finally, the picture of Horace drinking beneath the vine in C. 1.38 calls to mind the hedonist in C. 1.1, and both poems have a literary critical content: C. 1.1 as an explicit poetic manifesto, and C. 1.38 as an implicit statement of Callimachean aesthetics.

Fraenkel long ago argued from the poem's prominent placement that C. 1.38 espoused simplicity as an artistic ideal.[83] It is true that the epilogues to the other lyric books all have a poetic dimension: C. 2.20 and 3.30 proclaim Horace's poetic immortality, and C. 4.15 opens with a *recusatio*. But Nisbet and Hubbard argue that placement alone can never convey meaning.[84] Although they are correct, placement can alert us to meanings that are worked out in other ways. Thus, the basic contrast in the poem between grand and simple implies an aesthetic as well as an ethical choice. Elsewhere in the *Odes*, Horace's way of life is often synonymous with his type of poetry. This is made explicit in C. 2.16 where the poet's simple fare (*mensa tenui*, 14) corresponds to his simple Muse (*spiritum Graiae tenuem Camenae*, 38).[85] Here too, in C. 1.38, the luxury Horace rejects conjures up the grand style of poetry. Thus, *adparatus* (a hapax legomenon in Horace) can signify stylistic ornateness (cf. Cic. *De Orat.* 2.355, 3.92), and *Persicos* may be a subtle allusion to the *Aetia* prologue where Callimachus rejected the Persian measure, i.e. the criterion of length rather than quality (fr. 1.17–18 Pf.).[86] Similarly, Horace's garland functions as a metaphor for poetry earlier in the book (C. 1.1.29, 26.7–9), and the simple myrtle of which it is made up suggests not only the *tenuis* style but also the two most characteristic subjects of lyric, *convivia* and *erotica*, since myrtle is the plant both of Venus and of the symposiasts' crown. C. 1.38, then, is not just a summary of Horace's way of life but also an implicit manifesto of Callimachean aesthetics and, as such, a fitting conclusion to the first book of the *Odes*.

THIRTEEN

Book 1 has a very special character. Not only does it contain an irregular number of poems, thirty-eight as opposed to the other books' multiples of ten, but that number is also substantially larger, representing almost half (43%) of the poems in *Odes* 1–3. In addition, although chronology of composition does not appear to be the basis of arrangement for this or any other ancient poetry book, Book 1 contains more poems that can be dated to an early period in Horace's career.[87] In what is perhaps not an unrelated phenomenon, it also contains more experimental odes, like C. 1.14, 15, and 28. Finally, it is the most varied of the three volumes not only in its themes but also in its meters, containing ten out of the twelve that appear in the collection.

It is not surprising, then, that no satisfactory overall plan has emerged from the sequential reading of the book. There are, of course, certain signs of larger order such as the way the book opens with the Parade Odes, divides in the middle with a dedication to Maecenas, and concludes with an epilogue that has literary critical implications. The book is also framed, for the first three odes are balanced in reverse order by the last three. Beyond this, certain types of poems seem to be distributed at intervals. Hymns, for example, tend to occur every ten poems or so, at C. 1.10, 21, and 31. But these intervals are not exact, and, in any case, this pattern ignores C. 1.2 and 35 which are also hymnic. Thus, any idea, such as Salat's,[88] that the book is basically quadripartite is unconvincing because it depends on ignoring or regularizing such exceptions.

In a sense, the first book represents on a smaller and more dramatic scale the heterogeneity of Odes 1–3 as a whole. Here, as in the larger collection, unity is achieved not just by the static frames and balances noted above, but also by the dynamic movement of the book over time. As the roll gradually unfolds, the reader senses both the ad hoc groupings by which contiguous poems are related to one another and the interweaving of several important themes that run throughout the book. Love, for instance, frequently recurs, and Horace links his poems to specific girlfriends. When Glycera occurs at C. 1.30, a kletic hymn, the reader not only remembers her first occurrence at C. 1.19, a parody of a kletic hymn, but is also readied for her next appearance only three positions later, in the ode to Tibullus, C. 1.33. Or again, the Lydia poems, from C. 1.8 to 13 to 25, display a remarkable consistency in their portrayal both of Lydia's character and of the poet's way of relating to her. The political poems are linked in similar fashion. Combining encomia of Caesar with admonitions against renewal of the civil wars, they culminate with C. 1.37 which celebrates Caesar's definitive victory in those civil wars as a triumph over foreign foes.

The most important unifying concern, however, is not amatory but literary. It is appropriate that the first book of Odes attempts to define Horace's version of lyric and to formulate the terms on which his achievement should be judged. The Parade Odes initiate the process, setting Horatian lyric against satire, Greek lyric, and epic, and emphasizing not only his affiliation with these traditions but also his transformation of them. As the book progresses, the process of definition continues, and lyric is set against iambic in C. 1.16–17 and against elegy in C. 1.33. In addition to these comparisons with other genres, Horace also explores the function of lyric, announcing its consoling role in C. 1.26 and its ability to accommodate both public and private concerns in C. 1.32. Finally, the adaptation of Callimachean aesthetics to all these varied traditions and functions is suggested by echoes of the *Aetia* prologue that are distributed among the poems, particularly in C. 1.3, 6, and 38. Book 1, then, finds its most basic unity in its cumulative definition of lyric and of Horace's place in that poetic tradition.

THE SECOND BOOK

ONE

Odes 2 has impressed most readers as far more unified than the other books that surround it. Containing only twenty poems, all but two of them in Alcaics or Sapphics, it is remarkably economical even on a formal level.[1] More interesting, however, are the various signs of thematic coherence. Klingner, for instance, characterized the entire volume as "The Mean."[2] Although this is an exaggeration, moderation does inform not just the Licinius ode (C. 2.10) which enshrines the phrase *aurea mediocritas* (5), but also the injunctions to Dellius (C. 2.3) to keep a level head, and to Valgius (C. 2.9) and Quinctius (C. 2.11) to put an end to their immoderate indulgence of sorrow and anxiety respectively. The same message also underlies several of the odes in the second half of the book in which Horace attacks luxury by advocating not abject poverty but rather a middle ground, a life of simplicity and sufficiency.

Another important theme was identified by Verrall who claimed that "the book might almost be called a dirge," and by Wili who characterized it as "das eigentliche Todesbuch der römischen Lyrik."[3] Again, these are overstatements, though death is surely prominent in many odes. The lugubrious musings of C. 2.14 are addressed to the aptly named Postumus, and on three separate occasions the poet, in almost Propertian fashion, imagines himself as dead: in C. 2.6 where Septimius will weep over his ashes, in C. 2.13 where he will join the other poets in the underworld, and in C. 2.17 where he will keep Maecenas company on that final journey.[4] It may even be relevant that the third poem from the beginning of the book and the third from the end both contain in their penultimate strophes the observation that Orcus and his minions await rich and poor alike (C. 2.3.24, 18.34).

Politics provide another unifying feature of the book. The only political poem, in the strict sense, is C. 2.1, and even that ends with the poet reining in his Muse from further heroics:

> sed ne relictis, Musa procax, iocis
> Ceae retractes munera neniae,
> mecum Dionaeo sub antro
> quaere modos leviore plectro.   [C. 2.1.37–40]

But lest, wanton Muse, you abandon play and attempt again the task of the Cean dirge, seek with me in Venus's cave measures on a lighter lyre.

At the head of Odes 2, this abandonment of "dirge" (neniae) in favor of the "lighter lyre" (leviore plectro) signals a general avoidance of overtly political themes in the rest of the book.[5]

Yet Book 2 does have a political stance that goes beyond the usual safe advocacy of campaigns abroad (C. 2.9, 11, 12) and reforms at home (C. 2.15, 18). Verrall's quaint notion that a special importance attaches to the conspirator Murena[6] fails to convince not only for chronological reasons but also because Murena receives only one ode (C. 2.10).[7] But politics surface elsewhere, particularly in the first half of the book. As in Book 1, the first three poems are addressed to prominent citizens. It is not always appreciated, however, that for this very reason they are haunted by the memory of the recent civil wars. In C. 2.1 Pollio is represented as writing their history, a dangerous task as Horace reminds him (periculosae plenum opus aleae, 6). The civil wars are also implied in C. 2.2 which is addressed to Sallustius, an old republican turned Augustan, and which cites Proculeius as an example of liberality for having divided his fortune among his brothers who had lost theirs in the disturbances (5–8).[8] Finally, the advice given to Dellius in C. 2.3, that he keep a level head (Aequam . . . / . . . mentem, 1–2), most likely has some political resonance, for he changed sides so often that Messalla dubbed him "the acrobat of the civil wars."[9] With this personal background, the three poems become, in a sense, a testimonial to the clemency of the new regime. Pollio was permitted to remain neutral in the contest with Antony and thereafter to withdraw from public affairs into the security of a literary life.[10] And just as Horace sets the odes to Sallustius and Dellius side by side, so too Seneca couples both men together as recipients of Augustus's forgiveness.[11] It is perhaps not fortuitous that the book that opens in this fashion should also contain, after only a brief interval, the famous ode to Pompeius (C. 2.7) which celebrates an amnesty Augustus extended to the old republican faction.[12]

In addition to the mean, death, and politics, there are, of course, other recurrent concerns—in the second half of the book, for instance, patronage and the poet's special calling as an artist.[13] But because no single theme predominates, the reader inevitably looks for ways in which the various themes are interwoven. Any suggested arrangement of poems by which this is accomplished must take into account the two most obvious structural features of the book, which are also common to Books 1 and 3, namely an initial group of odes defined metrically and a midpoint dedication to Maecenas.[14] Thus, Wilhelm Port observed that the first half of the book is both metrically and topically a whole.[15] C. 2.1–11 alternate Alcaics and Sapphics. Then, within the framework constituted by the patron poems, C. 2.1 to Pollio and C. 2.12 to Maecenas, the rest are arranged in pairs according to subject matter, and these pairs in turn are disposed in rings.

```
┌── 1 (Alcaic)              —patron (Pollio)
│ ┌─ 2 (Sapphic) -  3 (Alcaic) —philosophical
│ │ ┌4 (Sapphic) -  5 (Alcaic) —erotic
│ │ │ 6 (Sapphic) -  7 (Alcaic) —friendship
│ │ └8 (Sapphic) -  9 (Alcaic) —erotic
│ └─10 (Sapphic) - 11 (Alcaic) —philosophical
└────12 (Second Asclepiadean)—patron (Maecenas)
```

Walther Ludwig has pursued this scheme further, exploring not only the verbal rivets that bind these poems together, but also the internal structure of the group.[16] The philosophical pairs seem to be ordered in parallel fashion: 2 and 10 urge the related ideals of equanimity and moderation, whereas 3 and 11 advise the addressee to enjoy life while he can. The erotic pairs, on the other hand, appear to be ordered chiastically: 5 and 8 offer complementary figures, Lalage who has no lover and Barine who has too many, whereas 4 and 9 offer amatory advice. Finally, the central poems, 6 and 7, are concerned with friendship—each actually ends with the word "friend" (*amici*, C. 2.6.24; *amico*, C. 2.7.28)—and constitute, in Ludwig's view, the poet's *sphragis* or personal seal. That this elaborate structure is not just decorative but functional is indicated by the poems' very position. Preceded and followed by thirty-eight odes, the group is centrally placed in the entire collection, for it gives expression to Horace's central concerns.

Although this interpretation is persuasive in its broad outlines and particularly in Ludwig's demonstration of the deeper connections that bind pairs of contiguous poems, there are certain weaknesses of detail and methodology. Some of the alleged parallelism and chiasmus seems overly subtle, and C. 2.6 and 7 are not technically a *sphragis*, for such seals include the author's name, which these odes do not, and they usually occur at the ends of poems or groups and not, as here, in the middle of a group.[17]

More problematic, however, is the identification of themes according to which pairs of poems are classified. Collinge, for example, notes that C. 2.11 cannot really be called philosophical "unless we are very broadminded about philosophy and swallow in its name, not only the last three hedonistic stanzas, but even what appears to be a direct injunction *not* to think at all (vv. 11 f.)."[18] In addition, this category tends to obscure the variety of the poems it embraces. Thus, the injunction in C. 2.3 to enjoy life while we can is basically Epicurean, even in its imagery of wine, perfumes, and flowers (13–16), whereas C. 2.2 quite explicitly casts its message in Stoic terms, as the classic paradox that only the wise man is truly rich, happy, and a king (17–24).

Just as the designation "philosophical" is too broad to be critically meaningful, the classification of love poetry is too arbitrary. For instance, the connection usually alleged between C. 2.8 and 9, that Barine is too faithless and Valgius too true, is overly facile.[19] Furthermore, the love interest in the latter is only a pretext for the exploration of another Horatian topic, acquiescence to the passage of time. As such, its true counterpart is not C. 2.8 but C. 2.11, a connection to which Horace calls our attention. Finally, in the analysis of the central pair, C. 2.6 and 7, context is again confused with theme. Although both poems are addressed to friends, this personal relationship is essentially background for the treatment of two very different subjects, as C. 2.6 explores the symbolic overtones of the Italian countryside[20] and (as we shall see) C. 2.7 celebrates political change, especially escape from a republican past.

Because the interpretation of Port and Ludwig is so illuminating, it is reasonable to ask why these inadequacies should exist in it. One facile explanation, that Horace tends to play against our expectations and so resists all attempts to impose an orderly plan upon his poems, perhaps begs the question. It is more relevant that no abstract pattern is likely to account perfectly for every poem unless all the poems were written initially with that pattern in mind. The *Odes*, however, appear for the most part to have been disposed after they were composed.[21] Furthermore, even if such perfection of design were easily achieved, Collinge notes that it would be apt to result in "aesthetic indigestion."[22] There may be, however, one other reason why the traditional interpretation of C. 2.1–12 does not account perfectly for all the material, namely the existence of a second principle of arrangement overlaid upon the first.

TWO

It has gone remarkably unnoticed that a cycle also exists in the center of the book. When C. 2.20 is excluded as an epilogue, C. 2.7–13 occupy the central position. Classified by general theme in a manner perhaps less arbitrary than Ludwig's, these poems describe concentric rings. A detailed analysis of the poems themselves not only clarifies this structure but also reveals its poetic effect or function.

```
┌─── 7 - escape: politics with a hint of poetry (Pompeius)
│ ┌─ 8 - love: faithless (Barine)
│ │ ┌ 9 - loss: living in the past (Valgius)
│ │ │ 10 - Golden Mean (Licinius)
│ │ └ 11 - anxiety: living in the future (Quinctius)
│ └─ 12 - love: faithful (Licymnia)
└─── 13 - escape: poetry with a hint of politics (Horace)
```

C. 2.7 and 13

In C. 2.7 Horace invites Pompeius, a comrade at the battle of Philippi, to celebrate the general amnesty granted by Octavian in 29 B.C. In C. 2.13 Horace recounts his brush with death beneath a falling tree, and vividly imagines the underworld scene into which he would have been received had he been killed. At first sight, the two poems seem to have little in common. Several small features, however, combine to establish a striking connection. Both share the same meter, the Alcaic, which at least alerts us to other possibilities. Then, there is a single verbal echo, the phrase *celerem fugam,* "swift flight," which occurs in both poems: in C. 2.7.9 it refers to the rout of the republican forces by Octavian at Philippi, and in C. 2.13.17 to the proverbially dangerous retreat of the Parthian cavalry. Though the particular context differs in each case, the phrase does point to a major connection between the two poems, one not of specific topic but of general theme: both recount the poet's escapes from death, in the first case from death in battle, in the second from death beneath the falling tree. There is the further similarity that in both the agency of his salvation is divine: Mercury rescues Horace from Philippi and, although his savior from the tree is not named in C. 2.13, the god is elsewhere identified as Faunus (C. 2.17), Bacchus (C. 3.8), or the Muses (C. 3.4). Most decisive, however, in the absence of any other verbal link between the poems is that Horace himself elsewhere couples the two salvations. In the fourth Roman Ode, as proof of the divine favor he enjoys and by virtue of which he presumes to advise Octavian, he lists a series of miraculous escapes from infancy onward. Among these, Philippi and the tree are brought into close association:

> non me Philippis versa acies retro,
>   devota non extinxit arbor   [C. 3.4.26–27]

The rout at Philippi did not destroy me, nor did the accursed tree.

Structure tends to reinforce the thematic resemblance. Each poem is bipartite, with the division in each corresponding to a change of time or tense. The first four strophes of the Pompeius ode, C. 2.7, recollect the past, both remote and recent (1–16). The slow (*morantem,* 6) day of peacetime is contrasted with the swift (*celerem,* 9) rout of battle, the frequent (*saepe,* 6) carousing before the war with the frequent (*saepe,* 1) dangers during it, and the drinking that used to "break up" (*fregi,* 7) happier days with the courage "broken" (*fracta,* 11) at Philippi. The last three strophes then shift from the past to the present and future: Pompeius must now pour the wine and unguents, and Horace will revel like a Bacchant (17–28). The injunction to Pompeius not to spare the casks (19–22) recalls the prewar wine (6), the unguent he is to pour (22–23) picks up the Syrian nard of those earlier days (8), and the garlands of parsley and myrtle (23–25) echo the garlands of peacetime (*coronatus*, 7). The present feast, in other words, is viewed as a reinstitution of past festivities which the war temporarily interrupted. Moreover, drinking in the past was literal, whereas that in the present and future is symbolic—the payment of a debt (*obligatam . . . dapem*, 17), a commitment to forget (*oblivioso . . . Massico*, 21), and a toast to the new order (*redde Iovi*, 17).

C. 2.13 is similarly bipartite, with the division again corresponding to a shift in time. The break, however, occurs now in the exact center of the poem. The first section (1–20) looks back to the past when the accursed tree was planted, and, just as the Pompeius ode divided the past into two categories, remote and recent, so too this poem makes a division between *arai* or execrations on the tree (1–12) and generalizations about the unpredictability of life (13–20). The second half (21–40) then moves, as did the Pompeius ode, to the future, in this case an imaginary reconstruction of the underworld as a sort of Poets' Corner where Horace might have joined his predecessors, Sappho and Alcaeus, who beguile the astonished shades with song.

These similarities between the two poems constitute a frame of reference from which the theme of escape is viewed from two very different points of view. In the Pompeius ode the context is primarily political: Horace's escape from Philippi signals his escape from a republican past. There is also, however, a suggestion of the role poetry played in this. It was, after all, as a poet that Horace was reconciled with the victor at Philippi, and Mercury, Horace's savior here, elsewhere appears as symbolic of that victor (C. 1.2.41–52) or as patron of poetry (C. 1.10.6, 2.17.28–30, 3.11.1–2).[23] In C. 2.13, on the other hand, the context of the escape is primarily poetic, a meditation on the immortality of the poet. Yet politics are at least suggested as a cause of this, both in the topics of Alcaeus's song (*dura navis, / dura fugae mala, dura belli*, "the hardships of sailing, the evil hardships of flight, the hardships of war," 27–28), and in the audience approval that this song wins (*pugnas et exactos tyrannos / densum umeris bibit aure volgus*, "the crowd packed shoulder to shoulder drink in with their ears [the song of] battles and the expulsion of tyrants," 31–32).

Both poems, then, explore the poet's divinely contrived escape from death, and this is reinforced by structural similarities. Yet each is, in a sense, a mirror image of the other: in C. 2.7 the escape is from politics with a hint of the power of poetry, whereas in C. 2.13 the context is poetic with a hint of politics.

C. 2.8 and 12

The coherence of the next pair, C. 2.8 and 12, is more immediately apparent. Both turn on love for a woman, Barine in the former poem and Licymnia in the latter. But the two women are very different. Barine is faithless as Horace demonstrates by reworking traditional amatory conventions.[24] She represents a familiar type to which Pyrrha in C. 1.5 is an almost exact parallel, all deceptive glitter (*enitescis*, C. 2.8.6; cf. *nites*, C. 1.5.13) and as changeable as the wind (*aura*, C. 2.8.24; cf. *aurae / fallacis*, C. 1.5.11–12). Licymnia, on the other hand, is perfectly faithful (*bene mutuis / fidum pectus amoribus*, C. 2.12.15–16), and thus is all the more pointed a contrast with Barine, since there is no exact parallel for such female fidelity in the *Odes*.

In erotic vocabulary, too, the similarity between the poems reveals the great difference between the two women. Only in these two odes does Horace refer to a woman in an amatory context as *domina*. In C. 2.8.19 the word means "mistress" and, as part of the specialized terminology of erotic elegy, it is qualified by the epithet *impiae* (19). In the Licymnia ode, on the other hand, the emphasis on fidelity and propriety (*nec . . . dedecuit*, "nor was it shameful," C. 2.12.17) also suggests the word's original and more domestic range of reference, *domina* not as erotic mistress but as mistress of the household (*domus*).[25]

Finally, Barine's effect on others is predictably negative: the men, young and old, are enslaved (*servitus*, C. 2.8.18) while the women, mothers and wives, fear for their men (21–24). On the other hand, Licymnia's effect is positive, not so much servitude as genial captivation, rendered by the oxymoron *facili saevitia* (C. 2.12.26). Furthermore, her effect is limited: exerted not over the entire population, male and female, young and old, but just over one man, it is a final confirmation of the fidelity that sets her apart from Barine.

It must be admitted that C. 2.12 is not just an erotic poem, for love here is also strategic, serving to reinforce a *recusatio*.[26] Licymnia is celebrated not only as a fitting object for love but also as a fitting subject for love poetry, a preferable alternative to the heroics Horace rejects. It is not surprising, therefore, that she should differ from

Barine because these differences are to some extent a function of the poems' different strategies. And yet, each woman is almost too precisely characterized as the opposite of the other. Barine is faithless, Licymnia faithful; Barine is a mistress, Licymnia almost a wife; Barine has a bad effect on everyone, Licymnia acts positively and on just one man. Insofar as the two women correspond so exactly in their points of disagreement, they suggest a deliberate attempt on Horace's part to represent two extremes of female love.

C. 2.9 and 11

Before comparing the poems in the next ring, it is necessary to consider briefly the context of C. 2.9. Porphyrion characterized it as a *consolatio* to Valgius on the death of Mystes, his *puer delicatus*. Yet the presence of stock erotic themes and the misuse of consolatory *topoi* make it at least as likely, if not more so, that Valgius lost Mystes not to death but to the affections of a rival suitor.[27] The poem becomes, then, an ironic treatment of the elegiac lover. Indeed, both Valgius's sorrow and the enjoined consolation are posed in literary terms. The vocabulary of grief consists of synonyms for elegiac poetry (*flebilibus modis*, 9; *amores*, 11; *mollium* / . . . *querellarum*, 17–18), and Valgius is urged to abandon this in favor of political panegyric (17–24).

This interpretation clarifies the position of the poem in the book. C. 2.8 and 9 now seem to be related not so much by the contrast usually alleged between the "all too faithless Barine and the all too true Valgius,"[28] but rather by the similarity between Barine and Mystes, both unfaithful beloveds. In other respects, however, the two poems differ: C. 2.9 is hortatory, not descriptive, and the emphasis remains on Valgius. Thus, the true pendant to C. 2.9 is not really C. 2.8 but C. 2.11, the ode to Quinctius. Although the poems are structured very differently,[29] the addressees resemble each other and so receive the same sort of advice in remarkably similar language.

Haunted by loss, Valgius lives in the past, whereas Quinctius, tormented by anxiety, lives in the future.[30] Both are familiar types in the *Odes*. Valgius's preoccupation, for example, is shared by Chloe who refuses to take a mate although she is ripe for love (C. 1.23), and by Lydia who refuses to give up lovemaking although her charms have fled (C. 1.25). Similarly, Quinctius's worries about affairs of state are virtually identical to those that trouble Maecenas and that Horace tries to dispel (C. 3.8, 29). C. 2.9 and 11, then, are not unique. But by casting these two poems as pendants to each other, Horace demonstrates that persons like Valgius and Quinctius suffer from what is essentially the same flaw: they deny the present by refusing to acquiesce to the passage of time. The poems explore this similarity by means of shared imagery, evoking nature as a moral metaphor.

In C. 2.9 Valgius's ceaseless mourning is counterpointed to the change of the seasons:

> Non semper imbres nubibus hispidos
> manant in agros aut mare Caspium
>   vexant inaequales procellae
>   usque nec Armeniis in oris,
>
> amice Valgi, stat glacies iners
> mensis per omnis aut Aquilonibus
>   querqueta Gargani laborant
>   et foliis viduantur orni:
>
> tu semper urges flebilibus modis
> Mysten ademptum nec tibi vespero
>   surgente decedunt amores
>   nec rapidum fugiente solem.   [C. 2.9.1–12]

Not always do the rains drop from the clouds on the shaggy fields, nor do the capricious winds disturb the Caspian Sea, nor on the borders of Armenia, O my friend Valgius, does the ice remain frozen for all the months, nor are the oaks of Garganus struggling with the North wind and the ash trees bereft of their leaves. But you always in tearful measures dwell on Mystes who was taken away, and your love songs cease neither when the evening star rises nor when it flees the swift sun.

Personification (e.g. *hispidos*, 1; *viduantur*, 8) alerts the reader to the human implications of the imagery,[31] and these become explicit in the third strophe where a verbal echo contrasts Valgius's constancy in sorrow (*tu semper*, 9) with nature's changeability (*Non semper*, 1). Valgius is out of harmony with nature and must learn to conform.

This is essentially the same advice Quinctius receives in C. 2.11:

> non semper idem floribus est honor
> vernis neque uno luna rubens nitet
> voltu. [C. 2.11.9–11]

Not always does the glory of spring's flowers remain the same,
nor does the blushing moon shine with a single face.

The evocation of nature here is far less extensive than in C. 2.9 and the season now is not winter but spring. Despite these differences, however, both poems share the same imagery—its source in nature, its phraseology (non semper), and its moral point that man should adapt to nature's changes.[32]

Within this general frame of resemblance, however, the two poems reverse or invert each other's stance. Both, for example, make political allusions, C. 2.9 to Scythians (17–24) and C. 2.11 to Scythians and Cantabrians (1–3). In the former, however, the political situation abroad is evoked as an alternative to brooding, whereas in the latter it is the subject and cause of it. Similarly, both poems betray a love interest. But in C. 2.9 love (of Mystes) is what Valgius must forget, whereas in C. 2.11 it is love (of Lyde, 21–24) that will make forgetfulness possible. Although the development of both poems is basically linear, they move in different directions: from love (and love elegy) to politics (and political poetry) in C. 2.9, but from politics to love in C. 2.11. Similarly, C. 2.9 moves forward in time from the past (grief for the lost Mystes) to the present, whereas C. 2.11 moves backward to the present from the future (worries about affairs of state). Both odes explore the theme of man's acquiescence to time and change, as expressed through a common imagery, range of political reference, and love interest. But these features are deployed differently, so that the poems constitute mirror images of each other.

C. 2.10

The final poem to be considered is the central one in the group, C. 2.10. Because its theme, moderation, was familiar from so much ancient philosophy, Horace's achievement here is not conceptual but aesthetic, the discovery of poetic vision within the commonplace. This is communicated at all levels, from the choice of a single word to the development of imagery. The key abstraction on which the poem turns provides a small but useful example of this. Elsewhere in Greek and Latin literature, the mean is usually qualified by another abstraction, "best."[33] Although it is now a cliché, the expression *aurea mediocritas*, "golden mean" (5), represents for its time an innovative attempt to render the abstraction not only concrete but also emotionally compelling.

In this attempt, however, Horace's greatest resource is the very structure of his poem which, as we shall see, is highly relevant to the poem's placement in the book. Virtually enacting his philosophical outlook, the structure does not so much convey as imitate the mean.[34] In the first two strophes the mean is not specified but is left to be supplied by the reader, who locates it between two negative extremes—neither pressing out to sea nor hugging the shore (1–4), neither a wretched hut nor a luxurious palace (5–8). The third strophe varies this procedure, as the images of lofty towers and tall trees represent only one extreme, excess. Yet the comparatives *saepius* (9) and *graviore* (10) pick up the first word of the poem, *rectius*, and imply an alternative sort of behavior: "The huge pine is shaken by the winds *more often* (sc. than smaller pines), and lofty towers fall with a *heavier* crash (sc. than shorter towers)" (9–11). This is not the opposite extreme, deficiency, but the mean itself.

Still unexpressed, the mean has so far either been located between two extremes or implied as the unstated alternative to one extreme. In the second half of the poem, it is at last explicitly defined, but again in terms of antithetical extremes. The fourth strophe specifies what constitutes moderation in different circumstances of life: hope in adversity and caution in prosperity, *sperat infestis, metuit secundis* (13). The changeability of fortune is then illustrated from myth: Jupiter brings bad weather but he also takes it away (15–17); Apollo shoots the bow but he also arouses the Muse with his lyre (18–20).

The final strophe, then, returns to the specific recommendations of the fourth. Not only the idea but also its phrasing and the parallelism of its expression are echoed as Horace advises courage when things go badly and wise restraint when they go well. This echo of the fourth strophe in the last rounds off the second half of the poem. But the entire ode is, in fact, in ring composition, for the final strophe also echoes the first. Excess is conveyed by the word *nimium*, identically placed in each strophe (3, 23); there is the same stylistic parallelism; and the imagery in each is drawn from the same nautical sphere.

This detailed reading of C. 2.10 bears on the poem's position in the book in at least three ways. First, placement reinforces theme: Horace urges the middle course of life in what is roughly the middle of the book.[35] Second, placement echoes the poem's structure. The internal framing of the poem by its first and last strophes is reiterated by an external frame, the three pairs of poems that surround it in rings. Finally, that these pairs consist of antithetical poems, mirror images of each other, reflects not just the ring composition of C. 2.10 but also, and more importantly, its inner dialectic, the series of antitheses through which the Golden Mean is imaginatively apprehended.

The disposition of the odes often approximates the composition of a single ode. The grouping of poems in concentric rings, for example, is analogous to the internal structure of a large class of odes that are individually constructed in terms of ring composition. In the disposition of C. 2.7–13, however, as in the arrangement of C. 2.1–12, Horace operates on a much larger scale than usual, because the framing extends beyond a triad to a long series of poems. In the central group, however, Horace goes even further in exploring the possibilities inherent in the technique, for the relationship between internal and external structure here is not just analogical but functional, serving to reinforce the meaning of a specific ode.

THREE

After considering the central group of poems, C. 2.7–13, it is now appropriate to return to the basic bipartite division of the book and to explore the arrangement of its second half. In the analysis of the first half, C. 2.12 had been assigned a prominent role in balancing C. 2.1: both address literary patrons and both refer to the writing of history. But the Asclepiadean meter of C. 2.12 is a sharp break from the alternation of Alcaics and Sapphics and sets the poem apart from the eleven odes that precede it. Also, its correspondence with C. 2.1 is less important in providing closure for the first half than it is in establishing a new beginning. Indeed, C. 2.12 is an apt introduction to the second half of the book at all levels. First, it rededicates the volume to Maecenas, the initial ode having been for Pollio. Then, by virtue of this dedication, it also serves as an overture to one of the major concerns of this section, patronage. Finally, a number of these poems explore the poet's vocation, and to this theme also C. 2.12 is a fitting introduction since, as a *recusatio*, it necessarily treats not only Horace's relationship with his patron but also his perception of himself as an artist.[36]

From C. 2.12 onward the book is unified in a number of ways. It contains roughly the same number of lines (284) as the first half (288), and, although the alternation of meters has given way, there is great metrical consistency. This may be symbolized by C. 2.13: just as Alcaeus takes precedence over Sappho in the underworld, so too the Alcaic meter is now predominant. There is only one Sapphic (C. 2.16) in the second half of the book and, aside from the two metrically anomalous odes (C. 2.12 in the Second Asclepiadean and C. 2.18 in the Hipponactean), all the others are in Alcaics.[37]

For the poems that follow C. 2.12, it is also possible to construct some sort of abstract pattern of arrangement comparable to that discovered for the first half. Perret, for example, succeeds not only in reproducing the effect of the earlier framing but also in locating friendship again in a roughly central position.[38]

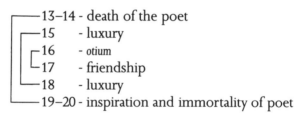

Alternatively, neat rings can be sacrificed to achieve consistent pairing of poems.

```
 ┌──13–14 - death
 │ ┌─15–16 - luxury vs. simplicity
 │ └─17–18 - patronage and friendship
 └──19–20 - denial of death: inspiration and immortality
```

These patterns, however, are less convincingly demonstrated for the second half of Book 2 than they are for the first half. There is, after all, no metrical reinforcement such as the alternation of Alcaics and Sapphics earlier provided. In addition, this section is topically less varied and more personal than the first half, so that each poem relates closely to several others and thus resists being assigned to a single partner in some neat design. In fact, the second half of Book 2 achieves a remarkably tight unity not only through its metrical consistency and the patterning of its poems but also, and more importantly, through the integration of two major and related themes: luxury and death, on the one hand, and poetry and immortality, on the other.[39]

C. 2.13 and 14

"The interaction of 2.13 and 2.14 is possibly more significant than that of any other pair in a Book which is, as is well known, almost entirely arranged according to paired poems."[40] Anderson's observation is just and is supported by specific connections such as the shared Alcaic meter and the topics of death and afterlife, piety, and the inevitability of fate. Anderson, however, pursues placement only insofar as it contributes to the rehabilitation of C. 2.14: "Carm. 2.13 is a recognized masterpiece ... [Horace] would hardly have juxtaposed to it an effort that he knew was juvenile, knew that his audience would feel inartistic. He planned that two good poems should interact."[41] Their interaction, however, can be explored further, since these two poems, taken together, constitute a thematic program for the remainder of Book 2.

Within the very categories of resemblance noted above, the poems nonetheless differ on details. It is precisely in these differences, rather than in their similarities, that the interaction between them takes place. Although death provides the occasion for each poem, it is presented as a specific threat to Horace in C. 2.13, but as a general necessity facing all men in C. 2.14. Similarly, though piety figures in each ode, in C. 2.13 it is a mark of distinction in the underworld (*sedes ... discretas piorum*, 23), whereas in C. 2.14 it is futile in the struggle against death in the world above (*nec pietas moram / rugis et instanti senectae / adferet indomitaeque morti*, 2-4). Again, whereas both poems describe the underworld in terms of its mythical inhabitants, C. 2.13 accommodates a cross section of that population, the *densum ... volgus* (32) comprised of gods, poets, and monsters, as well as the archetypal sinners, Prometheus, Tantalus, and Orion; in C. 2.14, on the other hand, only sinners—Tityos, the Danaids, and Sisyphus—are mentioned. Furthermore, whereas the latter is condemned to long labor (*damnatus . . . longi / . . . laboris*, 19–20), the sinners included in the more varied list in C. 2.13 are beguiled of their labor by song (*dulci laborem decipitur sono*, 38).

These differences in detail make it clear that, despite its basic resemblance to C. 2.13, C. 2.14 is a much gloomier poem. Indeed, the very first line sets the tone with its addressee's ostentatiously significant name, Postumus, to which attention is called by the rare gemination: *Eheu fugaces, Postume, Postume, / labuntur anni* (1–2). This somber tone is maintained to the end:

> absumet heres Caecuba dignior
> servata centum clavibus et mero
> tinguet pavimentum superbo,
>   pontificum potiore cenis.   [C. 2.14.25–28]

A worthier heir will consume the Caecuban that had been guarded with a hundred keys, and he will stain the pavement with magnificent wine, more potent than that served at the banquets of the priests.

This concluding vignette of the heir who squanders the wine he inherits surely points to a moral, that the wine (here, as so often in Horace, a symbol for life itself)[42] should not have been locked away but enjoyed by its original owner while he was still alive. Such a moral, however, is only implied. In Horace's other relevant odes, the idea of death's inevitability usually functions structurally as the basis for a direct or explicit injunction to enjoy life while one can. There is no such injunction in C. 2.14, which is unrelievedly pessimistic throughout.

This tonal disparity between C. 2.13 and 14 arises from what appears to be a basic thematic difference, that the former is about escape from death, whereas the latter is about death's inevitability. The inconsistency at this level, however, is only apparent. The escape in C. 2.13 is achieved through the immortality conferred by poetry upon its practitioners, and then C. 2.14 makes the complementary point that all other means such as piety (2–11) and material station (11–12) are useless to deter or even delay the coming of death. Both poems complement each other; taken together they not only introduce but also integrate the two basic themes of the second half of

Book 2. Luxury and death are associated, and set against them is the immortality of art by which death itself is overcome.

C. 2.15

Luxury is the theme of the next ode, C. 2.15. Its relevance to what has preceded is underscored by the meter, for C. 2.13, 14, and 15 constitute an Alcaic trio, a very rare phenomenon in a collection in which departures from metrical *variatio* always occur for a reason. The connection is particularly obvious between C. 2.15 and its immediate predecessor with which, coincidentally, it is run together in some manuscripts. The powerful image of extravagance with which C. 2.14 closes—the prodigal heir wasting wine on the pavement—makes an elegant transition to C. 2.15, which is all about extravagance. Perhaps even the mention of paving facilitates the transition, because the particular extravagance attacked in C. 2.15 is architectural.

The construction of large palaces, especially around Baiae and the Bay of Naples (cf. *Lucrino* / . . . *lacu*, 3–4), served as a familiar *topos* for the Roman moral writers who viewed it as an indicator of moral decline.[43] So firmly does Horace place himself in this tradition, that the poem has been read as a proem to the pessimistic sixth Roman Ode.[44] Like Sallust and Cicero, Horace assumes a primitivistic stance:

> non ita Romuli
> praescriptum et intonsi Catonis
> auspiciis veterumque norma:
>
> privatus illis census erat brevis,
> commune magnum; nulla decempedis
> metata privatis opacam
> porticus excipiebat arcton
>
> nec fortuitum spernere caespitem
> leges sinebant, oppida publico
> sumptu iubentes et deorum
> templa novo decorare saxo.   [C. 2.15.10–20]

Not so was it prescribed by the auspices of Romulus and unshorn Cato and by the custom of our ancestors. Private wealth among those people was slight, the public wealth great. No privately owned portico measuring tens of feet had a shady northern exposure, nor did laws allow people to spurn the handy turf, bidding them at public expense to decorate their towns and the temples of the gods with newly quarried stone.

In addition to the contrast between then and now, the passage also is structured around the antithesis of public (*commune*, 14; *publico*, 18) and private (*privatus*, 13; *privatis*, 15). Lavish expenditure is justified if it is in the public interest, but not if it supports the luxurious private existence these villas represent. Horace's attack, in other words, is not directed at opulence in general but only at its manifestations in private life. This too is consistent with the traditional stance of the Roman moralists as expressed, for instance, by Cicero: *odit populus Romanus privatam luxuriam, publicam magnificentiam diliget* (Pro Murena 76; cf. Pro Flacco 28).

Yet, Horace goes significantly beyond this tradition. The frequency with which the image of the villa recurs in the *Odes* attests to the poet's special fascination with it.[45] In C. 2.18, as we shall soon see, the pile that displaces the fish and juts out into the sea represents a transgression of natural boundaries and, thus, a denial of mortality. Here in C. 2.15 the pile infringes on the land, and the first half of the poem explores some, if not yet all, of the implications of such architecture:

> Iam pauca aratro iugera regiae
> moles relinquent, undique latius
>   extenta visentur Lucrino
>   stagna lacu platanusque caelebs
>
> evincet ulmos. tum violaria et
> myrtus et omnis copia narium
>   spargent olivetis odorem
>   fertilibus domino priori,
>
> tum spissa ramis laurea fervidos
> excludet ictus.   [C. 2.15.1–10]

Soon royal heaps will leave few acres to the plough; on all sides ponds will be seen stretching wider than the Lucrine Lake, and the solitary plane tree will oust the elms. Then violet beds and myrtle and the entire supply of perfumes will scatter their aroma

in olive groves that had been fertile for their previous owner.
Then dense laurel bushes will shut out the hot rays.

The villa is characterized as an assault upon nature (*evincet*, 5; *excludet*, 10). It threatens the land's fertility, leaving few acres to the plough (1–2). The elm, useful because vines could be trained on it, is ousted by the plane, a purely ornamental shade tree to which nothing can be grafted but the significant epithet, *caelebs* (4). Perfumes—even the artificially strained expression, *omnis copia narium* (6), imitates the artificiality of the plantings—spread their aroma among the olive groves, once but no longer fertile (*fertilibus domino priori*, 8). Finally, the thick laurel excludes the sun's warm (and generative?) rays (9–10). If the architecture is not yet explicitly associated with death, it is certainly depicted as imposing sterility upon a once creative landscape.

C. 2.16

The next poem, C. 2.16, pursues further the unsatisfactory nature of wealth, but differs only in the angle from which it views the subject. In C. 2.15 extravagance was perceived as an unnatural threat to the external landscape. In C. 2.16 wealth is now recognized as an internal threat as well, not just the desecration of the land but also a menace to human *otium* or peace of mind.

Although the poem's structure has been debated, its general movement is clear.[46] It opens with the picture of a sailor and a soldier, each of whom prays for *otium* in the restricted sense specific to his own case (1–8). That the sailor prays for calm weather and the soldier for peace, however, is ironic, for by their very choice of occupation both men not only betray their mistaken conviction that wealth can buy *otium*, but also effectively ensure that they will never achieve it, for the pursuit of wealth will lead them into dangers on the high seas or on the battlefield.

The third strophe then expands the definition of *otium* beyond these specific cases to something more general, peace of mind: wealth is insufficient to banish Cares which, personified as Harpies, circle around the paneled ceilings of the rich (9–12). But against this striking image Horace juxtaposes an alternative way of life:

> vivitur parvo bene, cui paternum
> splendet in mensa tenui salinum

> nec levis somnos timor aut cupido
>   sordidus aufert.   [C. 2.16.13–16]

He lives well on a little, who has an ancestral salt cellar shining on his modest table and whose gentle sleep is not stolen by fear and sordid greed.

The man who lives well has a table that is modest (*mensa tenui*, 14)—like Horace's poetic spirit later in the poem (*spiritum ... tenuem*, 38).[47] Although there is a sharp contrast with the wealth of the preceding strophe, Horace's point is not to advocate abject poverty, as we see from the presence of the (presumably silver) salt cellar on the humble board. *Parvo* (13) is the operative word, not "nothing" but "a little." Furthermore, *paternum* (13) adds another qualification: unlike gems, gold, purple, and the other products of the active quest for riches which destroys *otium*, the salt cellar is inherited. The life Horace advocates, then, is not just simple but unacquisitive. Thus, while the wealthy man is attended by *miseros tumultus / mentis et curas* (10–11), the man who follows Horace's advice enjoys a sleep undisturbed by *timor aut cupido* (15).

After further extensive reflection, Horace closes the poem with a pair of strophes, again contrasting wealth and simplicity:

> te greges centum Siculaeque circum
> mugiunt vaccae, tibi tollit hinnitum
> apta quadrigis equa, te bis Afro
>   murice tinctae
>
> vestiunt lanae: mihi parva rura et
> spiritum Graiae tenuem Camenae
> Parca non mendax dedit et malignum
>   spernere volgus.   [C. 2.16.33–40]

Around you a hundred herds of Sicilian cattle are mooing, for you the horse fitted for chariots neighs, you are clothed in wool dyed twice with African purple. To me, Fate that does not lie has given a small bit of the countryside and the slender spirit of the Greek Muse and a disdain for the envious crowd.

The echoes of the third and fourth strophes are striking: *vivitur parvo bene* there (13) is picked up here in *parva rura* (37); *mensa tenui* (14), as noted above, is now transformed into *spiritum ... tenuem* (38); and perhaps even the point of *paternum* (13) is resumed in Horace's reference to the Greek Muse as the Camena (38), which calls to mind the native Italian inheritance of song.

There are, however, two great differences between the earlier contrast of wealth and simplicity in the third and fourth strophes and the contrast as it is expressed now at the end of the poem. First, the juxtaposition of the two life-styles was generalized in the earlier part of the poem, whereas at the end it is personal, a contrast between the addressee, Grosphus, and the poet Horace. And second, the contrast in the third and fourth strophes was cast in purely material terms, a luxurious house with paneled ceilings as opposed to a frugal board, whereas in the last two strophes the contrast is between Grosphus's material wealth and Horace's inner resources, particularly poetry. The concluding passage, for instance, obeys the Callimachean injunction to feed one's sheep to be as fat as possible but to keep one's Muse slender (*Aetia* fr. 1.23–24 Pf.). Grosphus's wealth is expressed here in terms of three domestic animals—cattle, horses, and sheep—whereas Horace's riches are the small (*parva*) countryside, the slender (*tenuem*) Muse, and, like Callimachus in his *Hymn to Apollo* (H. 2.105–13), a scorn for envious detractors.

C. 2.17

The next poem, C. 2.17, resumes a theme that had been suspended since C. 2.12, the poet's relationship with his patron. Indeed, the last four poems in the book chart a gradual movement away from Maecenas. This will be demonstrated in greater detail in Chapter Seven, where the Maecenas odes of all three books will be studied as a group. For now it is necessary to view C. 2.17 only from the limited perspective of its role in the thematic structure of the second half of Book 2.

At this level, C. 2.17 follows naturally from its predecessor in the volume. Maecenas's fears of death provide the pretext for the poem, a request by the patron for Horace to reassure him. Maecenas is, then, a specific instance of those *curae* which wealth engenders and which banish *otium* in C. 2.16. In addition, though C. 2.17 ostensibly identifies the interests of the two men, particularly by means of the elaborate astrological apparatus which makes the point that the stars of both are linked (*consentit astrum*, 22),[48] it ends, as did C. 2.16, by contrasting Horace with his addressee:

> te Iovis inpio
> tutela Saturno refulgens
>   eripuit volucrisque Fati
>
> tardavit alas, cum populus frequens
> laetum theatris ter crepuit sonum:
>   me truncus inlapsus cerebro
>   sustulerat, nisi Faunus ictum
>
> dextra levasset, Mercurialium
> custos virorum. reddere victimas
>   aedemque votivam memento:
>   nos humilem feriemus agnam.   [C. 2.17.22–32]

The protection of Jove, outshining impious Saturn, rescued you and slowed the swift wings of Fate, when the crowded people thrice applauded gladly in the theater. The trunk of a tree falling on my head would have carried me off, if Faunus, the guardian of Mercurial men, had not deflected the blow with his right hand. Remember to offer victims and a votive shrine; we shall sacrifice a humble lamb.

The very incidents that demonstrate their common lot—the coincidence of Maecenas's recovery from illness and Horace's own escape from death beneath a falling tree—also serve, on another level, to set the two men apart. Their tutelary deities, for example, differ dramatically, with Jupiter looking after Maecenas but a minor woodland god protecting Horace. Again, Maecenas's recovery is greeted with applause, whereas there is no large audience for Horace's narrow escape. Finally, each man's thanksgiving offering varies with his lot in life, as Maecenas is invited to build a votive shrine, while Horace can only afford to sacrifice a humble lamb. Though honorific at one level, these contrasts are also very self-assertive.[49] As we have seen elsewhere, Horace's escapes usually betoken his status as a poet, and the details here—particularly the role of Faunus as the protector of Mercurial men, i.e. poets—are suggestive of poetry.[50] Indeed, Horace's sacrifice of a humble lamb (humilem ... agnam, 32) has Callimachean implications, for it conflates the Aetia prologue's fat sacrifice and slender (λεπταλέην) Muse and represents perhaps the poem itself. As he proclaims his intimacy with Maecenas, Horace also hints that the accord between them is not complete, for Horace is a poet and Maecenas is not.

This, we recall, was also the point behind the contrast between Horace and Grosphus at the end of C. 2.16. That poem also made Callimachean allusions and also ascribed Horace's talent to the Fates (37–40; cf. C. 2.17.13–16). The greatest similarity, though, is that the material disparity between the poet and his wealthy addressee is transformed in each case into a spiritual and artistic disparity, and, hence, into an emblem of the poet's superiority.

C. 2.18

The next poem, C. 2.18, makes the same point but it also serves as a summary statement of what has gone before, recapitulating and further developing ideas not just from the previous ode but from C. 2.15 and 16 as well. The poem opens as the poet disclaims any interest in palaces with ivory, gilded panels, Hymettian marble, African pillars, and clients trailing purple robes (1–8). The evocation of wealth in largely architectural terms recalls C. 2.15. Just as the *Attali / . . . regiam* (5–6) here looks back to the *regiae / moles* of C. 2.15.1–2, so the strategy behind the imagery is the same: in both poems lavish domestic architecture is an emblem of moral decline. In C. 2.15 the construction of the villa was represented as an act of violence imposing sterility upon a once fertile landscape. Now in C. 2.18 the connection between this sort of luxury and death is finally made explicit:

> truditur dies die
>   novaeque pergunt interire lunae:
>
> tu secanda marmora
>   locas sub ipsum funus et sepulcri
> inmemor struis domos
>   marisque Bais obstrepentis urges
>
> submovere litora,
>   parum locuples continente ripa:
> quid quod usque proximos
>   revellis agri terminos et ultra
>
> limites clientium
>   salis avarus? pellitur paternos
> in sinu ferens deos
>   et uxor et vir sordidosque natos.   [C. 2.18.15–28]

Day is driven out by day, and new moons hasten to wane. You contract for the cutting of marble at the brink of the grave, and forgetful of the tomb you construct a mansion, and not rich enough since the coast confines you, you hasten to build on to the shore of the roaring sea at Baiae. What of the fact that you take down the posts that mark your farm property and greedily leap over the boundaries of your clients? Both husband and wife are expelled, carrying in their embrace their paternal gods and grubby children.

The villa encroaches not only on the land, as it did in C. 2.15, but also on the lives of the pathetically dispossessed tenant farmers (23–28) and indeed on the sea itself (19–22). By thus denying social and natural boundaries, the rich man seeks to deny his own mortality: *sub ipsum funus et sepulcri / inmemor* (18–19). But as such a denial is not possible, the poem concludes with the powerful image of death awaiting all, rich and poor alike (29–40).

Although the link with C. 2.15 is very close, ideas from C. 2.16 and 17 are also picked up and developed in C. 2.18, particularly in the poet's prayer:

> at fides et ingeni
>   benigna vena est pauperemque dives
> me petit: nihil supra
>   deos lacesso nec potentem amicum
>
> largiora flagito,
>   satis beatus unicis Sabinis.   [C. 2.18.9–14]

But I have loyalty and a rich vein of talent, and the wealthy man seeks me out, a poor man. I ask nothing more of the gods nor do I request more of my powerful friend, since I am sufficiently blessed in my singular Sabine farm.

When Horace, content with what he already has, asks the gods for nothing more (11–12), his prayer stands in pointed contrast to that of the sailor and soldier in C. 2.16 who ask the gods for peace of mind (*Otium divos rogat*, 1), but whose active pursuit of wealth assures that they will never achieve it. Similarly, the contrast between rich and poor calls to mind the endings of C. 2.16 and 17. Now, however, it structures an entire poem, as lines 1–16 express Horace's rejection of riches and lines 17–fin. express the opposite way of life.⁵¹ The most important connection, however, is in the function of the contrast. In C. 2.16 and 17 Horace implied that his material poverty was a token of his spiritual and artistic riches. Now, in C. 2.18, these riches are explicitly set forth, as the poet, rejecting ivory, gold, and marble quarried from afar, vaunts his own fidelity and, maintaining the mining image, his rich vein of talent.⁵²

C. 2.19 and 20

It is this talent with which the last two poems are exclusively concerned. The shared Alcaic meter suggests that they should be read as a pair. In both odes Horace attempts to convey the quality of his experience as a poet in "mythic" terms, by representing it as a vision of Bacchus in C. 2.19 and as a metamorphosis into a bird in C. 2.20. Both myths are well chosen because they express certain fundamental aspects of Horace's creativity, not only its excitement but also its intense isolation and its transforming power.

Thus, C. 2.19 opens as Bacchus, accompanied by his Nymphs and Satyrs, inspires Horace on solitary crags. The loneliness of the landscape is reminiscent of other references to Bacchic experience in the Odes. In the very first poem, these same Nymphs and Satyrs set Horace apart from the people (secernunt populo, C. 1.1.32); the Roman Odes open with a disavowal of the crowd (Odi profanum volgus et arceo, C. 3.1.1); and in the other major Bacchus ode, C. 3.25, where the subject is political panegyric and not poetry in general, the poet still finds himself alone in groves, grottoes, and caves. The creative experience, in other words, is ultimately a private one. It is also transforming, for the god reveals his twofold nature to everyone with whom he comes into contact. On the one hand he causes Horace to tremble and rejoice (5–8), but he also calms the monster Cerberus in the striking image of art's power with which the ode closes (29–32).

An even more dramatic transformation is recorded in C. 2.20, as Horace is changed into a bird by virtue of his status as a poet. Again, the experience is an intensely private one, for when Horace soars aloft on his sturdy wings he abandons not only the cities of men (urbis relinquam, 5) but also the patron to whom the poem is addressed.⁵³ On one level, the relationship between C. 2.19 and 20 is one of cause and effect: Bacchus inspires Horace in C. 2.19, with the result that

Horace becomes immortal in C. 2.20. On another level, C. 2.19 may also supply the dramatic motivation for C. 2.20, as the poet's rather bizarre metamorphosis is perhaps to be understood as a hallucination induced by Bacchus. There may also be a literary connection between the two odes. Although the motif of the poet's winged flight is fairly common in Greek literature, it is particularly reminiscent of the dithyramb. Because that genre was closely associated with Bacchus, perhaps the placement of C. 2.20 after a Bacchus ode is intended to suggest that literary affiliation.[54]

Irony is the characteristic Horatian posture. One of its most common manifestations, the dying close, is familiar from individual odes such as C. 2.1 and 3.3, at the ends of which the poet checks himself. The same technique can also close an entire book. As we have seen, C. 1.38, a poem of small scale, simple theme, and expressed distaste for eastern opulence, follows upon a large and complex ode about an eastern queen. Similarly, at the end of Book 2, the comic elements in the picture of the poet as a bird qualify the high seriousness not only of that picture but also of the preceding Bacchus ode.[55] This does not mean that Horace in any way repudiates the special status that the images of inspiration and immortality convey upon him, but only that he bears his special status lightly—on wings.

FOUR

After this sequential reading, it is possible to formulate more precisely the unity of the second half of Book 2. The first half varied considerably in subject matter, and thus was held together by more schematic means, the patterning of its poems. For the second half, too, there is evidence of framing and of pairing at least at the beginning (C. 2.13–14) and the end (C. 2.19–20). But this should not obscure the fact that these poems are also a linear sequence. When read in their published order, they display a complex and tight thematic coherence, associating luxury and death and counterpointing to them poetry and immortality.

In C. 2.13 Horace, as a poet, is saved from death. Against this, neither the hoarding of Postumus in C. 2.14 nor the extravagance of the rich builder in C. 2.15 is effective. Indeed, as is clear from C. 2.16, wealth is not only ineffectual but is itself often the problem, for it banishes *otium*. Maecenas's anxiety about death in C. 2.17 is a perfect case in point, and reassurance comes from the poet whose vastly inferior material resources nonetheless stand for spiritual and artistic riches. It comes as no surprise, then, that Horace is sought out by the rich man in C. 2.18 but rejects the latter's offers of further enrichment. It becomes increasingly clear from the movement of these poems that wealth attempts to deny mortality but cannot, in the end, defy it. But against wealth stands talent, and against death abides art. This had already been suggested by the underworld vision in C. 2.13 and by the motif of the poet's salvation in that poem and in C. 2.17. It at last becomes explicit in the book's final two poems, which convey the fact of art's permanence through the fiction of the inspired poet's immortality.

THE THIRD BOOK
PUBLIC AND PRIVATE VOICES

ONE

Book 3 has the same basic structure as the other two books that precede it, opening with a metrical and thematic grouping, the so-called "Roman Odes" (C. 3.1–6), breaking in the middle with a dedication to Maecenas (C. 3.16), and concluding with a literary epilogue (C. 3.30). The book stands apart from the others, however, because of the special character of the Roman Odes as a major political statement. Explicitly political poems were missing from Book 2, the prologue of which restrained Horace's Muse from continued heroics (C. 2.1.37–40). Book 3, then, represents something of a return, not just to the political interests introduced in Book 1, but also to a problem raised by those interests, namely the tension between the public and private voices of the poet.

This tension, of course, has long been recognized as a defining characteristic of much Augustan literature. The *Aeneid*, for instance, has proved particularly hospitable to the sort of analysis that is represented by Adam Parry's influential essay elucidating "the continual opposition of a personal voice which comes to us as if it were Virgil's own to the public voice of Roman success."[1] Discordant notes have also been discovered in the elegists—in Tibullus who never mentions Augustus, in Propertius who actually vaunts his lack of sympathy with the new regime, and in Ovid whose celebrated wit often seems directed at the imperial family. Although individual interpretations, particularly of Tibullus and Ovid, are not always convincing,[2] the approach is at least invited by the very nature of these texts—by the characteristically un-Roman postures and values of erotic elegy, and by the complex symbolic interrelationship between myth and history that everywhere underlies the *Aeneid*.

It is not surprising, then, that the public and private voices should also be heard in Horace's *Odes*, where tensions have been detected at several levels. In the political poems, for instance, it is noted that the encomium of Augustus is rarely uncomplicated, that it is often tentative and shades into advice. Or again, with regard to the structural *variatio* of the collection as a whole, the way in which these political poems are set directly beside intensely personal ones has led some to conclude that "Horace's *Odes* teach us at least two different and incompatible lessons: energy and retirement, morality and voluptuousness, Roman toughness and Greek frivolity, religious conservatism and carefree Epicureanism, social and ethical reform and mild, unabashed hedonism. Aesthetically they are very nearly perfect; but morally, through them as through the work of every other poet of Horace's time, there runs a fundamental, an insoluble conflict."[3]

A conflict, yes; insoluble, no; and there precisely lies the difference between Horace and "every other poet of his time." That Horace was aware of a potential tension in his work is evident from Book 1 where, as we have seen, the invocation of classical Greek precedents represents an attempt to mitigate any such inconcinnity. Thus, in C. 1.32 Alcaeus is claimed as a model precisely because of his ability to harmonize the two voices. Though this is meant to apply to the *Odes*, the closest Horace has come to this ideal is in C. 1.31, the poem that precedes his tribute to Alcaeus. Against the background of the dedication of Apollo's temple, Horace celebrates the Meditrinalia, assuming a vatic role only to utter a personal prayer. This combination of public stance and private setting is an ingenious ploy. But the two concerns are not yet fully integrated within a larger conceptual framework.[4]

It is in Book 3, when the poet returns to politics, that a satisfactory integration is finally achieved, specifically in the poems that comprise the first half of the book. These include not only Horace's most definitive public statement, the Roman Odes, but also a strong private statement in the poems that immediately follow (C. 3.7–15). It can be shown, first, that the very structure of the Roman Odes enacts a tension, but that this is hardly the ambiguity toward Augustus which some other poets display; second, that the nine subsequent odes are themselves a unit and are meant to be read in close conjunction with the Roman Odes; and, finally, that the two groups do not contradict each other but are complementary and interdependent. Thus, Horace achieves here what none of the other Augustans quite manages or intends, the harmonizing of the public and the private voice in his art.

TWO

The title, "Roman Odes," was coined a century ago by Plüss,[5] but their connection was perceived much earlier: by Porphyrion who mistakenly read them as one poem, and perhaps also by Horace's contemporaries, Vergil and Propertius, who seem to have borrowed from them not only topics but also details of arrangement.[6] We have from antiquity, then, external evidence for the Roman Odes as a cycle.

Such testimony, however, which would be welcome in other cases, is not necessary here for the internal evidence of the poems themselves is overwhelming.[7] All six are in the Alcaic meter and are prefaced by two other Alcaic odes, on poetic inspiration (C. 2.19) and immortality (C. 2.20).[8] So extensive a metrical run is unparalleled and alerts the reader to more significant correspondences of subject and style.[9] Some of these are suggested in the first strophe of C. 3.1, which serves as an introduction to the entire cycle:

> Odi profanum volgus et arceo.
> favete linguis: carmina non prius
>   audita Musarum sacerdos
>   virginibus puerisque canto.   [C. 3.1.1–4]

I hate the uninitiated crowd and ward them off. Keep reverent silence. As priest of the Muses I sing to virgins and youths songs not heard before.

The poems offer something new (non prius audita). In them Horace assumes a lofty vatic stance (Musarum sacerdos) which the religious language reinforces (favete linguis). All are composed in an elevated, often Pindaric, style. None, moreover, is addressed to an individual but to the nation's youth (virginibus puerisque canto; cf. Romane, C. 3.6.2), and this depersonalization extends beyond the address to the subject matter which is consistently public.

Other poems, of course, display these features. Thus, not only C. 2.19 and 20 but also C. 2.15 and C. 3.25 have been read as proems to the cycle, and C. 3.24 has been dubbed the seventh Roman Ode.¹⁰ Such poems, however, are isolated in the collection, and it is only in the Roman Odes themselves that these features bind together a large group. But is the list of these features enumerated above exhaustive, or do the poems form a whole on any deeper level? The latter view is supported by the many attempts to discover schematic or thematic regularity in the group.

THREE

One possible schematic or architectural approach disposes the poems in concentric rings.¹¹

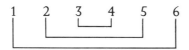

The cycle is framed by consideration of the ills that plague Roman society, wealth and ambition in C. 3.1 and sexual license in C. 3.6. The themes are closely related and both occur elsewhere in a single ode, C. 3.24, just as both derive from a single source, Vergil's second *Georgic* (G. 458–542).¹² Numerology reinforces the frame as both C. 3.1 and 6 are 48 lines long. The next ring is constituted by C. 3.2 and 5, which both treat aspects of military virtue and make specific reference to the nagging Parthian problem. Finally, C. 3.3 and 4 occupy the central position, for they are the longest and most Pindaric and treat the complementary themes of justice and mercy.

According to an alternative scheme, the group is divided into two halves.¹³

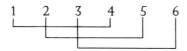

Even if the distinction between C. 3.1–3 as generally Roman and C. 3.4–6 as specifically Augustan is too fine, there are other signs of a break. The first three odes are set apart by their frame of Callimachean motifs—the first ode's initial disdain for the common crowd (cf. Call. *Epigr.* 28 = *AP* 12.43 = 1041 ff. G.-P.) and the third's concluding *recusatio*—and C. 3.4 does seem to mark a new beginning with its invocation of the Muse. The two halves are then related to each other in an interlocking design. As in the preceding scheme, C. 3.2 and 5 are again a pair. But now C. 3.1 and 4 are also coupled. Both begin with the Muses (*Musarum sacerdos*, C. 3.1.3; *regina . . . Calliope*, C. 3.4.2); in both the tone is religious, as Horace assumes a priestly role in the first and Bacchic frenzy in the fourth (*amabilis / insania*, 5–6); both are also characterized by a rare personal element, the poet's own lack of ambition in C. 3.1.41–48, his series of narrow escapes in C. 3.4.9–28, and his Sabine farm in both odes (C. 3.1.47–48; 4.21–22); and, finally, the Gigantomachy is mentioned in C. 3.1.5–8 only to be fully developed in C. 3.4.42–64. The last pair, C. 3.3 and 6, then, are the climax of their respective halves, a positive statement in the third ode where Juno gives her benediction to Rome's foundation, and a very negative one in the sixth where Horace presents a despairing vision of Rome's present and future state.

A third and final arrangement is also possible.[14]

```
1   —   2   3   4   5   6
        |   |_____|   |
        |_____|
```

The first ode is detached as an introduction, and the others are ordered in frames. The formulation of these as ethical (C. 3.2, 6), mythical (C. 3.3, 5), and mystical (C. 3.4) may be an oversimplification, but the general plan is interesting. C. 3.2 and 6 are moral exhortations and allude to Augustan reforms, the *collegia iuvenum* in the former and the temple restoration and marriage laws in the latter. Next, C. 3.3 and 5 seem calculated to frame the fourth ode. Both illuminate the present by the perspectives of history (the Trojan War in C. 3.3 and the Punic Wars in C. 3.5); both turn on massive speeches, by Juno and Regulus respectively; in both the name of Augustus occurs (C. 3.3.11, 5.3) which is elsewhere absent from the cycle; and both have a dying close, the poet's restraint of his Muse at C. 3.3.69–72 and the moving comparison of Regulus to a vacationing lawyer at C. 3.5.53–56. The fourth ode, then, stands majestic in the middle of the group, owing to the intrinsic grandeur of its subject, the Gigantomachy, the loftiness of its treatment, and the special relevance of the myth to Augustan politics. Its central position is reinforced not only by the frame of C. 3.3 and 5 but also by numerology:

it is the longest of all of Horace's odes (80 lines) and is surrounded by two equal masses (C. 3.2–3 = 5–6 = 104 lines).

To sum up: at least three different arrangements are possible for the Roman Odes. Each finds a parallel in Vergil's *Bucolics* where concentric framing, interlocking patterns, and division into halves have been discerned.[15] There is, however, another and more sobering parallel with that collection: no one scheme is entirely satisfactory, and any attempt to harmonize them by allowing for their overlapping or simultaneous operation[16] raises serious doubts, for the credibility of schematic arrangements seems generally to be in inverse proportion to their number and complexity.

FOUR

An alternative to the schematic approach is represented by attempts to discover a thematic coherence in the Roman Odes. Mommsen connected the cycle to the Senate's bestowal of the name "Augustus" on Octavian three days after he "restored the republic" in 27 B.C.[17] The odes would then celebrate the name, which occurs twice (C. 3.3.11, 5.3), and the ideas and programs associated with it. Domaszewski pointed to another closely related event, the Senate's dedication in the Julian Curia of a golden shield upon which were inscribed the four virtues of Augustus: *fortitudo, iustitia, clementia,* and *pietas*.[18] In alluding to this, the Roman Odes would resemble Vergil's *ekphrasis* on the armor of Aeneas (*Aen.* 8.628–70).

Though interesting, these interpretations are reductionist insofar as each argues for a single theme, whereas the person of Augustus and the concept of virtue are both crucial to the cycle. Moreover, there is no agreement among scholars on which odes should be paired with which virtues, or even which virtues are represented.[19] A further objection to these approaches is their excessive historicity. The odes make no reference to the events surrounding the restoration of the republic, and they are sparing with historical allusions in general.[20] This clearly signals that Horace's intent was to raise the relevance of the cycle above any specific events that might have occasioned its composition or collection, and to explore his themes on a larger and more timeless scale, that afforded by myth and tradition.

Ultimately, though, the search for a single thematic unity fails for the same reason that the search for a single schematic unity failed. Both approaches describe the cycle in static terms, as a pattern of rings or as variations on a single theme. But Horace can be shown to have conceived of the Roman Odes as a dynamic sequence. This has only occasionally been noted. Trenkel, for instance, speaks of the cycle's "gradually increasing earnestness," Collinge of its "increasing pessimism," and Silk of the movement "from hope through anxiety and despair."[21] These interpretations, however, focus only on the negative side and even that is not demonstrated fully. The sequential development of the Roman Odes can best be appreciated in two ways: first, by considering the gliding transitions that move the reader along from one poem to the next; and second, by tracing the movement of certain ideas which these surface transitions reinforce. At the heart of the cycle there is no static pattern or conceptual abstraction but rather a dynamic tension. This is perhaps best described in terms of an analogy with the drama:[22] against the backdrop of virtue, Horace plays out the melancholic counterpoint between the godhead of Augustus and the godlessness of his people.

FIVE

First, gliding transitions link contiguous poems. C. 3.1, which advocates a life of simplicity (*quod satis est*, 25), ends as Horace refuses to exchange his Sabine farm for burdensome wealth, *divitias operosiores* (48). Those final words are in pointed contrast with the first words of the next ode, *Angustam . . . pauperiem*. The first ode rejects wealth only to be followed by the second which embraces poverty.[23] A similar transition connects the end of this poem with the beginning of the third. The virtue extolled in C. 3.2 involves courage and loyalty, and at the end the man who does not possess these qualities is banished from Horace's company and stalked by Punishment: *raro antecedentem scelestum / deseruit pede Poena claudo* (31–32). This concluding image of the criminal is then contrasted with the very first words of C. 3.3, *Iustum et tenacem propositi virum*. Again, the verbal contrast underscores a shared moral vision.

The transitions thus far are so smooth that one can at least sympathize with mistaken views like Porphyrion's, that the Roman Odes are a single poem, or Howald's, that Horace practiced "block composition."²⁴ Collinge has more accurately likened them to the internal construction of a Greek sentence, "as if each ode ended with a μέν clause, to be picked up with an antithetical δέ clause in the next."²⁵ It is often assumed, however, that this mode of linkage ends with the third ode. It is certainly true, as was noted earlier, that the cycle seems to divide into two halves at this point. Yet even this sharpest of breaks is not absolute since the end of C. 3.3 is very closely related to the beginning of C. 3.4. In both places Horace calls upon his Muse (*Musa*, C. 3.3.70; *Calliope*, C. 3.4.2); in both the mode is imperative (*desine*, C. 3.3.70; *Descende*, C. 3.4.1); and in both she is associated with lofty poetry (*sermones deorum*, C. 3.3.71; *longum . . . melos*, C. 3.4.2). Of course, in the third ode the Muse is restrained from this sort of verse on Alexandrian aesthetic grounds (*magna modis tenuare parvis*, 72), whereas in C. 3.4 she is invoked as its patron. But there is no real contradiction; by setting the two addresses side by side, Horace signals that Callimachean principles have been reformed at Rome to accommodate public verse.²⁶

Between this and the next ode, C. 3.5, there are again surface connections. Both contain in their opening lines a reference to heaven, from which Calliope is urged to descend (*Descende caelo*, C. 3.4.1) and where Jupiter reigns (*Caelo tonantem*, C. 3.5.1). The divine locale may also provide another link to C. 3.3: although that poem does not actually contain the word *caelum*, it is all about getting to heaven, and Juno's speech on the subject is delivered there (*consiliantibus / . . . divis*, 17–18). More apparent, however, is that technique of linkage by which the end of one poem leads smoothly into the beginning of the next. Thus, C. 3.4 ends with the account of Jupiter's victory over the Giants in which Horace emphasizes the god's singular rule (*regit unus*, 48) and his power as manifested by the thunderbolt (*fulmine*, 44). The first sentence of C. 3.5 then follows like the conclusion to be drawn from the preceding Gigantomachy narrative, for it is a statement of faith in these same attributes of Jupiter: *Caelo tonantem credidimus Iovem / regnare*. Even the main verb, both in its meaning and its plural number, is suggestive, as if the knowledge of Jove's power expressed in the fourth ode (*scimus*, 42) has led to the religious conviction and assent of the fifth: *credidimus*. Finally, between this and the last Roman Ode there is a similar connection. C. 3.5 ends with the harangue of

Regulus, an ancestral Roman, who goes off to face death for his country. C. 3.6 then opens with ancestors, but of a very different and degenerate sort: *Delicta maiorum* (1).

These transitions are very smooth, connecting the end of one poem with the beginning of the next, and binding not just the first three odes but the entire cycle. Their literary function is to create a sense of coherence that is no less real for being on the surface, and that invites further investigation of the poems' deeper unity. This is accomplished by the dramatic interplay, noted earlier, between the godhead of Augustus and the godlessness of his people.

SIX

The godhead of Augustus is not a subject unique to the Roman Odes, but is treated by Horace in individual poems elsewhere in the collection. Ruler cult had been a familiar feature of eastern monarchy, and Hellenistic kings since Alexander had been celebrated as gods during their lifetime. Though such practices were foreign to the republican tradition, their acceptance at Rome was perhaps facilitated by certain established notions such as the sacrosanctity of certain offices, the guise of the *triumphator* as Jupiter, the belief in a personal *numen* and *genius*, the cult of *Roma* as a goddess, and the general tendency to worship abstractions and personifications. More important than these Roman elements, however, was the intellectual rationale for divinization which two Greek concepts were able to supply. The first was the theory of kingship according to which the ruler was the earthly counterpart and favorite of Zeus. The second was the concept of posthumous deification, that a man could qualify for heaven by performing great deeds while on earth.[27]

Consistent with both notions is Horace's strategy of deifying Augustus by associating him with other gods and demigods whose divinity was less problematic. The precise method of association varies greatly. In C. 1.2 it is a virtual identification with Mercury, who is incarnate in the person of Caesar. Usually, though, the association is less dramatic. In C. 3.14 it is an explicit comparison with Hercules, and in C. 1.12 an implied analogy with Jupiter and other gods. The Roman Odes, then, are not unique in deifying Augustus. But their treatment of the theme is novel in three other respects: first, they develop it not individually as unrelated poems but collectively; second, their movement is progressive; and third, the direction of this progress is toward a more explicit and unqualified statement of divinity than occurs elsewhere in Horace's first lyric collection.

The deification of the emperor is accomplished in three stages. The first two Roman Odes supply the intellectual bases for it. The Greek theory of kingship underlies the beginning of C. 3.1:

> regum timendorum in proprios greges,
> reges in ipsos imperium est Iovis,
>   clari Giganteo triumpho,
>   cuncta supercilio moventis.   [C. 3.1.5–8]

Terrifying kings have power over their own flocks. Over the kings themselves power belongs to Jove, famed for his triumph over the Giants and moving all things by raising his eyebrow.

The argument, that kings have authority over their subjects but that kings are subject to Jove, is only potentially relevant to Augustus (though the allusion to Jupiter's victory over the Giants points the analogy in that direction for it anticipates the allegorical Gigantomachy of the fourth ode). Expressed here only in very general terms, the theory is applied not to any one ruler in particular but to all as a class.[28] The same is true of the second ode's range of reference. After describing correct military conduct (1–16), Horace personifies such virtus opening the heavens for those who deserve not to die:

> virtus recludens inmeritis mori
> caelum negata temptat iter via
>   coetusque volgaris et udam
>   spernit humum fugiente pinna.   [C. 3.2.21–24]

Courage opening heaven to those who deserve not to die attempts a path denied to others and spurns the common crowd and the wet earth on soaring wings.

Just as the first Roman Ode drew on Greek political theory, this now espouses a theology of posthumous deification, and again Augustus is not mentioned.

It is in the next pair of poems that these concepts are applied, in reverse order, to the *princeps*, and in both he is associated with other deities. In C. 3.3 his virtue will enroll him among the demigods:[29]

> hac arte Pollux et vagus Hercules
> enisus arcis attigit igneas,
>   quos inter Augustus recumbens
>   purpureo bibet ore nectar,
>
> hac te merentem, Bacche pater, tuae
> vexere tigres indocili iugum
>   collo trahentes, hac Quirinus
>   Martis equis Acheronta fugit.   [C. 3.3.9–16]

This was how Pollux and wandering Hercules struggled and attained the fiery citadel. Among them Augustus will recline and drink nectar with his purple lips. In this way you, father Bacchus, deserved to be borne by your tigers, untaught to wear the yoke upon their necks. In this way Quirinus escaped Acheron on the horses of Mars.

This image of posthumous deification is then followed by C. 3.4, which is a full-scale allegory associating Jupiter's victory over the Giants with Octavian's victory over his enemies (42–80). The allegorical intent of the narrative is assured by the first half of the poem (1–42). Ostensibly a bit of autobiography, this section discreetly modulates from Horace, whom the Muses protect, to Augustus, whom they re-create with their *lene consilium* (37–42). The following Gigantomachy narrative, then, is itself an example of such counsel, for in it the leader can recognize his past achievements as well as the challenge of peace that confronts him in the future. And the allegory is signaled in other unmistakable ways as well. The Gigantomachy theme, for example, had traditionally admitted a political significance in art. Furthermore, Horace portrays the contest as one between the forces of restraint (*vim temperatam*, 66) and those of violence and disorder (*vis consili expers*, 65), and these were precisely the terms of the Augustan propaganda to which Vergil gave ultimate expression in the contrast between *pietas* and *furor* which shapes the *Aeneid*. Finally, even specific details support the allegory—not just the presence of *amatorem* . . . / *Pirithoum* (79–80) and other sexual criminals which may hint at Antony, the *amator* of Cleopatra, but most importantly the prominent role assigned to Apollo (60–64), by whose temple the battle of Actium was fought and won by Augustus who consequently claimed the god as his patron.[30]

The fifth Roman Ode then stands as the final statement of this development:

> Caelo tonantem credidimus Iovem
> regnare: praesens divus habebitur
>   Augustus adiectis Britannis
>   imperio gravibusque Persis.   [C. 3.5.1–4]

We have believed that Jove rules for he thunders in heaven. Augustus will be considered a god on earth when the Britons and the dangerous Parthians have been added to the empire.

Here, at last, both philosophies are united. The opening acclamation of faith in Jupiter recalls the kingship theory that was introduced in C. 3.1 and developed in the allegory of C. 3.4. Posthumous deification, which was introduced in C. 3.2 and applied to Augustus in C. 3.3, is now signaled by the future tense of the verb, *habebitur*. The ode, though, is not just a summary of what has gone before; it also represents the climax of the sequence, for Augustus is no longer deified by association with other gods but is acknowledged as a god-to-be, *praesens divus*, in his own right.

It has, understandably, disturbed some modern readers that a poet so constitutionally disposed to irony would fully assent to the proposition that a man was or could ever become a god. It may be offered in Horace's defense that the two ideas that supply intellectual respectability to the process (or at least mitigate its strangeness) are themselves qualifications of it. Posthumous deification, which accepts divinity but relegates it to the future, implies that immortality is a contingency rather than a certainty: Augustus is not now a god but will become one only after death, and only if he directs his vengeance at foreign rather than domestic foes.[31] Although it is true that posthumous deification may set some sort of limit to Augustus's godhead, this is a limit imposed not independently by the poet but by Augustus himself who discouraged people, at least in the west, from worshipping him as a god during his lifetime. The poet's use of kingship theory has also been read as a qualification, for it insists on the primacy of Jupiter to whom even Caesar is subject. Yet Jove's special jurisdiction over kings does not so much qualify as validate their rule on earth which is, by implication, analogous to his rule in heaven. To say that Augustus is second to Jupiter is to say that he is second to no one else.

In deifying Augustus, then, Horace is consistent with the party line. His originality in the Roman Odes consists not in subverting this, but in setting against it a pessimistic picture of the people Augustus rules.

SEVEN

The first Roman Ode is not just a personal advocacy of the simple life but also an attack on the majority of men who do not follow it. The rich landowner, the candidate for public office, the anxious millionaire, the impious contractor—after such a catalog, the opening words, *Odi profanum volgus*, take on added meaning. Their ritual and literary associations have long been recognized, the profane crowd suggesting both the uninitiated at the mysteries and the common audience Callimachus scorned. But in the context of the ode, the *volgus* also has a political relevance, for it suggests the irreligious mob whose single-minded pursuit of wealth is the poet's target.[32]

These sentiments recur in the next ode, expressed this time by the personified *virtus*:

> virtus repulsae nescia sordidae
> intaminatis fulget honoribus
>   nec sumit aut ponit securis
>   arbitrio popularis aurae:
>
> virtus recludens inmeritis mori
> caelum negata temptat iter via
>   coetusque volgaris et udam
>   spernit humum fugiente pinna.   [C. 3.2.17–24]

Courage, ignorant of sordid defeat, shines with untarnished honor, nor does it take up or put down the axes at the whim of the fickle people. Courage opening heaven to those who deserve not to die attempts a path denied to others and spurns the common crowd and the wet earth on soaring wings.

That *virtus* distrusts the *arbitrio popularis aurae* (20) echoes one category of ambition described and rejected in the first poem, the competition for public office (C. 3.1.10–14). Similarly, when *virtus* spurns the crowd, *coetus . . . volgaris* (23), the verbal echo to Horace's own earlier rejection of the *profanum volgus* is striking. Finally, the connection between Horace's stance in C. 3.1 and that of *Virtus* in C. 3.2 is made even more explicit toward the end of the latter poem when he rejects the man who has divulged—*volgarit* (27)—the Eleusinian mysteries. The passage repeats not only the personal voice of the first ode's opening, but also its language and religious cast. In the first two Roman Odes, then, there is a clear lack of confidence in the *volgus*. Expressed as Horace's own personal conviction in the first ode, it is validated by the agreement of the personified *virtus* in the second.[33]

The next three odes take a somewhat less direct approach. Although they make no explicit statement about the Roman *volgus*, all share an emphasis on the degeneration of a people. In C. 3.3 Juno's acquiescence to the foundation of Rome is bestowed on condition that Troy not be rebuilt but perish utterly, people and leader together, *cum populo et duce fraudulento* (24). Similarly, in C. 3.4 the account of the Gigantomachy focuses heavily on Jupiter's monstrous enemies perceived as a crowd, *inpios / Titanas immanemque turbam* (42–43). Finally, in C. 3.5 Regulus chides his fellow countrymen for their cowardice and complacency in dealing with the prisoners of war taken by Carthage.

In all three poems there is the further similarity that this negative characterization of a group suggests the Romans of Horace's own day. In C. 3.3 Troy represents the recent past flawed by civil wars.[34] In C. 3.4 the Titans and Giants who menace Jupiter stand allegorically for Octavian's enemies. Finally, in C. 3.5 the Romans whom Regulus harangues call to mind their Augustan descendants who also have an interest in foreign exploits (implied in the references to Britain and Parthia, 3–4) and who also lost prisoners of war (at Carrhae).

In these three odes, then, the negative treatment accorded a mass of people extends by implication to the Romans of Horace's own day. In this way, the poems are consistent with the outlook of the first two Roman Odes. There is, however, one other feature that sets them apart: the focus does not remain on the degenerate crowd, but each poem ends on an optimistic note. In C. 3.3 Juno's benediction far outweighs her anger which has been assuaged, in C. 3.4 Jupiter triumphs over his enemies, and in C. 3.5 our imagination is captured by the quiet courage of Regulus. It is in the sixth and final Roman Ode that Horace returns explicitly and single-mindedly to the theme of the Roman people's degeneracy. No longer concealed under the guise of Trojans, Giants, or third-century Romans, his target here is the same as in C. 3.1 and 2, the Romans of his own day, and the negative component in their treatment is now uppermost, the pessimism unrelieved.

This special quality of C. 3.6 can best be appreciated by comparing it with C. 3.5 with which it shares not only the surface transitions noted earlier, but also deeper structural correspondences. Both poems open with a generalization, progress to historical events, and finally move back in time to contrast the contemporary situation with an idealized past. At this point, however, the resemblance breaks down. The dying close of C. 3.5, where Regulus going off to certain death is likened to a lawyer quitting the city for the country (49–56), initially seems to be paralleled by the evocative description in C. 3.6 of the Sabine youths returning home from the fields at the close of day (41–44). But the latter poem does not end on that note, for Horace adds one last pessimistic strophe which returns to the decadent present and looks ahead to an even bleaker future:

> damnosa quid non inminuit dies?
> aetas parentum peior avis tulit
>   nos nequiores, mox daturos
>   progeniem vitiosiorem.   [C. 3.6.45–48]

What does decaying time not diminish? The age of our parents, worse than our grandfathers, bore us who are worse still and soon to produce offspring [even] more flawed.

The remarkably close structural correspondence between C. 3.5 and 6 emphasizes the ending of the latter, which stands outside this correspondence. The poem that opened with the sins of the Romans' ancestors, *Delicta maiorum*, closes with those of their even more corrupt descendants, *progeniem vitiosiorem*. The movement of this ode is, in a sense, a miniature of the progress of the entire cycle. The first ode, we recall, had looked toward the future, addressing the youth and exempting them from the general indictment: *virginibus puerisque canto* (4). By the end of the cycle, even that hope is shattered.

Like the positive treatment of Augustus, this pessimism about the Roman people may also reflect some of the emperor's own feelings, at least in the early years of the principate when he experienced frustration in his attempts to pass moral legislation.[35] Yet, for Horace to conceive of his most ambitious political poetry in terms of such a tension between Augustus and his people, and to end it on so pessimistic a note, goes far beyond any party line. It has been noted that "the Roman Odes end, as the *Aeneid* will, on a note of failure."[36] This is certainly true. But the quality of failure is different in each. At the problematic end of Vergil's poem it is Aeneas who, in a very real sense, fails; in Horace the problem lies not with Augustus but with his unregenerate people. Though a tension between public and private values animates both the Roman Odes and the *Aeneid*, Vergil locates this tension in the individual, whereas Horace locates it in society at large.[37] And there is one other difference: the *Aeneid* ends abruptly at this point, whereas the Roman Odes are followed by poems that attempt to resolve this tension.

EIGHT

Quid fles, Asterie? With that single question, which opens C. 3.7, the Roman Odes have come to an end. Alcaics yield to an Asclepiadean meter, and earnest nationalism to an ironic treatment of love. Yet there is consistency at another level. After the Roman Odes' concluding indictment of contemporary sexual degeneracy (C. 3.6.17–32), C. 3.7 may be seen to supply a specific case: Asterie, who is worried that her husband may be unfaithful while away on a business trip, is reassured by Horace but also warned to keep her own hands off her handsome neighbor, Enipeus! Breaking formally with the Roman Odes, but continuing to affirm their moral standards, C. 3.7 not only terminates that cycle but also creates a transition from it to the odes that immediately follow.

The cohesion of these subsequent poems and their relevance to the Roman Odes has occasionally been noted. Klingner, for example, identified a run of five love poems (C. 3.7, 9–12), interrupted only by an invitation (C. 3.8), and Mutschler has observed not only that C. 3.7 functions as an overture or prelude to the other four, but also that the placement of these amatory poems next to the Roman Odes effectively combines public and private modes of existence.[38] Though illuminating, these observations are incomplete. The intrusion of C. 3.8 into an otherwise erotic sequence is not satisfactorily explained. Also, whereas C. 3.7 is identified as a prelude to C. 3.9–12, the nearby ode with which it has most in common, C. 3.15, is overlooked. Finally, it has not been demonstrated exactly how public and private experiences are integrated apart from noting the collocation of the poems representing each. The problem, quite simply, is that criticism has stopped at C. 3.12 and has not also taken into account the three other odes, C. 3.13–15, which complete the first half of the book. And yet, it is this larger group that constitutes the fullest "answer" to the Roman Odes.

That C. 3.7–15 are the more natural and less arbitrarily defined unit seems assured by C. 3.16 which, like the midpoint poems of the other two books (C. 1.20, 2.12), rededicates its volume to Maecenas and so marks a new beginning.[39] In addition to being clearly demarcated in this fashion, C. 3.7–15 are further unified by their structure. There is, first of all, evidence of careful patterning in the disposition of the poems.

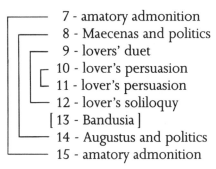

As noted earlier, the first and last poems are admonitions to a married woman by a detached observer of her love life. The poems of the next ring are addressed to patron and *princeps* respectively and downplay political worries. The third pair then returns to love, although the speakers are no longer detached as the form of each ode is mimetic, a duet and a soliloquy.[40] Finally, the central poems are both attempts by a man to persuade a woman, in the former by means of a *paraclausithyron* and in the latter by a cautionary tale about the Danaids. It will be noted that C. 3.13, the rustic dedication to the spring Bandusia, does not fit neatly into this scheme. But excessive neatness in such matters is rare among poets—it is apt to result in what Collinge has dubbed "aesthetic indigestion"—and suspect among critics.[41] Thus, while the pattern cannot be pressed too far, there certainly seems to be some attempt at concentric disposition.

As in the Roman Odes, however, there is also a dynamic principle of arrangement operative in the gliding transitions that link contiguous poems. Though no close verbal or motival connection is immediately apparent between C. 3.7 and 8, transitions among the other poems create a sense of movement and balance the effect of the static concentric framing. Thus, the final words of C. 3.8, *linque severa*, not only sum up Horace's advice to the anxious Maecenas, but also lead up to the next ode, C. 3.9, which surely abandons *severa* (i.e. political worries) to enact instead a lovers' quarrel and reconciliation. The concluding image of that duet, whereby Horace's volatile temperament is compared to the stormy Adriatic (21–24), then forges a link with the next ode which opens with a picture of a literal storm endured by the poet on Lyce's threshold (C. 3.10.1–8). Between that *paraclausithyron* and the following poem there is a general affinity of situations, as both represent a man's attempt to win a reluctant woman's affection. C. 3.11 does this by telling of the Danaids and ending with a speech by the one faithful Danaid who risked punishment by her father (*pater*, 45) for sparing her wretched (*misero*, 46) husband.

It is interesting that the next poem, C. 3.12, opens with the word *miserarum* (albeit with a different range of reference) and attributes unhappiness in love to a male relative, not a father now but an uncle (*patruae*, 2). At the end Neobule consoles herself by daydreaming about her boyfriend at his sports, the last of which is a wild boar hunt (11–12). This small detail provides a neat transition to C. 3.13 in which an animal is again killed, this time not a boar but a kid, and not in sport but in ritual. This private sacrifice, in turn, leads to C. 3.14, which opens with a call to a large public sacrifice that greeted Augustus on his return from Spain (4–8). Later in the poem, however, Horace shifts to preparations for his own private party: Neaera is to be invited, but, if her doorkeeper objects, the poet will not persist because he is no longer a hot-tempered youth (21–28). This concluding mention of old age leads smoothly into the last poem in the sequence, C. 3.15, which advises Chloris to do, in a sense, what Horace has just done, namely not to persist in love now that old age renders such interests indecorous.

So far we have seen that C. 3.7–15 are naturally defined by the demarcating function of C. 3.16, and are further unified by structural means, the patterned disposition of the poems into rings and the gliding transitions that simultaneously bind one poem to the next. The most striking bond uniting these odes, however, is that certain formal and thematic features which they share seem calculated to set them apart from the Roman Odes on that cycle's own terms. For example, the Alcaic meter which had persisted for so long is now abandoned, not to return until the second half of the book (C. 3.17 and thereafter only four times, in C. 3.21, 23, 26, and 29). The vatic stance is also replaced by the personal voice. For this reason the tone is no longer lofty but often ironic and familiar. Consistent with this is the shift in models from the choral lyric of Pindar to monody and Hellenistic epigram.[42] Even the audience has changed, from the youth and general public of the Roman Odes to named individuals.[43] Finally, as Klingner observed, a love interest predominates, although in the larger group, C. 3.7–15, there are not five such odes but six, and so there is even a numerical balance to the Roman Odes. These six poems explore the emotion through several different literary forms and from every vantage point. Horace moves through *paraenesis* (C. 3.7, 15), mime (C. 3.9), *paraclausithyron* (C. 3.10), mythical narrative (C. 3.11), and soliloquy (C. 3.12). Similarly, his perspective shifts from that of the detached observer (C. 3.7, 15) to that of both participants together (C. 3.9), and of the man (C. 3.10, 11) and woman (C. 3.12) separately. Insofar as these six odes give a sample of virtually every sort of love poem in the collection, they balance the Roman Odes not only in their number but also in their message, a definitive expression of the private voice, just as the Roman Odes were of the public. It only remains to see how these two voices are integrated and not merely juxtaposed.

NINE

This is accomplished by C. 3.8 and 14. In subject these odes at first seem to have little in common: C. 3.8 is a familiar, even somewhat teasing, invitation to Maecenas to celebrate the anniversary of Horace's deliverance from the falling tree, whereas C. 3.14 is a grand celebration of Augustus's return home from an expedition to Spain. And yet, that the two are meant to be read together is assured not only by their symmetrical placement (as noted above), one position in from each end of the group, but also by numerous similarities in detail and structure. Both are, after all, celebrations, each characterized by the poet in the same words as "festive" (dies . . . festus, C. 3.8.9, 14.13); both open with a ritual, a sacrifice to Bacchus in C. 3.8 and a procession (and presumably sacrifice) to iustis . . . divis (6) in C. 3.14; and in both the occasion is one of thanksgiving for safety, for Horace's in C. 3.8 (sospitis, 14) and for the nation's soldiers' in C. 3.14 (sospitum, 10). Of equal length, both poems are even structured in the same way, in the A-B-A pattern familiar from other odes containing an uneven number of strophes. Thus, the first three strophes of C. 3.8 describe the poet's celebration and the reason for it, the middle one invites Maecenas to join in, and the last three support the invitation by reassuring Maecenas that his worries for the state are groundless. Similarly, in C. 3.14 the first three strophes describe the public celebration of Augustus's return, the middle strophe proclaims the poet's freedom from worry now that Augustus is back in control, and the last three move on to plans for a private party.

The greatest similarity, however, is that these two odes, alone in the group of nine, have an explicit political content. But they treat political concerns in a way very different from the Roman Odes. Specifically, both poems label them curas (C. 3.8.17, 14.14), troublesome worries that are best dismissed. This is the burden of the message to Maecenas in C. 3.8.[44] As in C. 1.31, public and private are again combined in the poem's setting: it is the official holiday, the Matronalia, but Horace is celebrating a private anniversary, his escape from the falling tree. Unlike C. 1.31, however, this poem actually integrates public and private concerns in its injunction to Maecenas, who is urged to put aside his worries for the state (civilis . . . curas, 17) and become a private citizen (privatus, 26). Here the relation between public and private ways of life is not represented as one of simple contrast but rather of interdependence. This is made explicit in the fifth and sixth strophes which support the injunction by providing a rundown of imperial trouble spots (11–24). In the Roman Odes, as in the political odes of Book 1, Horace referred to foreign nations only to urge expeditions against them. Now, in C. 3.8, the Dacians, Parthians, Spaniards, and Scythians no longer pose a threat to Rome. In other words, the private life enjoined upon Maecenas has been made possible by the Augustan peace.

This is even more explicit in C. 3.14.[45] In the first section (1–12), the poet assumes a vatic stance to outline plans for a grand public celebration of Augustus's return. So unmistakable is the public voice here that this section resembles the Roman Odes in a number of ways. The addressee is the same, the Roman people (*o plebs*, 1), especially the youth (*o pueri et puellae / non virum expertae*, 10–11); the opening association of Augustus with Hercules (*Herculis ritu*, 1) recalls the posthumous deification of Augustus in the Roman Odes, particularly by association with Hercules at C. 3.3.9; and the religious language (*male ominatis / parcite verbis*, 11–12) resembles the ritualistic opening of C. 3.1 (*favete linguis*, 2).

Later in the poem, however, the public persona to which these echoes of the Roman Odes contribute is replaced by Horace's own personal voice. Shifting his address to a slave boy (*puer*, 17), Horace makes plans for a private party (17–28). Even here, however, the details are politically charged. The wine Horace will serve remembers the Marsian Wars and the rebellion of Spartacus (18–20). Similarly, the slave who is to invite the lovely Neaera should not persist if her doorkeeper is obstinate, as Horace is no longer the contentious youth he once was in the consulship of Plancus, i.e. in the year of Philippi (27–28). Thus, embedded in the personal section of the ode are references to the sort of civil strife that was finally ended by Augustus, whose public honors the first part of the ode recorded. This is the point of the central strophe which mediates between these two major sections of the poem, between the public and the private voices:

> hic dies vere mihi festus atras
> exiget curas: ego nec tumultum
> nec mori per vim metuam tenente
>   Caesare terras.   [C. 3.14.13–16]

This day, truly festive to me, will drive away black cares. I shall fear neither civil war nor death by violence so long as Caesar holds the earth.

Here, as in C. 3.8, public and private ways of life are not so much juxtaposed as interrelated. The day can be festive for Horace precisely because Caesar rules the earth.

To conclude, both of these poems raise political concerns only to dismiss them—not as unimportant but as no longer urgent. The private life does not take priority over the public life, but is instead guaranteed by it, for the military and political successes of Augustus have at last made the world safe for music, drinking, and love. These successes and their impact on the lives of men will be a dominant theme of Book 4 of the *Odes* published ten years later. But the relationship between the two was already worked out in the first lyric collection. In a very real sense, these private joys follow as naturally from the Augustan achievement as *Odes* 3.7–15 follow from the Roman Odes. Here in Horace, as in Vergil's *Aeneid*, we hear both the public and the private voices of the poet. In the *Odes*, however, they are made to sing in harmony. There will always be those who prefer Vergil.

THE THIRD BOOK
THE POETICS OF CLOSURE

ONE

Like the other two books that precede it, Book 3 is divided at its midpoint with a dedication to Maecenas. That poem, C. 3.16, is a moral sermon on the danger of wealth and the poet's own blessed sufficiency, and is fully discussed in Chapter Seven with all the other odes addressed to the patron.[1] For now, however, it is worth noting that one emblem of wealth, a Laestrygonian wine cask (34–35), may forge a link with the next poem in which the addressee's family is said to be descended from the king of the Laestrygonians (C. 3.17.1). If such a link is not fortuitous, however, it is certainly very slight. In general, C. 3.16 is less closely related to its immediate neighbors than it is to the other Maecenas odes, particularly C. 3.29 together with which it frames the second half of the book. It is with the poems enclosed by this frame, namely C. 3.17 to 28, that the collection begins to wind down. Just as the first half of the book is a self-contained group in which the public and private voices are juxtaposed and then harmonized in a vision of Augustan peace, so the poems in the second half, when read sequentially, achieve a satisfactory closure for the volume and, indeed, for the collection as a whole.

TWO

The first three poems after the central Maecenas ode are held together by season and setting: all celebrate winter festivals.[2] In C. 3.17, an invitation to Lamia, the storm (9–12) and hearth fire (14) suggest a time at the end of the year, just as the reference to the *genius* (14) marks the occasion as a birthday party. In C. 3.18 Horace enjoys a country holiday, the Faunalia, which is precisely dated in the text to 5 December (*nonae . . . Decembres*, 10; cf. *pleno . . . anno*, 5). Finally, C. 3.19 celebrates the adlection of Murena into the college of augurs, and temporal indicators include not only references to heated water (6) and Paelignian cold (8), but three toasts—to the new moon, midnight, and Murena (9–11)—which point specifically to midnight, 31 December, when the new augur would have taken office.

These techniques of seasonal and contextual linkage are employed elsewhere. Book 1, for instance, ends with three drinking poems (C. 1.36, 37, 38), and its opening Parade Odes seem to progress from spring's thaw (C. 1.4) to wintry snows atop Mount Soracte (C. 1.9).[3] The poems under discussion from Book 3, however, differ in that their season and occasion are fixed with far greater precision. Interconnection depends not merely on a shared sympotic setting or the inference of season from problematic details. Rather, the poems present explicit internal dates—a birthday, the Faunalia, and New Year's Eve.

Such precision, which sets these poems apart as a triad of sorts, also raises the question of whether this superficial linkage hints at any deeper connection. There are, in fact, tonal, structural, and thematic resemblances between the two end poems, C. 3.17 and 19.[4] The former opens with an elaborate parenthesis on Lamia's mythological pedigree:

> Aeli vetusto nobilis ab Lamo—
> quando et priores hinc Lamias ferunt
>   denominatos et nepotum
>   per memores genus omne fastus
>
> auctore ab illo ducis originem,
> qui Formiarum moenia dicitur
>   princeps et innantem Maricae
>   litoribus tenuisse Lirim
>
> late tyrannus—. . .   [C. 3.17.1–9]

Aelius, nobly sprung from ancient Lamus—for since men say that both the Lamiae of old are named after him and the whole line of descendants in the family records, you trace your origin to that founder who is said to have been the first to hold the walls of Formiae and the Liris which floods Marica's shores, a wide-ranging ruler—. . .

Because the Aelii Lamiae were still equestrians in Horace's time,[5] the genealogy, if taken at face value, resembles the royal descent with which the Augustan poets equipped Maecenas. It is more likely, however, that Horace is here burlesquing the fashion (legitimated by Varro and Vergil) by which Roman families claimed Trojan descent, for Lamia's Homeric ancestor is not a noble warrior but the king of a tribe of cannibals in the *Odyssey*.

This good-natured joke, however, also has a strategic function when set against more timely concerns:

> cras foliis nemus
> multis et alga litus inutili
>   demissa tempestas ab Euro
>   sternet, aquae nisi fallit augur
>
> annosa cornix: dum potes, aridum
> conpone lignum: cras genium mero
>   curabis et porco bimenstri
>   cum famulis operum solutis.   [C. 3.17.9–16]

Tomorrow a storm sent down by the east wind will litter the grove with many leaves and the shore with useless seaweed, unless the ancient crow, augur of rain, deceives me. While you are able, gather dry firewood. Tomorrow you will care for your Genius with wine and a two-month-old pig, and your slaves will be freed from their chores.

In contrast to the first part of the poem, the only thing that is old here is the crow, and its age merely attests to its powers of predicting the future. The emphasis has clearly shifted from the past to the present and future, from reminiscence to injunction, from nostalgia to preparation and enjoyment. The reader can now appreciate why the first half of the poem was cast as a parenthesis. Not only a parody of honorific modes of address, the genealogy's grammatical subordination also reflects its moral subordination, for Horace is proposing not a drink to yesterday but a toast to tomorrow.

The reference to the crow as augur (12) of tomorrow's storm perhaps establishes a surface link with C. 3.19, which is about a party for an augur. A more meaningful connection, however, is established by the contrast with which C. 3.19 opens:

> Quantum distet ab Inacho
>   Codrus pro patria non timidus mori,
> narras et genus Aeaci
>   et pugnata sacro bella sub Ilio:
>
> quo Chium pretio cadum
>   mercemur, quis aquam temperet ignibus,
> quo praebente domum et quota
>   Paelignis careum frigoribus, taces.   [C. 3.19.1–8]

On the time span between Inachus and Codrus, unafraid to die for his country, on the family of Aeacus and the battles fought under sacred Troy: you discourse. On the price of a jar of Chian wine, on who will warm the water with fire and at whose house and at what hour I may be rid of Paelignian chills: you are silent.

These lines are probably addressed to Telephus (only named at line 26) who, like Lamia, is gently teased for living in the past. Even the subjects of his antiquarian research recall the Lamia ode. The first two (the time span between two kings and the family tree of the Aeacids) are essentially genealogical, and the second and third are Homeric as well (since the Aeacids included Achilles who fought at Troy). About these useless matters Telephus discourses (*narras*, 3), but about what really matters he is silent (*taces*, 8): the price of wine, the location of the party, and the hour when it is to begin. For the rest of the poem, Telephus is urged to abandon his scholarship and drink deeply, following the poet's lead (9–12). Others can drink three ladles of wine, but Horace will have nine—one for each Muse!—and there will be flute music, revelry, and roses in December (13–20).

C. 3.17 and 19, then, balance each other very closely in tone, structure, and thought. Playfully teasing their addressees, both turn on the contrast of past with present and future, and both invest that contrast with hortatory significance. A similar A-B-A pattern occurs in other triads concerned with the passage of time. In Book 1, for instance, admonitions to the youthful Chloe who fears love (C. 1.23) and the aging Lydia who refuses to give it up (C. 1.25) aptly frame a poem on death, in which Vergil is chided for his excessive grief (C. 1.24).[6] Similarly, in Book 2, poems rebuking Valgius for living in the past (C. 2.9) and Quinctius Hirpinus for living in the future (C. 2.11) surround the ode to Dellius (C. 2.10), which enjoins the Golden Mean.[7] In each case, two related poems about the passage of time pivot around a thematic core. C. 3.17, 18, and 19, however, are defined as a triad not only by the central poem, which shows Horace enjoying the leisurely existence he preaches to Lamia and Telephus, but also by the fact that all three celebrate winter festivals. This is not a superficial connection, after all, for setting and theme are actually related. The poems' dramatic date at the end of the year gives particular point to their injunction to forget yesterday and to live in the here and now.

After this triad, the next few poems are more loosely attached by a general affinity of topic. C. 3.19 ends by describing three very different pairs of lovers: the ill-matched Lycus and a neighboring woman (*vicina*, 24), the well-suited Telephus and Rhode, and Horace himself with Glycera (22–28). This concluding vignette not only marks an internal transition within the ode from an early to a late stage in the festivities, i.e. from drinking to lovemaking,[8] but it also facilitates a transition to the next poem, C. 3.20, which is all about love. Furthermore, because the last two lovers illustrate a lingering (*lentus*, 28) and impassioned (*torret*, 28) affair, they lead into the specific topic of C. 3.20, unrequited love, experienced now not by Horace but by two rival suitors who compete for the affections of the indifferent youth, Nearchus.[9] After this amatory excursion, the subject of drinking returns in the next poem, the witty hymn to the wine jar, C. 3.21, though here too love is incorporated into the final strophe where references to Bacchus, Venus, the Graces, and the return of Phoebus (i.e. morning) tell of a night devoted not only to wine but also to women and song.[10]

This smooth but superficial movement prepares the way for another distinctive triad. Norden long ago observed that C. 3.21, 22, and 23 are all to some extent religious.[11] He did not investigate further and the interconnection of the poems has received only very occasional and perfunctory acknowledgment.[12] It is possible to demonstrate, however, that the odes are much more carefully arranged than even Norden realized, and also that they have a functional connection with the poems that follow.

Though C. 3.21 is technically addressed to a wine jar (*pia testa*, 4), it is really intended for Messalla Corvinus whose call for a drink (*Corvino iubente*, 7) provides the pretext for the poem. Like Lamia and Telephus a few odes earlier, Messalla is also teased. Horace jokingly assimilates the great man's philosophical interests to his well-known fondness for the grape by describing him as "soaked in Socratic writings" (*Socraticis madet / sermonibus*, 9–10).[13] The real point of the poem, however, is not a personal but a literary joke, the sophisticated generic play involved in casting a sympotic poem into hymnic form. Norden's discussion remains classic, demonstrating how the parody is worked out at all levels[14]—stylistically, with the postponed vocative and asyndeton; lexically, with puns on religious terminology; even structurally, as the poem is delineated in terms of traditional aretalogy and includes not only the prayer proper but also the god's (here the wine jar's) lineage, titles and powers, past achievements, and attendant deities.

This literary joke is reinforced by the ode's position just before C. 3.22, a dedication to Diana of a pine tree on Horace's property. The two poems are related by more than their common religious coloring. The parody of hymnic form in C. 3.21, for example, leads smoothly into the elaborate hymnic address which opens C. 3.22. Similarly, Apollo concludes the catalog of deities attendant on the wine jar in C. 3.21, and indeed *Phoebus* is the last word of that poem; that C. 3.22 should then address Diana is apt, since the two gods, brother and sister, are often coupled together, as in Horace's other Diana ode (C. 1.21) and the *Carmen Saeculare*. Both poems, furthermore, recall Catullus's hymn to Diana (34), the former borrowing from it the liturgical escape clause *quocumque . . . nomine* (C. 3.21.5; cf. Cat. 34.21–22), the latter echoing Catullus's invocation of the goddess in her multiple aspects (C. 3.22.1–4; cf. Cat. 34.9–20). There are also limited precedents for both odes in Greek epigram, for C. 3.21 recalls Posidippus's sympotic address to a wine jar (AP 5.134 = 3054–57 G.-P.), and C. 3.22 resembles the dedications in the sixth book of the *Greek Anthology*. Finally, both poems involve Horace personally, as the wine was bottled in the year of his birth and the pine tree hangs over his house.

Though C. 3.21 and 22 are closely related in these ways, C. 3.22 also introduces something that sets them apart, the element of rusticity which is missing from the urbane hymn to the wine jar. Thus, the ritual enacted in C. 3.22 is a dedication to woodland Diana, and even the sacrifice is suited to the ostensible occasion, for it is a wild boar rather than the domestic pig that we are led to expect by the fact that this is a yearly ritual.[15] This rustic element, moreover, leads smoothly into the next poem, C. 3.23, in which Horace offers religious advice to Phidyle, a girl who comes from the country (*rustica*, 2) and who prays for the land's fertility (5–8). Although the sacrifice here is narrated rather than enacted as in the Diana dedication, there is nonetheless a very close similarity of detail because both descriptions evoke pathos for animals. The device is as old as Homer's description of Odysseus's dog (*Od.* 17.290–327). However, Horace innovated by applying it not to a pet but to a sacrificial victim, first in the Bandusia ode (C. 3.13.2–7), and a bit later in these two adjacent poems. In the Diana dedication the boar is killed as he practices his thrusting (C. 3.22.7), and in the Phidyle ode the animal's happier past is juxtaposed with the image of his blood on the priests' axes (C. 3.23.9–13).

As it shares these rustic touches with C. 3.22, the Phidyle ode also introduces a new subject of its own, simplicity and frugality. Horace's general theme is that the gods do not require elaborate sacrifices. The contrast between the priests' large offering in the third strophe and Phidyle's inexpensive ones in the fourth eloquently makes the point. Even small details are controlled by this theme. The girl's very name, for example, derives from the Greek φείδομαι, "to be sparing." Again, that the gods to whom she sacrifices are "tiny" (*parvos* . . . / . . . *deos*, 15–16) may be more than a humorous conflation of the gods with their images, for their diminutive size assimilates the gods themselves to Horace's theme.[16]

In conclusion, C. 3.21, 22, and 23 are bound by their common religious coloring. They differ in form and tone, though even these differences tend rather to smooth than to obstruct the transitions from one poem to the next. The first two, for instance, are prayers, but the third is a sermon on how to pray. Again, the first poem is parodic, but the second and third are cast as expressions of faith. Finally, the poems embody a progression not only of tone, from parody to seriousness, but also of theme. The first introduces the common religious element and the others each add one new idea, rusticity in C. 3.22 and simplicity in C. 3.23. The effect of such tonal progression and thematic augmentation is, at least in part, to create an inner dynamic, strongly urging the reader forward in the book.

This movement leads to C. 3.24, which may be summarized briefly. "Wealth is of no avail in the face of death. The simple virtue of the nomads is better than our luxury. The man who will be called 'father of cities' (*pater urbium*, 27) must curb this license. Words will not help; strong action is needed. Let us discard our gems and gold, root out evil, and train the young more strenuously. Nowadays they and their fathers will commit any crime for money, which always grows but never satisfies." This poem is often compared to the Roman Odes. Although its pessimism is particularly reminiscent of C. 3.6 (and perhaps dates both poems to the failure of Augustus's first attempt at moral legislation in 28 B.C.),[17] that entire cycle is recalled by the lack of a specific addressee, the inclusion of Caesar, albeit unnamed, in the very center of the poem, and the generally moralistic tone assumed throughout. These affinities give point to the poem's placement in the book. Just as the Roman Odes were introduced by the religious strophes of C. 3.1.1–8, and perhaps even by the Alcaic odes on divine inspiration and immortality that close Book 2 (C. 2.19, 20),[18] so C. 3.24 is preceded by a "religious" triad that serves as a prelude to its lofty sentiments.

The last poem in the triad is particularly relevant. C. 3.23 closes with a picture of the worshipper "touching" (*tetigit*, 17) the altar with a giftless hand. Then the very first word of C. 3.24 is *intactis*, referring to the "untouched" riches of Arabia and India. The verbal echo, if not fortuitous, would seem to underscore a shift in topic, from simplicity to opulence; this is reinforced by formal differences, as the brevity and stylistic simplicity of the former ode is far removed from the lengthy moralizing of the latter. Yet both poems share the same basic moral outlook: C. 3.23 preaches simplicity and frugality, and then C. 3.24 goes on to attack luxury. As elsewhere in Horace, the relationship between the two poems is one not only of topical contrast but also of attitudinal affinity. Both odes approach the same moral center but from different directions, C. 3.23 from the positive side and C. 3.24 from the negative. In addition, the focus broadens, from the Phidyle ode's Italian setting to the wealth of the Orient in the next poem, and from the essentially private nature of Horace's message to the girl to the more public injunction that follows as Horace calls for simplicity not only in one's relationship with the gods but also in one's entire way of life.

The next poem, which is addressed to Bacchus, is in the same meter as C. 3.24. As one of the very rare departures from metrical *variatio*, it alerts us to the many other ways in which it is related to C. 3.24. For example, it too has affinities with the Roman Odes. Horace's role here as votary of Bacchus is akin to his earlier vatic stance as *Musarum sacerdos*, "priest of the Muses" (C. 3.1.3). The novelty of his undertaking here (*dicam insigne, recens, adhuc / indictum ore alio*, "I shall sing something special, new, as yet unsung by any other mouth," C. 3.25.7–8) also resembles the claim of originality made for the Roman Odes (*carmina non prius / audita*, "songs not heard before," C. 3.1.2–3). Finally, if the promise of lofty poetry in C. 2.20.1–2 (*Non usitata nec tenui ferar / pinna*, "I shall be borne on no ordinary or slender wing") refers to the Roman Odes,[19] there would be a further connection between that cycle and C. 3.25, for the latter also promises *nil parvum aut humili modo, / . . . loquar*, "I shall sing nothing slight or in humble measure" (17–18).

C. 3.24 and 25, then, are similar in that they both echo the Roman Odes. They are most closely related, however, not only to the Roman Odes but also to each other, by their treatment of Caesar. Though he is not mentioned by name in C. 3.24, Caesar is clearly present there:

> o quisquis volet inpias
>   caedis et rabiem tollere civicam,
> si quaeret pater urbium
>   subscribi statuis, indomitam audeat
> refrenare licentiam,
>   clarus postgenitis, . . .   [C. 3.24.25–30]

O whoever wishes to end impious slaughter and mad civil war, if he seeks "Father of Cities" to be inscribed on his statues, let him dare to restrain our unbridled license and win fame among future generations . . .

The Bacchus ode then follows, explicitly identifying this man as Caesar and further specifying his reward. Recalling the potential deification of Caesar in the Roman Odes (C. 3.3.9–12, 5.1–2), the Bacchus ode represents Horace planning to set the emperor among the stars in his poetry:

> Quo me, Bacche, rapis tui
>   plenum? quae nemora aut quos agor in specus
> velox mente nova? quibus
>   antris egregii Caesaris audiar
>
> aeternum meditans decus
>   stellis inserere et consilio Iovis?
> dicam insigne, recens, adhuc
>   indictum ore alio. non secus in iugis
>
> exsomnis stupet Euhias
>   Hebrum prospiciens et nive candidam
> Thracen ac pede barbaro
>   lustratam Rhodopen, ut mihi devio
>
> ripas et vacuum nemus
>   mirari libet. [C. 3.25.1-14]

Whither, Bacchus, are you rushing me filled with your spirit? Into what groves or caves am I driven swiftly with a new mind? In what hollows shall I be heard rehearsing to set Caesar's eternal glory among the stars and the council of Jove? I shall sing something special, new, as yet unsung by any other mouth. Just as a sleepless Bacchant on mountain ridges looks out in awe over Hebrus and Thrace white with snow and Rhodope traversed by barbarian feet, so it pleases me as I wander to marvel at the banks and the empty grove.

It is this explicitly political content that most dramatically distinguishes this Bacchus ode from the earlier one in the collection, C. 2.19. There Horace attempted to convey the excitement of poetry in general, whereas C. 3.25 is specific to political poetry. Thus, Horace conceived of his task in C. 2.19 as the celebration of the god, but in C. 3.25 as the celebration of Caesar. Excited by Caesar's glory, he is also excited by his own ability to create it. Whereas the Bacchants appear in C. 2.19 as the god's attendants, here in C. 3.25 the solitary votary takes on a symbolic meaning of her own. She forms the subject of the majestic simile on which the poem turns and provides an analogue for the poet's own creative impulse.[20]

These Bacchic raptures, then, follow naturally as a commentary on the preceding ode's seriousness and particularly on its central Caesarian strophe. This sort of retrospective commentary calls to mind the endings of several other political poems. In C. 2.1, for instance, the poet brings to an end his meditation on the civil wars by checking his Muse:

> sed ne relictis, Musa procax, iocis
> Ceae retractes munera neniae,
>   mecum Dionaeo sub antro
>   quaere modos leviore plectro.   [C. 2.1.37–40]

But lest, wanton Muse, you abandon play and attempt again the task of the Cean dirge, seek with me in Venus's cave measures on a lighter lyre.

The account of Juno's speech in C. 3.3 is abruptly terminated in similar fashion:

> non hoc iocosae conveniet lyrae.
> quo, Musa, tendis? desine pervicax
>   referre sermones deorum et
>   magna modis tenuare parvis.   [C. 3.3.69–72]

This will not suit the jovial lyre. Where, Muse, are you heading? Stop obstinately reporting the speech of the gods and demeaning great matters in humble measures.

Here, the very phrasing of the question, *quo, Musa, tendis?* (70), resembles the opening gambit of C. 3.25, *Quo me, Bacche, rapis?* "Whither, Bacchus, are you rushing me?" (1). Of course, in C. 2.1 and 3.3 this backward glance at the political content of the ode is appended as the ode's final strophe, whereas the commentary on C. 3.24 takes up a separate poem, C. 3.25. Also, these other examples are essentially *recusationes*: Horace is apologizing for his political fervor, as it is "not suited to the jovial lyre" (*non hoc iocosae conveniet lyrae*, C. 3.3.69) and can even be "a task full of dangerous risk" (*periculosae plenum opus aleae*, C. 2.1.6). By C. 3.25, however, such writing has been rehabilitated to a "sweet peril" (*dulce periculum*, 18), and so the Bacchus ode is not so much a palinode for the preceding poem as a retrospective commentary on it, on the source of inspiration for political poetry and on the excitement such poetry is capable of generating.[21]

It is in light of this excitement that the next poem can best be understood. In C. 3.26 Horace retires from love as if from an occupation by dedicating to Venus the tools of the *exclusus amator*.[22] In moving to this from the Bacchus ode, Horace has clearly shifted to a lighter form, from dithyramb to dedication, and to a lighter topic, Venus instead of Bacchus, the warfare of love (*militavi*, 2; *arma*, 3) rather than Caesarian exploits. There is consistency in the poet's attitude, however, since C. 3.25 expresses enthusiasm for politics and then C. 3.26 follows up on that commitment by abandoning love:

> Vixi puellis nuper idoneus
> et militavi non sine gloria:
>   nunc arma defunctumque bello
>   barbiton hic paries habebit,
>
> laevom marinae qui Veneris latus
>   custodit . . .   [C. 3.26.1–6]

Recently I lived fit for girls and I fought not without glory; now this wall which guards the left side of sea-born Venus will display my weapons and my lyre discharged from service.

When C. 3.25 and 26 are read in succession, the contrast of past and present with which the latter opens appears to be reflected in the placement of the poems themselves. *Nuper*, "recently" (1), looks back to the time evoked in C. 3.25, i.e. before Horace's Bacchic discovery of politics and political poetry, and *nunc*, "now" (3), to the time after. Until recently he lived for girls, but now that lighter side of his existence is over. Even the final strophe, in which Venus is asked to flick Chloe just once with her lash (9–12), is consistent with Horace's renunciation of love, for the prayer is not a request for one last fling (as the traditional view goes), but rather, as C. P. Jones has convincingly argued, a request for revenge, that Chloe be made to experience the same pain that she has inflicted on the poet.[23]

The dependence of C. 3.26 on C. 3.25 is reinforced by one final and problematic detail in C. 3.26, the choice and treatment of the cult sites by which Venus is invoked:

> o quae beatam diva tenens Cyprum et
> Memphin carentem Sithonia nive. . . .   [C. 3.26.9–10]

O goddess, you who rule over blessed Cyprus and over Memphis which is lacking in Sithonian snow. . . .

There are two problems here: why is an unfamiliar town on the River Nile included in the same context as the goddess' famous shrine at Cyprus, and why is that town characterized by the obvious fact that it lacks Sithonian, i.e. Thracian, snow?

Kiessling and Heinze suggested that Venus is here identified with Isis, the Egyptian goddess whose worship was popular among Augustan *hetairai* like Chloe.[24] Also, since a certain (the same?) Chloe is elsewhere said to come from Thrace (C. 3.9.10), it may be relevant that Venus was worshipped at Memphis as *Aphroditē Xeniē*, goddess of foreigners.[25] Another, and simpler, explanation is that Memphis was chosen primarily for its sweltering climate, to which attention is drawn by the unnecessary reminder that it is without Thracian snow. The heat of Memphis, suiting the passionate Venus, is in symbolic contrast with Chloe who is cold not just in her Thracian origins but also in her disposition (*arrogantem*, 12).[26]

There is, however, one other possible explanation. In C. 3.25 the poet's enthusiasm for politics and political poetry was compared to that of a Bacchant ranging over Thracian snows (8–14). The explicit absence of Thracian snow in the very next poem, then, recalls and contradicts this Bacchant simile. When the retired Horace consigns Chloe to her passion in C. 3.26, it is fitting that he should address his prayer to the Venus of Memphis, for sultry Memphis represents the world of love from which Horace withdraws and which is far removed by climate and location from the Bacchic landscape into which he has painted himself in C. 3.25.

C. 3.26, then, is a logical sequel to the Bacchus ode. It is also, however, closely related to the two poems that follow it. Although they vary in tone and length—C. 3.26 and 28 are short and light, whereas C. 3.27 is long and allegorical—all three share details which, in turn, point to deeper connections. Kiessling and Heinze noted that each involves a woman: Chloe, Galatea, and Lyde respectively.[27] It might be added that all three end with Venus: C. 3.26 with a prayer to the goddess, C. 3.27 with her address to Europa, and C. 3.28 with Horace and Lyde singing her praises. Finally, the sea figures in each poem: in C. 3.26 Horace makes his dedication to *marinae . . . Veneris* (5); C. 3.27 is a *propempticon* that recounts Europa's voyage over the waves; and C. 3.28 celebrates the Neptunalia, the feast day of the god of the sea.[28]

The presence of women and Venus in the three poems might

initially seem inconsistent with the pretext of the first, that Horace has given up love. Yet a deeper link binds the poems together: all make allusions to closure. The phenomenon has been amply documented for English literature by Barbara Herrnstein Smith who observes that, although explicit statements of ending are rare (since they generally do not fit a poem's thematic structure or level of dramatic immediacy), covert references are fairly common: "The most casual survey of the concluding lines of any group of poems will reveal that in a considerable number of them there are words and phrases such as 'last,' 'finished,' 'end,' 'rest,' 'peace,' or 'no more,' which, while they do not refer to the conclusion of the poem itself, nevertheless signify termination or stability."[29] Equally interesting is another form of closural allusion, "references not to termination, finality, repose or stability as such, but to events which, in our nonliterary experiences, are associated with these qualities—events such as sleep, death, dusk, night, autumn, winter, descents, falls, leavetakings and homecomings."[30]

We have already observed the technique, perhaps, in the end-of-year settings of C. 3.17, 18, and 19. Here, at the end of the sequence those three poems introduce, there are again closural allusions, for C. 3.26, 27, and 28 are all cast as farewells of a sort. This is explicit even in the literary forms of the first two, a retirement dedication and a bon voyage. But a sense of finality also informs C. 3.28, as we shall see, and in all three odes the farewell Horace makes is, in a sense, to poetry itself.

Just as C. 3.25 expressed enthusiasm not only for politics but also for political poetry, so C. 3.26 retires Horace not only from love but also from love poetry. The metaphor of dedication is an apt one: in *Epistle* 1.1.4–6, for example, Horace explicitly signals his retirement from lyric by comparing himself to an aged gladiator hanging up his arms to Hercules. That C. 3.26 has the same literary relevance is suggested perhaps by the inclusion of the lyre among the poet's offerings. It is also the point behind the correspondence of C. 3.26 with C. 1.5, the Pyrrha ode. Fifth poem from the beginning of the collection and fifth from the end, both involve dedications to a god of the sea (C. 1.5 a past thank offering, C. 3.26 a present retirement offering), and both view love in terms of an occupational metaphor (sailing in C. 1.5 and housebreaking in C. 3.26). That C. 3.26, which renounces love, should so pointedly recall the first love ode in the collection is an unmistakable signal to the reader that the collection is coming to an end.³¹

The same programmatic implications underlie the Galatea ode, C. 3.27. According to the traditional interpretation, Galatea is a girlfriend of Horace who is deserting him for another man. Thus, the poem is Horace's farewell to Galatea and, if the Europa myth parallels her case, Galatea's farewell either to her virginity or her fidelity.³² But Ross Kilpatrick has more convincingly argued that Galatea is not Horace's girlfriend but the sea goddess, that the Europa myth parallels the anonymous traveler's experience, and that this traveler is none other than the poetry book itself—like Europa, starting out rashly, then suffering fear and self-reproach, but finally achieving fame.³³

This leaves C. 3.28 which, though not in its form a farewell, nonetheless is intelligible in these terms. Horace and Lyde are celebrating the Neptunalia by singing of the gods in alternate song (*invicem*, 9) and, at the end, hymning in unison Venus and the hypostasized Night:

> summo carmine, quae Cnidon
>   fulgentisque tenet Cycladas et Paphon
> iunctis visit oloribus,
>   dicetur merita Nox quoque nenia.   [C. 3.28.13–16]

In the last part of the song [we shall sing] of her who rules over Cnidos and the gleaming Cyclades and visits Paphos with her yoked swans; Night also will be sung in a well-deserved coda.

The Loeb editor's unwitting pun—"Night also shall be celebrated with a fitting lay"—at least expresses the erotic connection we would expect between the two subjects of the song. Though *nox* indicates the time for lovemaking, however, its range of reference is not restricted to this, but extends to another familiar Horatian concern, the passage of time:

> inclinare meridiem
>   sentis et, veluti stet volucris dies,
> parcis deripere horreo
>   cessantem Bibuli consulis amphoram?
>   [C. 3.28.5–8]

Do you sense that midday is waning and, as if the swift day were standing still, do you hesitate to snatch from the storeroom the amphora lingering there from the consulship of Bibulus?

The swiftness of the day, *volucris dies* (6), is imaged by the ode's very structure, its swift movement from the real noon in which it is set (*meridiem*, 5) to the night imagined at the end. If it is not possible to maintain that this poem, toward the end of the first lyric collection, already anticipates the love odes of Book 4 in which concern for the passage of time overrides any explicit erotic interest, nonetheless there does seem to be more here than the melancholy reminder of time's flight, which is conventional in sympotic and erotic verse. We recall that Vergil concluded his *Bucolics* at nightfall, withdrawing from pastoral with the observation, "Let us arise, for the shade is often harmful to singers": *surgamus: solet esse gravis cantantibus umbra* (Buc. 10.75).[34] That the Horatian *nox* has the same symbolic potential as an allusion to closure is suggested by the terms Horace uses to speak of his song about it, *summo carmine* (13) and *nenia* (16). The former has its usual partitive sense, "the end of the song," and the latter takes on a meaning suited to this context, "coda" or "finale."[35] Both terms, in other words, signify the last section of the hymn. But *nenia*, significantly placed as the last word of the poem and perhaps preserving a hint of its primary meaning, "dirge" (cf. C. 2.1.38, 20.21), conveys more general connotations of finality. Because it is followed only by the great Maecenas ode (C. 3.29) and the epilogue (C. 3.30), there is a sense in which the poem is itself the coda or last song, *summum carmen*, of the book. For all intents and purposes, the collection has come to an end.[36]

THREE

This sequential reading of the poems suggests a more comprehensive plan behind the second half of Book 3.

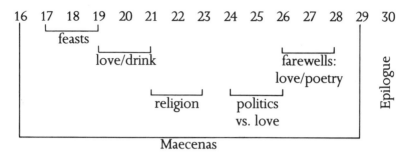

Though Horace's approach to arrangement is never just schematic, the diagram nonetheless can serve as a convenience, enabling one to visualize such important structural features as the large frame constituted by the two Maecenas odes, the tendency of the poems within that frame to cluster in groups of three, and the existence of rings both within triads (C. 17 and 19 frame 18) and among them (C. 3.19–21 balance 26–28). But such symmetry is rather loose and inconsistently applied, and the arrangement is not rigidly triadic since several poems overlap between groups (C. 3.19, 21, 26). In any case, the most meaningful structural principle operative here is not static but dynamic, not framed or triadic disposition but sequential ordering. This is the effect of the overlapping which facilitates the transition from one group of poems to the next. The movement is so smooth that the poems from C. 3.21 onward can almost be read without a break. Thus, tonal progression and thematic augmentation lead the reader through three odes (C. 3.21, 22, 23) which, because of their religious coloring, serve as an apt prelude to the moralizing of C. 3.24. That poem's political stance is then explained retrospectively by C. 3.25, which celebrates Bacchus as the source of inspiration for Horace's political verse. Horace's retirement from love and love poetry then follows naturally in C. 3.26, and a sense of finality is reinforced by C. 3.27, a farewell poem, and C. 3.28, which ends with the poet's song at the close of day.

It is not difficult to understand why Horace chose to conclude his poetry book in this way. On one level, the arrangement of the poems enriches their meaning. Thus, the programmatic function of C. 3.26 can be fully appreciated only when that poem is read in conjunction both with C. 3.25 and C. 1.5. On another level, though, sequential ordering also fulfills an important aesthetic function: the creation of momentum to carry the reader forward from one poem to the next and on, ultimately, to the end of the collection. In this respect, the poems in the second half of Book 3 are the concrete realization of the aesthetic implicit in the physical format of the book roll. Finally, they serve to convey what Frank Kermode has called, in a different context, "the *sense* of an ending"—not just actual cessation but a perception on the part of the reader that structural expectations have been fulfilled, that the work has arrived at a stable and satisfying close.[37] And it has, for only the two epilogues remain. These poems, C. 3.29 and 30, stand apart from the preceding sequence and will be discussed in detail in the next chapter.

THE ENSEMBLE

ONE

The preceding investigation of the individual books leads inevitably to consideration of some aspects of design that span the ensemble. Although the formal and thematic heterogeneity of the *Odes* precludes any simple underlying unity, the collection resembles the three books that make it up in that various and shifting criteria of arrangement are employed to establish both static and dynamic structures.

At the most basic level, the cohesive effect of certain balances and symmetries is undeniable. Just as the midpoint of each book is marked by a poem to Maecenas, so the collection as a whole is also anchored at its center. Whether or not one fully accepts Ludwig's analysis of C. 2.1–12 as concentrically arranged thematic pairs,[1] the alternation of Horace's two most important meters and the thematic comprehensiveness of these poems establish their status as a group. Placed in the exact center of the collection, with thirty-eight odes preceding them and thirty-eight following, they serve not only to open the second book but also to stabilize the entire ensemble.

If there is centerpinning, there is also framing. Just as the ends of Book 1 are individually linked by poems that balance each other, so the collection as a whole is surrounded by rings.[2]

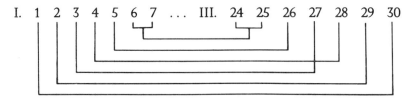

The correspondence of the first and last poems is well known. The only examples of the First Asclepiadean meter in Odes 1–3,[3] C. 1.1 and 3.30 treat the subject of poetic immortality. Though the poems in the second position from each end of the collection do not display so close a formal relationship, they are nonetheless addressed to the two persons who figure most prominently in the Odes, Augustus and Maecenas respectively, and they mention political concerns. The odes in the third and fourth positions also link up with one another, but in chiastic fashion: C. 1.3 and 3.27 are both *propemptica* for metaphorical journeys, and C. 1.4 and 3.28 both celebrate religious feast days, the Faunalia and Neptunalia respectively. Even more obvious is the connection between the poems in the fifth position, for both are metaphorical dedications by a lover to a god of the sea. Next, in C. 1.6 and 3.25 Horace expresses his views on political poetry, at first refusing to write it but then responding enthusiastically to the challenge. Finally, even the immediately adjacent poems are consistent with these two stances: C. 1.7 continues the *recusatio* initiated in the preceding ode, and C. 3.24 prepares for the Bacchus ode that follows by introducing Caesar (as yet unnamed) in its central strophe.

In assessing the significance of these structures that span the three books, it is important to observe that they are not, in fact, exclusively static. The framing at the ends of the collection actually charts a dramatic progression in Horatian poetics. C. 1.1 and 3.30, for example, both treat poetic immortality, but the former prays for it whereas the latter boasts that it has at last been achieved. Similarly, though C. 1.2 and 3.29 both refer to politics, such concerns are cause for anxiety in the former poem, but by the end of the collection Maecenas is advised to forget them since they are no longer troublesome. Again, the journey in C. 1.3 stands for the composition of Vergil's *Aeneid*, whereas the final *propempticon*, C. 3.27, seems to have some relevance to the publication of Horace's own poetry book.[4] The same sort of movement is apparent in the feast-day poems and the dedications: the spring setting of C. 1.4 and the poet's first treatment of love, C. 1.5, make possible allusions to the poetry book's inception, whereas the melancholy celebration of the Neptunalia in C. 3.28 and the poet's renunciation of love in C. 3.26 clearly allude to its closure.[5] Finally, while both C. 1.6 and 3.25 respond to the challenge of writing political poetry, the shift in Horace's position which they record reflects the intervening poems that worked out a viable accommodation between public and private values.

Even apparently static patterns, then, serve to mark the dynamic movement of *Odes* 1–3 as a whole. Thus, it is not surprising to find that in the collection, as in the individual books, sequences play the most important role in relating poems to one another. C. 2.19 and 20, for example, provide a lead-in to the Roman Odes and so link Books 2 and 3.[6] More crucial, however, are sequences of noncontiguous poems such as those operative in individual books, particularly Book 1.[7] A good example of the use of the technique on a larger scale is the progression of the groups with which each book opens. The Parade Odes introduce many of Horace's meters and themes; the first half of Book 2 then alternates the two most important meters, although thematic variation is continued to some (lesser) extent; finally, the Roman Odes are restricted to a single meter and put forth a remarkably consistent message. In a sense, these initial groupings prefigure the overall personality of their respective books, the highly diversified contents of Book 1 and the more coherent, though still varied, character of Books 2 and 3. More importantly, though, the three opening groups also reflect in their own movement the ensemble's progress toward greater formal and thematic definition.

This sort of movement is felt at all levels. Indeed, the reader who attempts to trace a given theme or addressee through the collection is left with the unmistakable impression that the collection develops over time. Best known, perhaps, is Horace's growth in poetic self-confidence, from his prayer for immortality in C. 1.1, to his amusing form of survival in C. 2.20, and finally to the more serious statement of his achievement in C. 3.30. The political odes chart a similar movement—Book 1 mixing the encomium of Caesar with the admonition to fight foreign wars; Book 2 then overtly avoiding political themes; and Book 3, finally, returning to politics, confident that the civil wars are over and that Augustus has brought a lasting peace.

Among the most interesting but least recognized sequences are those determined not by theme but by addressee. The total body of Horace's love odes, for example, does not seem to be disposed according to any overall plan, symmetrical or sequential. Yet certain odes to named individuals, though physically separated, tend to group themselves together. Thus, while the mere repetition of a woman's name does not guarantee that the same character is meant, and while most of Horace's female addressees are, in any case, probably imaginary,[8] there are at least several women whose poems seem to be disposed according to some progressive design. The characterization of Lydia, for instance, is consistent in the four odes Horace addresses to her; these odes have Catullan models and move from open hostility (C. 1.8, 13, 25) to tentative reconciliation (C. 3.9). Similarly, it does not seem accidental that Glycera, whose first appearance is in a parody of a kletic hymn (C. 1.19), should next appear in a real kletic hymn (C. 1.30), and that her third occurrence should be only three poems later (C. 1.33). In addition to this linkage by poetic genre and proximity, the Glycera odes, like the Lydia odes, display an emotional continuity, for though Glycera is the object of Tibullus's unrequited love in C. 1.33, C. 1.19 and 30 presume some amatory interest on Horace's part, and her final occurrence, at C. 3.19, is as the poet's own "lingering" (*lentus*, 28) passion.[9]

Examples of this phenomenon can be multiplied, and not just with human addressees. We have already noted, for example, Silk's interesting suggestion that the Bacchus odes present a pattern of conversion in three stages, from initial skepticism (C. 1.18), to sudden revelation of the god's power (C. 2.19), and thence to enthusiastic acceptance and ecstasy (C. 3.25).[10] Rather than pursue a great number of examples to make what should, by now, be an obvious point, it may be more instructive to focus in some detail on a single sequence. Defined both by addressee and theme, the eight Maecenas odes comprise the largest of all the sequences and explore not only Horace's relationship with his patron, but also his views on the nature and extent of his own artistic achievement. As such, these poems are the most dramatic and effective of the many structures that span the three books, and are a fitting conclusion to this discussion of the collection's larger design.

TWO

The relationship between Horace and Maecenas has long fascinated scholars because of its unusually copious documentation and its intrinsic human and literary interest. Although it is generally agreed that the personal element outweighed the professional in their friendship, interpretation of Horace's poems to Maecenas must nonetheless take some account of the realities of patronage in the Augustan Age.

The old view of Maecenas as "Minister of Propaganda" and of the poets that gathered around him as paid agents of the regime was put to rest long ago.[11] Among literary critics, biographical reconstruction has given way to an appreciation of the formal, possibly even fictive, nature of the texts. Thus, *recusationes* are explained not only as refusals of actual patronal requests for epic but also, and primarily, as manifestos of Callimachean aesthetics.[12] Similarly, there is increasing recognition that a patron's external role (if any) in occasioning a poem is far less important than his literary role within the larger poetic design.[13] On the historical level, too, there has been a significant revaluation. It is well known that, as *equites*, most of the poets did not need regular financial support.[14] Recent study has further clarified their material and social position by showing that literary patronage was but one aspect of a much larger institution, *amicitia*, by which Roman society at all levels was organized into a network of reciprocal exchanges.[15]

These various approaches agree in deemphasizing the uniqueness and completeness of the poet's dependence on his patron. Although questions of personal, political, and artistic integrity were bound to arise, given the expectations of both sides, poets were able to cope by devising ingenious strategies of independence. These ranged from Tibullus's habitation of an insulated pastoral-erotic landscape to Propertius's outright refusal to celebrate the new regime.[16] Horace had other, more subtle, ways of reconciling his need and affection for Maecenas with his own autonomy. Critics have generally focused on the most obviously relevant works, the *recusationes*, and poems like *Satire* 2.6 and *Epistle* 1.7 which can be labeled declarations of independence. But Horace's most comprehensive attempt to define his relationship with Maecenas is represented by the eight poems addressed to the patron in the first collection of *Odes*.

The arrangement of these poems is usually explained in terms of static patterning. The compliment Horace elsewhere bestows on Maecenas—*Prima dicte mihi, summa dicende Camena* (*Epist.* 1.1.1)—can almost serve as a statement of this principle, for, when the epilogue is excluded, the first and last odes are addressed to the patron (C. 1.1, 3.29).[17] Also, the center of each book is occupied by a rededication to him (C. 1.20, 2.12, 3.16). Finally, Maecenas closes Book 2 (C. 2.20) and opens Book 3 at the first practical opportunity after the Roman Odes

(C. 3.8).¹⁸ But this symmetry at beginnings, middles, and ends is not exact. C. 2.17, for instance, is addressed to Maecenas but stands outside the scheme; it should also be noted that, while Maecenas occurs at the midpoint of each book, that position is calculated roughly by line totals in Book 2 (C. 2.1–11 = 288, 12–20 = 284), but in Books 1 and 3 by the total number of poems.¹⁹ In any case, static symmetry is not the only or the most important principle of arrangement. The Maecenas odes are also dynamically disposed to chart the poet's gradual movement toward greater independence.

C. 1.1 has already been examined as a formal and thematic overture. But it also serves another function, to dedicate the entire collection to Maecenas. Some have objected to the fulsome praise of Maecenas, as others have complained that its insertion only at the beginning and the end of the ode is mechanical and gratuitous.²⁰ These objections, however, ignore the patron's function in the larger structure of the poem. On one level, this is a poetic testament, retrospective in affirming moral continuity with the *Satires*, and programmatic in establishing new generic expectations.²¹ The patron's role in this process may perhaps be clarified by comparison with Catullus's first poem. Catullus proclaims his neoteric standards not to distinguish himself from Nepos but, rather, to exploit some striking resemblances between himself and his friend. Both men, as writers, are innovative (*novum*, 1 = *ausus . . . unus*, 5); the works of both are refined (*pumice expolitum*, 2 = *doctis . . . et laboriosis*, 7); and, finally, both compose on the small scale (*libellum*, 1, and *nugas*, 4 = *tribus . . . cartis*, 6). In other words, Catullus sets up an analogy between himself and Nepos by implying that they share an allegiance to Callimachean literary standards.²²

Although Horace does not compare himself with his patron, his poetic program is also inseparable from, and indeed accomplished by, the personal dedication. Deferential and dependent, it is framed by effusive compliments for Maecenas. The opening address extols the nobility of his Etruscan lineage in grandiloquent language, and the flattery is enhanced by the likelihood that it stretches the truth:²³

>   Maecenas atavis edite regibus,
>   o et praesidium et dulce decus meum . . .   [C. 1.1.1–2]

Maecenas, sprung from royal ancestors, o my protection and sweet glory. . . .

The *priamel* that follows enumerates a number of the occupations in which men glory (*palma* ... / ... *evehit ad deos*, 5–6; *honoribus*, 8) or take delight (*iuvat*, 4; *gaudentem*, 11; *iuvant*, 23). But Horace has already indicated that his glory and delight (*dulce decus*, 2) is Maecenas, and so we are prepared for the end of the ode where the proclamation of the poet's superiority prompts the patron's reappearance:

> quodsi me lyricis vatibus inseres,
> sublimi feriam sidera vertice. [C. 1.1.35–36]

But if you enroll me among the lyric bards, I shall strike the stars with my uplifted head.

At the end of his first poem, Catullus had prayed that the Muse allow his poetry to survive "for a century or two" (*plus uno maneat perenne saeclo*, Cat. 1.10). Though Horace's hope for immortality in the canon of lyric poets is surely more audacious, it is also qualified by being contingent upon the approval not only of the Muses (32–34) but also of the patron, who is the recipient of his prayer and the agent of his apotheosis.

Maecenas next appears in C. 1.20 where Horace invites him for a drink. The poet's tone has already become less formal and more familiar. The encomium, for instance, is no longer direct as in C. 1.1, but oblique. Thus, Maecenas's Etruscan heritage is only hinted at, as the Tiber, whose source is in Etruria, is dubbed his "paternal river" (*paterni / fluminis*, 5–6). Similarly, the title *eques* (5) becomes, in context, an oblique compliment, for it alludes to the privileged seating enjoyed by the knights at the theater. Even the wine that Maecenas is offered is invested with indirect encomiastic significance. Its modesty (1–2) sets up an honorific contrast with the luxurious vintages to which the wealthy Maecenas is accustomed (9–12). Its bottling by the poet when Maecenas's recovery from illness was applauded in the theater attests to the public and private devotion the great man inspires. That the wine is Sabine (2) implies the poet's gratitude as well, for it alludes to the gift of the Sabine farm. Finally, the very image of Italian wine in a Greek jar (*Graeca* ... *testa*, 2) calls to mind Horace's descriptions of his poetic achievement as a synthesis of Greek and Roman elements (e.g. C. 3.30.13–14; *Epist.* 1.19.21–34), and the vocabulary (e.g. *conditum*, 3) and motifs here are often calculated ambiguities, applying to poetry as well as to wine.[24] The drink is ultimately suggestive of Horace's own poetry which Maecenas, as its guarantor, is invited to imbibe.

It is not, however, just in the oblique and sometimes symbolic quality of its encomium that C. 1.20 differs from the first ode. It also introduces a number of motifs and themes that will recur in undeniably self-assertive odes farther along in the sequence. These include the patron's recovery from illness (cf. C. 2.17), his equestrian status (cf. C. 3.16), the invitation to drink (cf. C. 3.8, 29), the Etruscan river (cf. C. 3.29), and the social and material disparity between the rich man and the poet (cf. C. 2.17; 3.16, 29). When they recur in subsequent poems, these elements will be exploited to establish the poet's independence from his patron. As yet, however, they have only the honorific function that has been observed. The Maecenas odes are an ordered sequence, and, though C. 1.20 facilitates the distancing process, we can read too much into the poem by reading too far ahead.[25]

Basically, then, the first book of *Odes* acknowledges, directly in C. 1.1 and obliquely in C. 1.20, Horace's respect for and dependence on Maecenas. In Book 2, however, this deferential and dependent stance is much qualified. It is significant that Maecenas does not open the volume (C. 2.1 is for Pollio), and that his first appearance is in a *recusatio*, C. 2.12. Horace's strategy here is to co-opt his patron to his own position. This is accomplished by the very first word, Nolis: Horace refuses to write heroics not because he is unable to do so (the usual gambit, as in C. 1.6), but because Maecenas is unwilling. Other details contribute to the co-option of the patron. For example, when Maecenas is urged to take on the literary task himself—an unlikely eventuality in light of his neoteric tastes—he is portrayed as writing not in poetry but in prose (*pedestribus* / . . . *historiis*, 9–10). Similarly, the rest of the poem (13–28) celebrates Maecenas's love for a certain Licymnia who may be a cover for his wife, Terentia, but who, in any case, has a symbolic function. Her name is a Greek translation, from λιγύς and ὕμνος, of a phrase in the poem, *dulcis* . . . / *cantus* (13–14). Licymnia, then, incarnates an alternative to politics and political poetry—for Maecenas love and for Horace love poetry.[26]

This analogy between poet and patron which Horace exploits to assert his independence is further developed, and then broken down, in the sequence of four poems with which Book 2 closes.[27] In C. 2.17 Horace calms Maecenas's fears of death. As evidence that their stars are linked (*consentit astrum*, 22), two biographical details are adduced: Maecenas's recovery from illness (22–26) and the poet's own miraculous escape from death when a tree nearly fell on his head (27–30). These salvations were introduced independently at C. 1.20 and 2.13 respectively, but their conjunction here in the same poem expresses the closeness of the association between the two men. And yet, there are already some discrepancies. Although Maecenas is called, in words that recall the opening of C. 1.1, the glory and prop of the poet's existence (*mearum / grande decus columenque rerum*, 3–4), his anxiety and constant requests for reassurance which prompt this ode (*Cur me querelis exanimas tuis*, 1) belie the compliment and anticipate the role reversals we shall observe in Book 3 in which the patron becomes dependent on his client for support. Even more interesting are the details of salvation. It was great Jupiter who rescued Maecenas from illness (22–25), whereas Horace was protected from the falling tree by the minor woodland deity, Faunus (28–30). Similarly, Maecenas is advised to build a votive shrine in thanksgiving (30–31), but Horace can only sacrifice a humble lamb (*humilem ... agnam*, 32). Though appropriate to the rustic context here, Faunus elsewhere in Horace is also suggestive of the poet's literary inspiration,[28] and the "humble" lamb is transparently Callimachean, a conflation of the *Aetia* prologue's fat sacrifice and slender Muse (fr. 1.23–24 Pf.), and so represents (as elsewhere in Horace) the poem itself.[29] At the end of an ode ostensibly comparing poet and patron, these contrasts are also a subtle indication of where the resemblance ultimately breaks down.

This is made explicit in the very next ode. C. 2.18 is not strictly a Maecenas ode: the patron is not addressed by name and *tu* (17) is ostensibly an unspecified second person. Nisbet and Hubbard, however, argue very strongly for the ambiguity of *tu*, noting a striking number of possible covert allusions to Maecenas in the poem. Thus, the mention of the heir of Attalus (5–6) conjures up not only Maecenas's wealth but also his Etruscan heritage (as Attalus's Lydian realm was the alleged origin of the Etruscans), the rich man's clients trail Etruscan-style garments (7–8), the luxurious architecture (17–28) calls to mind the *turris Maecenatiana* (which will be mentioned openly in C. 3.29), and the emphasis on death and the underworld (18–19, 29–40) is appropriate to Maecenas's own morbid preoccupations.[30] It might be added that the change in addressee from Maecenas in C. 2.17 to *tu* in C. 2.18 is paralleled by the internal structure of several individual poems (e.g. C. 1.1, S. 1.1, Epist. 1.1) which move from Maecenas to an unspecified second person who suggests both the general reader and the patron.

Finally, whatever view we take of the second person, there are unmistakable third-person allusions to Maecenas in one passage. Having rejected wealth, Horace proclaims that his riches are invested elsewhere:

> at fides et ingeni
>   benigna vena est pauperemque dives
> me petit: nihil supra
>   deos lacesso nec potentem amicum
>
> largiora flagito,
>   satis beatus unicis Sabinis.   [C. 2.18.9–14]

But I have loyalty and a rich vein of talent, and the wealthy man seeks me out, a poor man. I ask nothing more of the gods nor do I request more of my powerful friend, since I am sufficiently blessed in my singular Sabine farm.

In so personal a passage, references to a rich man who pursues Horace, to a powerful friend who grants his request, and, finally, to the Sabine farm can only point to Maecenas. Here, as in the preceding poem, there is a hint of role reversal, as the rich man seeks out the poor client: *pauperemque dives / me petit*.[31] Similarly, the contrast between poet and patron which was symbolized in C. 2.17 by their different tutelary deities and thank offerings is now made explicit, specified as the difference between material wealth and the spiritual and poetic riches that infinitely surpass it.

The next ode, C. 2.19, is a hymn to Bacchus which attempts to convey through Dionysiac imagery the essence of this poetic experience, its isolation, excitement, and mystical power. But this excludes Maecenas who is not a poet and who is neither addressed nor mentioned here. He does, however, receive the final ode in the book, C. 2.20. The poet has moved from inspiration to immortality, from cause to effect. Although the imagery of a bird metamorphosis is humorous, the conception behind it is basically serious and striking. The poet, soaring aloft on newly sprouted wings, leaves his patron grounded far below:

> non ego, pauperum
> sanguis parentum, non ego, quem vocas,
> dilecte Maecenas, obibo
> nec Stygia cohibebor unda. [C. 2.20.5–8]

The offspring of poor parents, I shall not die, I, whom you call upon, beloved Maecenas, nor shall I be held in by the waters of the Styx.

In C. 2.17, we recall, Horace had announced that he and Maecenas would die together. By C. 2.20 the analogy between the two men has broken down completely, and Horace boasts that, as a poet, he will not die at all: *non ego, . . . / . . . obibo* (6–7).

After such a bold assertion, Book 3 fully develops a role reversal in its portrayal of the patron-client relationship, as Maecenas becomes spiritually dependent on Horace.[32] This had been anticipated, as we have seen, in Book 2 where a role reversal is implicit in the context of two poems: in the patron's requests for reassurance at C. 2.17.1, and in the rich man's active pursuit of the poet at C. 2.18.10–11. Now, however, role reversal is accomplished by the poem's content, as Horace extends the paraenetic function of ancient lyric by venturing not only advice but also explicit criticism, and by setting himself up as a model for Maecenas.

C. 3.8 is a drinking song like C. 1.20. But whereas that poem was honorific, this is playful. Horace teases his patron in the opening address for his useless learning (1–5), and even the language may parody Maecenas's precious literary style:[33]

> Martiis caelebs quid agam kalendis,
> quid velint flores et acerra turis
> plena miraris positusque carbo in
>   caespite vivo,
>
> docte sermones utriusque linguae:
> voveram dulcis epulas et album
> Libero caprum prope funeratus
>   arboris ictu. [C. 3.8.1–8]

What I, a bachelor, am doing on March first, what the flowers mean and the box full of incense, and the coal placed on living turf—do you wonder at this, who are learned in the lore of both languages? I had vowed sweet banquets and a white kid to Liber when I was nearly killed by the falling tree.

In C. 1.20 Maecenas had been invited to drink in celebration of his own escape from death, but now in C. 3.8 he is to toast his client's health. In a similar reversal, the wine which was honorific in C. 1.20 now takes on a hortatory significance,[34] for Horace advises Maecenas to enjoy life and to cease worrying about the state:

> mitte civilis super urbe curas:
> . . . .
> neglegens, ne qua populus laboret,
> parce privatus nimium cavere et
> dona praesentis cape laetus horae:
>   linque severa.   [C. 3.8.17, 25–28]

Put aside political worries about the city.... Unconcerned about whether the people are anywhere in trouble, as a private citizen stop worrying too much and happily take the gifts of the present hour. Leave serious matters behind.

In light of this injunction, the setting and mode of address are not only humorous but also programmatic. *Docte sermones utriusque linguae* (5): though "learned in the lore of both tongues" (i.e. Greek and Latin), Maecenas is at a loss to explain why his friend, a bachelor, should be celebrating 1 March, the Matronalia. But Horace informs him that he is not observing that public holiday but rather a private anniversary that just happens to coincide with it, his deliverance from the falling tree. This is precisely what Maecenas must learn to do, to put aside public matters (*civilis* . . . *curas*, 17) and become a private citizen (*privatus*, 26). Horace functions, then, as a model for his patron to emulate.

   The middle poem of the book, C. 3.16, goes further, taking as its subject not the cares of state but rather the cares that are engendered by wealth which are equally burdensome. Drawing from myth (Danae, 1–11), heroic legend (Amphiaraus, 11–13), Greek history (Philip, 13–15), and recent Roman history (if *navium* / . . . *duces*, 15–16, alludes to Menas who was twice enticed by money to desert from

Sextus Pompeius to Octavian), Horace illustrates not just the destructive power of wealth but also its capacity to produce anxiety and greed, and then he dissociates himself from this way of life:

> crescentem sequitur cura pecuniam
> maiorumque fames: iure perhorrui
> late conspicuum tollere verticem,
>   Maecenas, equitum decus.   [C. 3.16.17–20]

Care follows upon increasing wealth, as does hunger for greater riches. With good reason I have shrunk from raising my head conspicuously, Maecenas, glory of the knights.

Here too the mode of address is functional: alluding to Maecenas's equestrian status, Horace implies that his own preference for the simple life resembles his patron's lack of worldly ambition. This looks at first like the old strategy of co-option. But what follows is problematic:

> quanto quisque sibi plura negaverit,
> ab dis plura feret: nil cupientium
> nudus castra peto et transfuga divitum
>   partis linquere gestio,
>
> contemptae dominus splendidior rei.
>   [C. 3.16.21–25]

The more each man denies himself, the more he will receive from the gods. Naked I seek the camps of those who desire nothing, and as an exile I long to desert the quarters of the rich, a more splendid master of the wealth I despise.

As the "glory of the knights," *equitum decus* (20), Maecenas would presumably qualify for inclusion among the rather vaguely expressed *nil cupientium* (22) whom Horace seeks out. Yet, as a very rich man, he is at least a potential member of the camp from which Horace deserts. R. J. Shork has demonstrated, for instance, that the examples of flawed wealth with which the poem opens are all at least marginally relevant to Maecenas. All are cases of fraternal, dynastic rivalry and involve the use of money for political bribery. Maecenas's wealth must have recommended itself to Augustus for similar reasons in the years of his contested ascent to power. Thus, the address to Maecenas follows as almost the last item in the catalog, "the fifth *exemplum*, by no means parallel to the previous four, but a personal and contemporary reminder to Horace of the dangers inherent in wealth."[35] And so, Horace ends by rejecting more help from his patron:

> inportuna tamen pauperies abest
> nec, si plura velim, tu dare deneges.
> . . . .
> multa petentibus
> desunt multa: bene est cui deus obtulit
> parca quod satis est manu.   [C. 3.16.37-38, 42-44]

But troublesome poverty is absent, nor would you refuse to give me more if I wanted it.... To those seeking much, much is wanting. He fares well to whom the god with a sparing hand has given what is enough.

This is more than a polite acknowledgment of gratitude made necessary by the awkward circumstance of dedicating a poem on poverty to one's benefactor. Horace's attitude throughout has been ambiguous, his gratitude tempered with wariness; and, while he compliments Maecenas for his willingness to provide further assistance, he also precludes the acceptance of any such offer.[36]

The final Maecenas ode, C. 3.29, recapitulates themes and motifs from throughout the collection, especially from the other Maecenas odes. But now advice gives way to a critique more thoroughgoing than that contained in any of the preceding poems. Maecenas is yet again invited for a drink, but the poet's tone betrays impatience. That the wine is untouched (non ante verso, 2) and has long been awaiting Maecenas (iamdudum, 5) implies that previous invitations have gone unheeded—not just the literal summonses of C. 1.20 and 3.8, but also the larger philosophical messages contained therein. This is confirmed by the picture of the unreconstructed Maecenas that follows. Gazing wistfully from his tower at the Campagna (9-12), he nevertheless delays his arrival there, still subject to the same distractions:

> fastidiosam desere copiam et
> molem propinquam nubibus arduis:
>   omitte mirari beatae
>   fumum et opes strepitumque Romae.

. . . .

> tu civitatem quis deceat status
> curas et urbi sollicitus times,
>   quid Seres et regnata Cyro
>   Bactra parent Tanaisque discors.
>   [C. 3.29.9–12, 25–28]

Abandon cloying abundance and the pile that reaches to the lofty clouds. Stop marveling at the fumes, riches, and noise of blessed Rome. . . . You are concerned about the state's proper condition and, anxious for the city, you fear what the Chinese are planning and Bactria ruled by Cyrus and the quarrelsome Scythians.

Just as the patron's cloying wealth (*fastidiosam . . . copiam*, 9) recalls the theme of C. 3.16, so his political anxieties here are familiar from C. 3.8. It is, of course, honorific to show Maecenas concerned with affairs of state. But in C. 3.8 his anxiety was shown to be groundless (18–24), and now in C. 3.29 Horace states explicitly that it is impious as well, for it runs counter to the intent of the god who has shrouded the future in darkness:

> prudens futuri temporis exitum
> caliginosa nocte premit deus
>   ridetque, si mortalis ultra
>   fas trepidat.   [C. 3.29.29–32]

Prudently god hides the outcome of the future in dark night and laughs if mortals fear more than is right.

This leads to an almost perfunctory injunction to enjoy life, which is tailored to Maecenas by means of one striking and strategic image:

>   quod adest memento
>
> conponere aequos: cetera fluminis
> ritu feruntur, nunc medio alveo
>   cum pace delabentis Etruscum
>   in mare, nunc lapides adesos
>
> stirpisque raptas et pecus et domos
> volventis una, non sine montium

> clamore vicinaeque silvae,
>   cum fera diluvies quietos
> inritat amnis. [C. 3.29.32–41]

Remember calmly to set in order what is at hand. The rest is carried away like a river which now flows peacefully in mid channel down into the Etruscan Sea, but now catches up in its rush worn stones, uprooted tree trunks, and the flock and houses all together, making noise in the mountains and the neighboring woods when the wild flood enrages quiet rivers.

To convey the changeability to which Maecenas should be immune, Horace evokes the erratic course of the Tiber, identified as the river "flowing into the Etruscan Sea" (35–36). The rare hypermetron whereby the word *Etruscum* does indeed flow into the next line's *in mare* is not just a neat mimetic trick but also alerts us to the significance of the description.[37] In the opening address Maecenas had been reminded of his Etruscan lineage (*Tyrrhena regum progenies*, 1), and in C. 1.20 the Tiber was, for this reason, called his "paternal river" (5–6). The river image in C. 3.29, then, gives point to the opening address and personalizes the injunction by implying that Maecenas should learn from his heritage. And perhaps not only the Etruscan but also the regal aspect of that heritage is exploited in the very next words:

>   ille potens sui
>   laetusque deget, cui licet in diem
>   dixisse "vixi." [C. 3.29.41–43]

That man will live happily as master of himself who can say each day "I have lived."

In C. 2.18 Horace thanked, but set himself apart from, his *potentem amicum* (12), and in C. 3.16 wealth's destructive power (*potentius*, 10) is rejected by Horace who has thereby become its master (*dominus*, 25). Liberated from materialistic associations, the word *potens* takes on a new, more spiritual meaning in C. 3.29. Maecenas claims regal descent; however, true power is not that wielded by kings over their subjects, but that exercised over oneself, *potens sui* (41).

At this point the patron disappears from the poem, the rest of which consists of a long monologue by one who has achieved this mastery of himself. His impassioned advocacy of a life of simplicity and acquiescence to Fortune is not consistent with the previous negative picture of Maecenas. But it is a familiar Horatian theme, and the first person narrator is inevitably identified by the reader as Horace himself.[38] The poem then concludes with one final, charming image:

> tunc me biremis praesidio scaphae
> tutum per Aegaeos tumultus
>   aura feret geminusque Pollux.   [C. 3.29.62–64]

Then the breeze and Castor and Pollux will bear me safely through Aegean waves protected in my two-oared skiff.

This subtle modulation from patron to poet imitates the movement of the entire collection. In the very first ode, Maecenas had been characterized as the poet's support, *praesidium* (C. 1.1.2). Now, in the last poem addressed to him, Maecenas gradually fades away and the word *praesidio* (62) describes the poet's own craft which enjoys divine protection.

This brief survey of the Maecenas odes has necessarily been schematic, focusing only on one aspect of the poems. Although the complexity of the individual odes has thereby been simplified, their dramatic progress as a group is now apparent. In Book 1 Horace is deferential and dependent, emphasizing the material differences between himself and his patron. In Book 2 these differences acquire a spiritual dimension as Horace's poverty becomes symbolic of the artistic riches that set him apart from others, including Maecenas. Finally, in Book 3 the distinction between the two men is mainly philosophical, the superiority of Horace's very way of life to his patron's anxiety-ridden existence. Their roles are reversed as Horace becomes, in a sense, the spiritual patron of Maecenas. Because this order of publication does not seem to coincide with that of composition, it is not possible to trace in this sequence of poems the history of the relationship. Their clear movement toward independence may be based on an historical or psychological development, but is ultimately an aesthetic effect. While consistently affirming Horace's sincere affection for Maecenas, these odes, by their dynamic disposition, create a certain distance and enable their author to maintain a high degree of personal and artistic freedom.

It is precisely this freedom that makes possible the achievement celebrated in the final poem of the collection:

> Exegi monumentum aere perennius
> regalique situ pyramidum altius,
> quod non imber edax, non aquilo impotens
> possit diruere aut innumerabilis
>
> annorum series et fuga temporum.
> non omnis moriar multaque pars mei
> vitabit Libitinam: usque ego postera
> crescam laude recens, dum Capitolium
>
> scandet cum tacita virgine pontifex:
> dicar, qua violens obstrepit Aufidus
> et qua pauper aquae Daunus agrestium
> regnavit populorum, ex humili potens
>
> princeps Aeolium carmen ad Italos
> deduxisse modos. sume superbiam
> quaesitam meritis et mihi Delphica
> lauro cinge volens, Melpomene, comam. [C. 3.30.1–16]

I have built a monument more enduring than bronze, more lofty than the royal mound of the pyramids, which neither corrosive rain nor the furious north wind can destroy, nor the countless succession of the years and the flight of time. I shall not entirely die, but a great part of me will escape Libitina [the goddess of death]. I shall grow ever fresh with future praise, as long as the Pontifex climbs the Capitol with the silent Vestal Virgin. Where the raging Aufidus thunders and where Daunus, poor in water, ruled over countryfolk, I who have risen from humble origins to become powerful shall be said to have been the first to bring Aeolian song to Italian measures. Take up the proud honor that has been deserved, Melpomene, and willingly crown my hair with Delphic laurel.

It is often noted that just as Horace's other boastful epilogue, C. 2.20, is qualified by its humor, so here too Horace is a bit self-deprecatory. This is perceived in the double hypallage (if such it be) of the boast itself (13–14),[39] and in the very structure of the poem, its threefold downward movement. Horace's achievement is first said to be immune from the elements and time itself (3–5), but is soon qualified as coterminous not with nature but with the nation (8–9), and, finally, it is circumscribed within even narrower boundaries, those of Horace's native Apulian countryside (10–11).[40] But this movement is not necessarily downward, and the initial boast may be enhanced rather than diminished by these subsequent details. Thus, the reference to the Capitol calls attention to the political resonance of *princeps* (13), which suggests that Horace is to poetry what Augustus is to the state. Similarly, Horace's local pride corresponds to the very nature of his achievement, which was to have transferred Greek song *ad Italos / . . . modos* (13–14).

The epilogue is certainly a proud document and, as such, it follows quite smoothly from the preceding ode to Maecenas. Horace's boast of self-sufficiency there, *potens sui* (C. 3.29.41), leads up to *ex humili potens* here (12), just as his triumphant *vixi* in C. 3.29.43 is now taken one step further by *non omnis moriar* (6). In moving from C. 3.29 to 30, the poet has moved from the satisfaction of having lived fully in this world to the assurance of life beyond it in his poetry. This was the prayer for immortality that Horace had addressed to Maecenas in the first ode (C. 1.1.35–36). Now it is finally answered, though it is not Maecenas who grants it, but the Muse, Melpomene, an emblem of the poet's own creative power.[41] This power and endurance, we should note, are proclaimed not for the individual poem but for the collection of *Odes* 1–3 as a whole. It is the poetry book which has become, finally, a monument more enduring than bronze.

CONCLUSIONS

ONE

Before formulating some general conclusions about Horace's techniques of arrangement and their relevance to the interpretation and appreciation of his poetry, it will be useful to summarize briefly the results of the preceding investigation of the *Odes*.

Recent papyri finds and critical advances have necessitated a revaluation of the evidence regarding the origin and development of the poetry book. Several widely held beliefs can now be challenged, such as the alleged genealogy of the poetry book from Alexandrian editions of classical authors, or the overriding importance attached to *variatio* as a principle of design. Most important for the understanding of Horace's *Odes*, however, is the distinction between them and the other Augustan poetry books which are relatively homogeneous in meter and content. The *Odes*, on the other hand, are far more heterogeneous, closer perhaps to Hellenistic and Roman republican collections (insofar as their organization can be reconstructed). Like these predecessors, the *Odes* are not likely to be structured around any single principle of organization. On the other hand, a poem-by-poem reading reveals that Horace's exploitation of the random linkage, whether superficial or at some deeper level, is more thoroughgoing than has been thought.

The first book appears to be the most diversified in all respects. Its nine initial Parade Odes constitute an implicit poetic for the whole, setting Horatian lyric against satire, Greek lyric, and epic, especially Vergil's *Aeneid*. The rest of the poems in the book then group themselves into a number of smaller units, and the whole volume is tied together by the recurrence of certain basic themes such as Augustan politics, love, and poetry.

In contrast with this opening book, the second is the most tightly unified of the three. The metrical alternation of Sapphics and Alcaics in the first eleven poems underscores their grouping by theme into pairs of poems concentrically arranged. Though the second half of the book resists such neat analysis, it too is carefully arranged, as static patterning is abandoned in favor of a dynamic sequence of poems exploring the twin themes of luxury and death, and poetry and immortality. Finally, C. 2.7–13 constitute a third group located in the center of the book and overlapping both halves. They combine both static and dynamic techniques, since the disposition of contrasting poems into concentric frames enacts the inner dialectic of the central poem, C. 2.10, in which the Golden Mean is apprehended in terms of antithetical extremes.

The two Alcaic odes on inspiration and immortality that close Book 2 lead nicely into the Roman Odes that open Book 3. Although schematic and thematic structures have been proposed for these six poems, their arrangement is also dramatic: against a backdrop of virtue, Horace plays out the tension between the godhead of Augustus and the godlessness of the people he rules. The rest of the poems in the first half of the book then break from the Roman Odes, for they are either about love or else easily assimilated to such a lighter mood. In a sense, the first half of Book 3 resembles the *Aeneid* in that it juxtaposes two voices, the public and the private. Unlike Vergil, however, Horace creates C. 3.8 and 14 in which the two voices are made to sing in harmony. The second half of the book then works toward a speedy conclusion, for it not only makes frequent allusions to closure but is also structured sequentially, so that one poem leads to the next and on, ultimately, to the end of the book.

Turning, finally, from the individual books to the three-book ensemble, we see that the same sort of arrangements are operative, only on a much larger scale. Thus, there are static patterns such as the framing of the collection by at least seven poems at the beginning and seven at the end. But there are also sequences of noncontiguous poems, the most important of which is the series of eight odes addressed to Maecenas and enacting the poet's gradual independence from his patron.

TWO

From even this bald summary it is possible to derive some general principles regarding the criteria according to which poems are related to one another, and about the forms that these relationships can take. At the most basic level, two or more odes are related by the fact of similarity or difference with regard to one or more poetic features. It is noteworthy, however, that Horace never avails himself of certain rather obvious possibilities. Chronology, for instance, seems to play no significant role in the disposition of the poems apart from the somewhat puzzling fact that Book 1 contains more of the poems that can be dated to an early period. Equally unimportant is narrative and argumentative discourse; that is, poems are not linked by continuity of plot or explicit argument, presumably because such features are more suited to epic or didactic poetry than to lyric verse. Instead, meter, theme, and verbal reminiscence provide the most obvious points of contact between odes. Tone or atmosphere is also very important, and odes can even be related by very specific and tangible details. Thus, the first odes of Books 1 and 2 have addressees who are not only prominent Romans but also prime examples of the new regime's co-option of and clemency toward the old republican faction. Many other poems are connected not by their addressees but by imagery, particularly when they share nature as a moral metaphor. Structural similarity also seems to be a factor in the positioning of poems: C. 1.27 and 28, for instance, are both dramatic monologues, and C. 3.5 and 6 have similar movements, from the vision of a degenerate present to the remembrance of a different past. A particularly common method of linkage is, of course, by literary model: a pair like C. 3.21 and 22, for example, shares a debt both to Catullus and the Greek epigrammatists, whereas more public utterances such as the Roman Odes seem to recall Pindar. Finally, even a slight detail such as a poem's setting or occasion can serve to establish connections, as in the case of C. 3.17, 18, and 19, all of which celebrate winter festivals.

Examples could be drawn from the earlier chapters of this study to illustrate further each of these features or to suggest new ones. But the variety of criteria according to which poems are related should by now be clear. It is worth noting, however, that odes can be related at one level while differing with regard to other criteria. C. 3.7 is an excellent example: in meter, tone, address, and literary models, it breaks from the preceding Roman Odes; but its basic theme, adultery, clearly relates it not only to the general moralizing of that earlier cycle but also to a specific concern of C. 3.6, sexual degeneracy. A second important point should also be kept in mind: although the variety of organizational criteria may be great, not all criteria are equally important. Some, like thematic and verbal reminiscence, are sufficient in themselves to establish a connection between poems. Others, however, can only reinforce. Thus, those very rare collocations of poems in the same meter invariably call attention to some other connection, usually thematic, between the poems. The same limitations apply to numerology which, when pursued as an end in itself, usually leads to unsatisfactory results. Yet the midpoint break in Book 2, which is otherwise perceptible by a change in meter, theme, and addressee, is reinforced by the nearly exact line totals of the two halves of the book, and by the position of C. 2.1–12 in the exact center of the collection. Similarly, the thematic resemblance between C. 3.1 and 6 is reinforced by the equal length of the poems, just as the importance of C. 3.4 is signaled both by its status as the longest of all the odes and by the fact that it is surrounded by two masses of equal length (C. 3.2–3 = 5–6 = 104 lines).

Once odes are related to one another on the basis of these features, they are then disposed in one of three ways. The first and most basic is *variatio*, the avoidance of certain obvious collocations, particularly of meter and addressee. *Variatio*, however, is essentially a negative consideration, and Horace avails himself of two other, more positive organizational principles. These are static patterning, either framed (ABBA) or interlocked (ABAB), and dynamic sequences (ABCD). Horace's use of these is characterized by several features. First, the same types of arrangement are capable of structuring everything from small groups of contiguous poems to series of noncontiguous odes that span a whole book or even the three-book ensemble. Second, of the two structural possibilities, static and dynamic, the latter are far more common, interesting, and critically significant. Indeed, this is borne out by the third major characteristic of Horatian practice, the way in which static and dynamic structures are often interdependent. In other words, even the most abstractly patterned groups are often capable of a sequential reading. Thus, C. 1.1 and 3.30 balance each other and frame the collection; but they also mark a real progression, from the poet's prayer for poetic immortality to his final boast that it has been achieved in his art. Finally, it is not possible to fit each and every poem into some definite structure. A good case in point is C. 3.13, the Bandusia ode which, as we have seen, stands outside the concentric disposition of C. 3.7–15. But the presence of some neutral material in the collection should not be surprising, since an attempt to dispose every poem according to some design would have resulted in what Collinge has aptly dubbed "aesthetic indigestion." The pursuit of artistic strategy by poet and reader must always allow for some fortuity.

THREE

From the criteria according to which odes are related, and the forms that these relationships can take, we pass, finally, to the question that prompted this study in the first place, namely the literary function of arrangement. In other words, apart from any private delight in virtuosity that the author might derive from it, does the arrangement of the *Odes* make any real difference to the reader?

On one level, placement clearly has some bearing on the actual meaning of the poems. This is not to say that we must abandon the excellent critical principle so often stressed by Fraenkel, namely that each ode is self-sufficient and contains within itself all the information necessary for its interpretation.[1] And yet, even Fraenkel departed slightly from his own principle when he based his interpretation of C. 1.38 as a literary manifesto on nothing more than its prominent position as the epilogue to its book. Fraenkel's intuition has been validated by more recent scholarship which has argued on the basis of internal evidence that literary critical implications are latent in the piece. If placement, then, cannot by itself convey meaning, it can at the very least encourage us to look more carefully at a poem's meaning than we might ordinarily be inclined to do. At the very most, it can even enhance meaning. Thus, we have seen that the close structural similarity between the two dramatic monologues, C. 1.27 and 28, helps to clarify the mise-en-scène of the latter which is difficult to recognize initially owing to Horace's experimental treatment of his models. Or again, many poems that at first reading appear to be straightforward take on an unmistakable programmatic significance when read in conjunction with other poems. Thus, C. 3.26, an apparently simple lover's dedication, is recognized as an allusion to closure when it is read as the sequel to C. 3.25 and the balancing poem to C. 1.5. Finally, progressive cycles such as the Roman Odes or the Maecenas odes convey a meaning largely independent of that conveyed by any one member of the cycle: the former group explores the tension between the ruler and his people, the latter group Horace's gradual growth toward poetic independence. In these instances, the whole is truly more than the sum of its parts.

Arrangement, however, is not just an intellectual but also an aesthetic device; its function is not only to enhance meaning but also to create and maintain certain effects, impressions, and moods. *Variatio*, for example, prevents the reader from becoming bored; static patterns enliven the whole through surface artifice; and dynamic sequences create momentum and, at last, a sense of closure. Ultimately, though, these techniques impart a sense of unity and coherence to what would otherwise have been a hopelessly heterogeneous collection. Thus, even the most negative strategy, *variatio*, contributes greatly to this effect, for its most important function is not so much to diversify an already varied body of poems as it is to tie it together: insofar as similar poems are separated, they serve almost as leitmotivs, any one occurrence of which will conjure up those that precede and anticipate those that follow. If we may adapt a common ancient metaphor for poetic activity, they are the threads out of which the poetic texture is woven. Or, to use a metaphor from Horace's own epilogue, they are the individual stones out of which a single monumental edifice is constructed. Horace has woven, or built, so successfully, that his three books do not appear to be a medley of discrete poems but almost one large poem.

Thus, composition and disposition are at last revealed to be related activities. It had always been suspected that Horace might have composed certain odes, or at least revised them, with an eye on their eventual placement in the larger publication.[2] It is not possible to confirm this, however, and in any case the more interesting relationship between composition and disposition is not really chronological but qualitative. In other words, an analogy obtains between the structural principles upon which the individual ode is built and those operative in the creation of the larger collection.

Of course, the unity that the collection possesses is a unity in diversity which necessarily differs from the extraordinarily tight coherence—*simplex et unum*—of the individual ode. Nevertheless, the collection resembles the latter in a number of ways—for example, in the simultaneous operation (or co-operation) of static structures (such as frames) and dynamic ones (such as sequences); in the *callida iunctura* which the latter display, particularly the "juxtaposition coloring" a poem can exert over its neighbors, just as a word can color the word next to it, even though they are not syntactically related;[3] and in techniques of closure, for C. 1.38 and the second half of Book 3 bring their respective volumes to the sorts of conclusion familiar from many individual odes.

In his essay, "The Philosophy of Composition," Edgar Allan Poe remarked that "What we term a long poem is, in fact, merely a succession of short ones."[4] Perhaps the reverse is also true, that a succession of poems can approximate a single entity. Certainly T. S. Eliot suggested as much in his account of the genesis of some of his larger works. Speaking of "Ash Wednesday," he observed that "like 'The Hollow Men,' it originated out of separate poems.... That's one way in which my mind does seem to have worked throughout the years poetically—doing things separately and then seeing the possibility of fusing them together, altering them, and making a kind of whole of them."[5] The same could almost be said of Horace's *Odes*, for, though they do not add up to a single poem, their unity approximates that state. The arrangement of the collection, no less than the internal structure of each poem in it, is the product of artistic sensibility and taste. As such, it is relevant to a full understanding and appreciation of the poems. In a sense, what critics as diverse as Nietzsche and Petronius have found to admire in the individual ode applies equally well to the larger collection, its resemblance to an intricate mosaic and its incomparable *curiosa felicitas*.[6]

NOTES

PREFACE

1. I deviate from Klingner in three places: C. 2.1.37 (*Musa procax, iocis*), 3.14.6 (*divis*), and 11 (*male ominatis*).

CHAPTER ONE

1. This chapter derives from my article in *Arethusa* 13 (1980). I have taken this opportunity not only to update it but also to discuss methodology more fully and to revise (esp. in the notes) some of my earlier views.
2. Von Christ, "Über die Verskunst," pp. 1–44; Kiessling, "Horatius I," pp. 48–75.
3. A roughly chronological survey of such theories with some refutation was provided by Raiz, "Die Frage nach der Anordnung," pp. 43–56; see also Simon, *Zur Anordnung der Oden*; Häusser, Review of Raiz and Simon, pp. 362–66. When meter was abandoned as the sole criterion for order in favor of verbal or thematic links, the results were equally fanciful: see Simon, ibid.; Verrall, *Studies Literary and Historical*, pp. 90–120 and passim; Belling, *Studien über die Liederbücher des Horaz*. Many of these studies, however, at least had the advantage of noting verbal echoes, for which see now Huber, *Wortwiederholungen in den Oden des Horaz*.
4. See Draheim, "Die Anordnung der Gedichte," col. 1268.
5. Duckworth, *Structural Patterns and Proportions*; Dalzell, Review of Duckworth, pp. 314–16. For general remarks on numerology see Wilkinson, *Georgics of Virgil*, pp. 316–22.
6. Segal, "Ancient Texts," p. 13. The entire article is interesting, and on the larger questions it raises see also Wilkinson, "Ancient Literature," pp. 13–26.
7. A remarkable exception is Dettmer, *Horace: A Study in Structure*. In a complicated exposition illustrated by over 150 charts and diagrams, Dettmer attempts to show that all 88 odes are arranged by theme in a ring com-

position which is occasionally interrupted at parallel intervals by smaller groups that may or may not be themselves symmetrically arranged. Utilizing a complex terminology that distinguishes between "outer-ring" and "inner-ring" poems, and between "structural" and "non-structural" ones, Dettmer searches for verbal, numerological, and metrical "clues" that the poet furnished to point up his complicated "thematic concatenation." Such ring composition, finally, is alleged to be the "predominant organizational pattern" not just of *Odes* 1–3 but of all the Augustan poetry books as well as of the Catullan corpus. A strange throwback, this approach suffers in general from the same deficiencies as the earlier scholarship discussed above, namely problems of methodology, probability, and conception. For a more specific critique of this, see p. 210, n. 2, below; see also the review of Dettmer by Syndikus, pp. 11–15. Because our ways of reading are so fundamentally opposed, I have for the most part chosen to engage in a dialogue with Horace rather than with Dettmer, whose argument the reader may evaluate independently. I have, however, cited Dettmer on points of agreement or information.

8. Apart from Dettmer, *Horace: A Study in Structure*, the only other comprehensive and systematic study of the collection was published sixty years ago by Port who, more judiciously, espoused no monolithic theory ("Die Anordnung," pp. 280–308, 427–68). For a briefer account of the Augustan poetry book that omits Horace and stresses ring composition, see Michelfeit, "Das augusteische Gedichtbuch," pp. 347–70. Other, briefer overviews include Stemplinger, "Horatius," col. 2372; Schanz and Hosius, *Geschichte der römischen Literatur* 2:126–27; Wickham, *Works of Horace* 1:25–30; Perret, *Horace*, pp. 80–84; M. Schmidt, "Die Anordnung der Oden," pp. 207–16; Giardina, "Sulla struttura delle odi," pp. 44–55; Silk, "On Theme and Design," pp. 47–54; Collinge, *Structure of Horace's Odes*, pp. 36–55 (with the review by Ludwig, pp. 171–77). I regret that it has not been possible for me to obtain the thesis of Fontaine, *Enchaînement et groupement*, which is mentioned by Collinge, ibid., p. 36 n. 2. More common than overviews, finally, are useful observations on specific groupings and collocations, especially in the introductions to individual poems by Kiessling and Heinze, *Oden und Epoden*; in random remarks in Commager's *Odes of Horace*, Fraenkel's *Horace*, Pöschl's *Horazische Lyrik*, and Wili's *Horaz und die augusteische Kultur*; and in the periodical literature. All of these will by cited where appropriate in the notes below.

9. Wilkinson, *Horace and His Lyric Poetry*, p. 15; Dawson, "The Iambi of Callimachus," p. 140.

10. Nisbet and Hubbard, *Horace: Odes, Book I*, p. xxiii; see also ibid., p. xxiv: "It is only too easy to imagine some subtle principle either of similarity or difference in every juxtaposition, not to mention more complicated sequences and cycles. Most of these suggestions seem completely fanciful, and equally ingenious reasons could be adduced to justify any arrangement." The

same authors' later commentary on Book 2 is somewhat more moderate: "The book contains 20 odes ... and as usual is arranged with a measure of design.... The organization is most apparent in the first half, particularly in the formal aspect of metre; otherwise Horace may have noticed some superficial resemblances, which may or may not now be divined, but even then he was likely to have been left with a few poems that did not fit any scheme precisely. After all he was not composing a cycle of odes, but in ancient terminology 'arranging a garland'" (Horace: Odes, Book II, pp. 5–6).

11. G. Williams, Third Book of Horace's Odes, p. 23; see also his Horace, p. 35: "The arrangement of the odes has attracted increasing attention—to little purpose." For the inadequacies of the treatment of arrangement generally in Williams's Tradition and Originality, see the review by Otis, pp. 316–30.

12. It should perhaps be noted at this point that there is no good reason to doubt that the order of the Odes as we have it is the poet's own. Whereas the position of the lyrics with relation to Horace's other works varies in the manuscripts, there is unanimity regarding the placement of individual lyrics, with only occasional dissension about poem divisions. Testimonia concur in this numeration. Finally, Horace may himself allude to a presentation copy of this work in Epistle 1.13, where the description of the contents as carmina (17) and the references to plural volumes (volumina, 2; libellis, 4; chartae, 6) would suit Odes 1–3 very well.

13. A convenient survey of theories on the Bucolics may be found in Rudd, Lines of Enquiry, pp. 119–44; to this should now be added Van Sickle, Design of Virgil's Bucolics; Dettmer, Horace: A Study in Structure, pp. 2–14. For Tibullus, see the listing in Harrauer, Bibliography to Tibullus, pp. 45–46; to this should be added Powell, "The Ordering of Tibullus Book I," pp. 107–12; Leach; "Poetics and Poetic Design," pp. 79–96; Dettmer, ibid., pp. 14–22; Mutschler, Die poetische Kunst Tibulls, pp. 157–200, 279–302. For Propertius, studies of arrangement are complicated by the textual transmission—see Ullman, "The Book Division of Propertius," pp. 45–52; and, more recently, the novel suggestion of Butrica, "The Propertian Corpus," p. 6. The extensive literature is listed in Harrauer, Bibliography to Propertius, pp. 101–2; to this should be added Barsby, "Composition and Publication," pp. 128–37; King, "Propertius' Programmatic Poetry," pp. 108–24; Putnam, "Propertius' Third Book," pp. 97–113; Dettmer, ibid., pp. 22–32; Hutchinson, "Propertius and the Unity of the Book," pp. 99–106; Stahl, Propertius, passim.

14. On the Iambi see Carrubba, Epodes of Horace. On the Sermones see Ludwig, "Komposition der beiden Satirenbücher," pp. 304–25; Jensen, "Secret Art," pp. 208–15; Rambaux, "Composition d'ensemble du livre I," pp. 179–204; Dettmer, Horace: A Study in Structure, pp. 32–35; and the series of lengthy articles by van Rooy under the general title "Arrangement and Structure of Satires," listed in the bibliography.

15. Although we are concerned with the precedents available to Horace, it

should be noted that interest in arrangement persists in later books: see, for example, Ludwig, "Anordnung des vierten Horazischen Odenbuches," pp. 1–10; Putnam, *Artifices of Eternity*; McGann, *Studies in Horace's First Book of Epistles*, pp. 33–87; Buchheit, *Studien zur Corpus Priapeorum*, pp. 43–53; Loercher, *Aufbau der drei Bücher von Ovids Amores*; Evans, *Publica Carmina*, passim; Jacobson, *Ovid's Heroides*, passim; Newmyer, *Silvae* of *Statius*, pp. 45–58, 122–30. Not unrelated to the poetry book is the disposition of episodes in the *Kollektivgedicht*: see, for example, Ludwig, *Struktur und Einheit der Metamorphosen Ovids*; Otis, *Ovid as an Epic Poet*, pp. 45–90; Galinsky, *Ovid's Metamorphoses*, pp. 79–109.

16. E.g. Otis, Review of G. Williams's *Tradition and Originality*, p. 326: "So far as we can tell, this sort of collection or poetical context was Roman and not Greek. There is, for example, no indication that Hellenistic poetry books were constructed in this way"; Otis, "Propertius' Single Book," p. 38 n. 8; Ross, *Backgrounds to Augustan Poetry*, p. 49, who seems to suggest that Gallus came up with the idea.

17. For a general account of the transition in Greek culture from the oral to the written word, see Havelock, *Literate Revolution in Greece*; Pfeiffer, *History of Classical Scholarship*, pp. 16 ff.; Davison, *From Archilochus to Pindar*, pp. 86–128. It should be noted that, even after the rise of the book, reading was largely done aloud: see Balogh, "Voces Paginarum," pp. 84–109, 202–40, with supplements by Hendrickson, "Ancient Reading," pp. 182–96, and correctives by Knox, "Silent Reading," pp. 421–35.

18. Kroll, *Studien zum Verständnis*, pp. 225–46.

19. For a description of this edition see Wilamowitz-Moellendorff, *Textgeschichte der griechischen Lyriker*. That Horace used it is likely because his placement of C. 1.2, which ends with Mercury as political savior, seems to recall the Alcaeus edition in which the second position was also occupied by Hermes: see below, pp. 21–22, with p. 187, n. 27. It should be noted, however, that not every poet's text might have achieved such fixity in antiquity. For instance, the common assumption that the Ambrosian list of Pindar's seventeen books reproduces the order of a standard Alexandrian edition is called into question by the existence of other dissenting lists: see Race, "POxy 2438 and the Order of Pindar's Works," p. 106.

20. On the remote possibility that the division of Sappho's work is older than the Alexandrian edition because the sticho-metrical subscript of POxy 1231 is in Attic notation rather than the Milesian in use in Egypt at the time, see Lobel, Σαπφοῦς Μέλη, pp. xiii–xvii.

21. See Page, *Sappho and Alcaeus*, p. 126, for the principles behind the disposition of the Epithalamians.

22. See Lobel, Σαπφοῦς Μέλη, pp. xv–xvi; see also Daly, *Contributions to a History of Alphabetization*, p. 23 n. 3.

23. See Daly, ibid., p. 23, with literature there cited.

24. This does not mean that other factors could not also have been operative. *Olympian* 1, for example, may owe its prominent placement to its popularity in antiquity (Lucian, *Gallus* 7), the centrality of its myth to the Olympic Games, and the importance of its occasion. But an editor's occasional appreciation of such niceties is not the same as a poet's truly aesthetic design.

25. There is no evidence to suggest that the distinction between choral lyric and monody (Plato, *Laws* 6.764d-e) or between monostrophic and triadic systems (*Schol. Epimetr. Pind.* III, p. 310.27 Dr.) played any part in arrangement: see Harvey, "Classification of Greek Lyric Poetry," pp. 157–75.

26. This conclusion seems valid not only for the lyric poets whom we have been considering, but also for the other early writers from whose works one occasionally receives the impression of organization. For instance, the elegiacs attributed to Theognis are clearly by several hands, and their collection and arrangement was the work of a later editor: see M. L. West, *Studies in Greek Elegy and Iambos*, pp. 40–64. For Mimnermus's *Nanno* also there is no evidence of aesthetic design because the fragments are very varied in content, and the idea that the poet's love for the girl provided a thematic unity may well be a Hellenistic invention on analogy with Antimachus's *Lyde*: see West, ibid., pp. 74–76. Finally, though the Attic *scolia* (Ath. 15.693–5) may have constituted a book from which uninventive guests could select a poem to recite at the symposium (see Wilamowitz-Moellendorff, *Aristoteles und Athen*, 2:316–22), the variety of social and political constituencies represented by the poems precludes any real aesthetic unity, and such grouping as has been observed seems editorial: see Bowra, *Greek Lyric Poetry*, pp. 375–76; Cuartero, "Estudios sobre el escolio ático," pp. 5–38.

27. For a general discussion of *poikilia/variatio* as a larger feature of all aspects of composition, see Deubner, "Ein Stilprinzip hellenistischer Dichtkunst," pp. 361–78; Schulze, "Über das Princip der Variatio," pp. 857–78. It should perhaps be noted here that structural studies often use familiar technical terms in new or more specific meanings. Thus, *variatio* is used to refer to the diversification of poems that are placed together and not just to the practice of "theme and variation." Similarly, "ring composition," which usually refers to the archaic Greek style whereby the beginning and the end of a poem are temporally linked, can also refer to the disposition of poems in concentric frames.

28. See Dawson, "The Iambi of Callimachus," pp. 1–168; Clayman, *Callimachus' Iambi*.

29. It is commonly assumed with little real authority that this prologue headed a second, collected edition of Callimachus's *Aetia* and other works: see Pfeiffer, "Ein neues Altersgedicht," pp. 339–41, and his *Callimachus*, 2: xxxvi–vii. For an alternative view, however, see Eichgrün, *Kallimachos und Apollonios Rhodios*, pp. 64 ff., where the idea of consequential publication is

rejected. The entire question is reexamined and Pfeiffer's theory is rejected by Alan Cameron in a forthcoming monograph, *Callimachus and His Critics*.

30. According to the new reconstruction of the *Aetia* by Parsons, "Callimachus: Victoria Berenices," pp. 1–50, the last two books were also framed, by poems in honor of Berenice.

31. This does not mean that there was a collected edition in which the *Iambi* followed the *Aetia* as they do in POxy 1011 and in the Milan Diegesis: see above n. 29. On the meaning of πεζὸν . . . νομόν, see Van Sickle, *Design of Virgil's Bucolics*, pp. 104–5.

32. Lawall, *Theocritus' Coan Pastorals*. While Lawall's arguments do not prove the existence of poetry books by Theocritus or Herodas, the interconnections he observes among poems are very illuminating and have great interpretive value in other respects.

33. For an account of the MSS see Gow, *Theocritus*, 1:xxx ff. A detailed critique of the presuppositions underlying Lawall's interpretation is provided in the review by Giangrande, pp. 170–73. For an alternative sense in which the poems constitute a libellus, see Segal, "Thematic Coherence and Levels of Style," pp. 35–68, reprinted in his *Poetry and Myth*, pp. 176–209. On the relationship between the collection of the corpus and ancient awareness of genre, see Van Sickle, "Theocritus and the Development of the Conception of Bucolic Genre," pp. 18–44; and, for more general definition of the genre, see Halperin, *Before Pastoral*.

34. See Cunningham, *Herodas: Mimiamboi*, p. 160; on the possibility of pairing see Cunningham, "Herodas 6 and 7," pp. 32–35.

35. On the history of the epigram see Fraser, *Ptolemaic Alexandria*, 1:553–617 and 2:791–869, with literature abundantly cited. For a list of papyrus anthologies of epigrams from the Hellenistic period see Pack, *Greek and Latin Literary Texts*, p. 92. To this should now be added PKöln 204 which contains the remains of six epigrams by Mnasalkes which are arranged into pairs by theme. Dating to the middle of the second century B.C., this is the earliest extant collected edition of an epigrammatist. For more detailed discussion of this and other collections, see Cameron, *The Greek Anthology*.

36. Reitzenstein, *Epigramm und Skolion*, pp. 94 ff.

37. Lloyd-Jones, "The Seal of Posidippus," pp. 75–99.

38. See Webster, *Hellenistic Poetry and Art*, p. 45, who argues for this meaning by citing as a parallel the use of the word at Theocritus 7.155, a literary harvest; see also Gow, *Theocritus*, 2:169. It should at least be noted, however, that, while the notion of winnowing can be supplied from the Theocritean context, the word σωρός usually conveys only the undifferentiated quality of a heap.

39. A third-century B.C. papyrus appears to be the beginning of a collection of Posidippus (the *Soros*?): see Lasserre, "Aux origines de l'Anthologie, I,"

pp. 222–47. The MS bears the title *Symmeikta Epigrammata*, which may carry literary critical implications parallel to those detected in the title *Soros*; see Webster, *Hellenistic Poetry and Art*, p. 46: "Symmeikta seems from its uses elsewhere to mean 'mixed' rather than 'blended'; it emphasizes the variety of the contents rather than the choice of each epigram to suit its neighbor."

40. Cameron, "Garlands of Meleager and Philip," pp. 323–49.

41. These principles were discovered by Radinger, *Meleagros von Gadara*, pp. 88–107, and Weisshäupl, "Zur den Quellen der Anthologia," pp. 184–88.

42. Gow and Page, *The Greek Anthology*, 2:597.

43. On metrical *variatio* in Lucilius see Puelma-Piwonka, *Lucilius und Kallimachos*, pp. 364–67.

44. The publication of prose letters would seem initially to offer another parallel. Pliny, for example, tells us (*Epist.* 1.1) that his letters are not chronologically arranged but occur as they came into his hands, which suggests conscious *variatio* and which calls to mind his insistence on variety in his lyric poetry (*Epist.* 4.14.3, 8.21.4). Furthermore, though elaborate schemes are not convincing, there is evidence that "[in] each book Pliny sought to include a representative collection of the major themes, but he did not bind himself to an arithmetical proportion" (Sherwin-White, *Letters of Pliny*, p. 50; and see the full discussion of distribution on pp. 20–56). But Pliny is much later than Horace. The earlier letters of Cicero are not relevant either, for they seem to have been published posthumously and their organization displays no real aesthetic design: see Shackleton Bailey, *Cicero's Letters to Atticus*, 1:59–76, and his *Cicero: Epistulae ad Familiares*, 1:2–24.

45. See, for example, Ferguson, "Catullus and Horace," pp. 1–19; van der Paardt, "Catullus en Horatius," pp. 287–96; Lee, "Catullus in the Odes of Horace," pp. 33–48.

46. It is interesting that Vergil's *Bucolics*, Horace's *Sermones* 1, and Tibullus 1 all contain ten poems, and that Horace's *Iambi* divide after the first ten poems, which are all in the same meter. In this concern for the number ten, as in other respects, Vergil may have influenced his fellow poets: see van Rooy, "'Imitatio' of Vergil," pp. 69–88; Leach, "Vergil, Horace, Tibullus: Three Collections of Ten," pp. 79–105.

47. Pliny compares a dead friend, Pompeius, to Catullus who is said to have placed harsh poems among light ones (*inserit sane . . . mollibus levibusque duriusculos quosdam*). Whether or not this accurately describes Catullus's methods and although it does not indicate which poems are involved, it does imply some sort of organized collection.

48. Wilamowitz-Moellendorff, *Sappho und Simonides*, p. 292, translated by Quinn, *Catullus: An Interpretation*, p. 11.

49. On the distinction between neoteric and non-neoteric see Ross, *Style and Tradition in Catullus*.

50. See, for example, E. A. Schmidt, "Catulls Anordnung," pp. 215–42; Wiseman, *Catullan Questions*, pp. 1–31; idem, *Catullus and His World*, pp. 136–75, 265–66; Quinn, *Catullus: An Interpretation*; Skinner, *Catullus' Passer*; Most, "On the Arrangement of Catullus' Carmina Maiora," pp. 109–25. Those who support the view that the entire corpus was arranged by the poet may find support in Macleod, "Catullus 116," pp. 304–9, reprinted in his *Collected Essays*, pp. 181–86, where the last poem is treated as a suitable Callimachean epilogue; see also Van Sickle, "Poetics of Opening and Closure," pp. 65–75.

51. Of course, the papyrus roll and the literary book are not to be equated: the physical capacity of the former could exceed the length arbitrarily fixed for the latter. For full discussion see Van Sickle, "The Book Roll," pp. 5–42, with literature there cited.

52. See Clausen, "Catulli Veronensis Liber," pp. 37–43.

53. Ellis, *Commentary on Catullus*, pp. xlviii–ix, uses this very fact to cast doubt on the discovery of conscious design in Catullus. On the other hand, Quinn, *Catullus: An Interpretation*, p. 16, draws a very different conclusion: "Indeed, I think it likely that the illusion of a work unfinished, of a collection made up in large part of fragments of poems which are too short, too abrupt in the way they begin or end to be felt as complete poems, but which plainly belong together—snatches of conversation, as it were, in an easily imagined context—was one of the principles adopted by Catullus in putting his collection together. Rather as a modern painter or sculptor leaves his painting or bust at a stage where it is, by normal standards, unfinished (the likeness just emerging from the marble, say) because it is finished for him; or because to finish it off means robbing it of life."

54. E.g. 5/7 (*basia*), 21/23 and 24/26 (Furius and Aurelius), 37/39 (Egnatius). Such separated pairs also occur outside the *polymetra* (e.g. the famous Lesbia poems, 70/72) where they may be taken as traces of the poet's own conscious design, now lost, or as the work of a perceptive editor.

55. An example of a surface glide occurs early in the *polymetra*: poem 9, on Veranius's return from Spain as a member of Piso's cohort, leads into 10 which alludes to Catullus's own experiences in the Bithynian cohort of Memmius, and thus introduces 11 which opens with a travelogue (see Kinsey, "Catullus 11," pp. 537–44; Ferrero, *Interpretazione di Catullo*, p. 221). An example of a less superficial sequence occurs at the end of the *polymetra*: poem 50, an account of the *otiosi* Catullus and Calvus, is followed by 51, the last strophe of which condemns *otium*, and thus prepares for 52–54, a return to the *negotium* of politics (see Wiseman, *Catullan Questions*, p. 15). As was the case with A-B-A patterns, sequences of contiguous poems also occur after the *polymetra* (e.g. 88–91, on Gellius, the longest run of contiguous poems on a single individual) and may be viewed either as the work of an editor or (in some cases at least) as traces of a now lost original design by the poet. For

useful lists of such clusters throughout the corpus see Ellis, *Commentary on Catullus*, pp. xlv–l; Kroll, *C. Valerius Catullus*, p. x.

56. Barwick, "Zyklen bei Martial," pp. 284–318; Segal, "Order of Catullus, Poems 2–11," pp. 305–21.

57. The Alexandrian influence was first explored in great detail by Pasquali, *Orazio lirico*, pp. 141–641.

58. The question naturally arises at this point of whether the *Odes* were written to occupy their positions in the collection or whether placement was a subsequent activity. For certain collections like Vergil's *Bucolics* and the other homogeneous books of ten, it is possible that some elements of overall design preexisted the composition of individual poems. The *Odes*, however, are so numerous and varied that it is probably safer to assume that, in most cases, arrangement came later. Thus, the poems of even the most cohesive cycle, the Roman Odes, give evidence of having been composed at different times. That disposition followed composition, however, does not mean that it was an afterthought, an unrelated or less important creative activity (as we shall see). Also, we need not exclude the possibility that at least a few poems might have been reworked to suit their context in the collection, and that a few might even have been written with an eye on their placement. This hypothesis certainly suits C. 1.1 and 3.30 and perhaps also pairs like C. 1.31 and 32, which read as if they were a single poem (see the discussion on pp. 69–72). Such pairs certainly exist in Ovid (e.g. *Amores* 1.11–12) and Propertius (e.g. 3.4–5). On the whole question see now Hutchinson, "Propertius and the Unity of the Book," pp. 99–106.

59. Rosenthal and Gall, *Modern Poetic Sequence*; Vendler, *Odes of John Keats*.

CHAPTER TWO

1. See, for example, Callimachus frs. 226–29 Pf.; Theocritus *Id.* 28–30; Cercidas *Meliambi* (Powell, *Coll.Alex.*, pp. 201–12); Laevius (Morel, F.P.L., pp. 55–62); Catullus 11 and 51 (in Sapphics). Admittedly, much literature has been lost. Thus, Asclepiades gives his name to one of Horace's favorite metrical groups, but only his epigrams survive. On the development of the lyrical impulse outside of monody see H. Parry, *Lyric Poems of Greek Tragedy*; for its development in epigram, see p. 182, n. 35, above.

2. First described by von Christ, "Über die Verskunst," pp. 1–44; for further bibliography and the attempt to extend the group to the first twelve odes, see pp. 42–43 below.

3. Messalla at the end of his talk with Tibullus in the first series of *Imaginary Conversations*; for interesting discussion of the *marginalia* in Landor's copy of Horace, see Ruoff, "Landor's Criticism of Horace," pp. 189–204.

4. For echoes to the *Satires* and also to that most "satiric" of the *Iambi*, number 2, see Musurillo, "The Poet's Apotheosis," pp. 230–39; for their larger significance, see Shey, "The Poet's Progress," pp. 185–96.

5. For an interpretation of the poem emphasizing the importance of the hedonist, see Pomeroy, "A Man at a Spring," pp. 34–50.

6. For full discussion of the form see Race, *The Classical Priamel*, esp. pp. 122–23 on C. 1.1.

7. For the literary overtones of such elements see, for example, Troxler-Keller, *Dichterlandschaft*; Commager, "The Function of Wine," pp. 68–80; Mette, "*Genus tenue* und *mensa tenuis*," pp. 136–39.

8. For other structural approaches to the ode, see Collinge, *Structure of Horace's Odes*, pp. 108–9, with literature there cited. To this should be added Schoenberger, "Horatius, Carm. I,1," pp. 388–412; Pasoli, "Per una rilettura," pp. 323–35; Ghiselli, "Lettura dell'Ode 1,1," pp. 103–46; La Penna, "A proposito della struttura," pp. 326–30; Setaioli, "Il proemio dei Carmina oraziani," pp. 1–59; Vretska, "Horatius, carm. I,1," pp. 323–35.

9. See D. West, *Reading Horace*, pp. 79–80, where another Pindaric hint is detected in the mention of the Olympic victor in lines 3–6; for Callimachus, see Nisbet and Hubbard, *Horace: Odes, Book I*, p. 14. It should perhaps be noted that while *tibia* is usually translated "flute," it was, in fact, a reed instrument.

10. It is not possible, therefore, to agree with Johnson, that "Horace displays his technical virtuosity in prosody by placing twelve poems in twelve different meters at the beginning of Book 1, and the sheer skill that this variety requires is uniformly sustained throughout the first three books of the *Odes* and does not weaken in the fourth book" (*Idea of Lyric*, pp. 123–24). Incidentally, even if the Parade is extended beyond the first nine poems to the twelfth (see n. 2 above), only ten meters are represented, because C. 1.2, 10, and 12 are all Sapphics. Johnson's point about the variety of Book 4, though, is correct, for its fifteen poems encompass eight meters.

11. See the discussions of C. 1.2, 4, and 7 below.

12. See Zetzel, "Poetics of Patronage," p. 95, for the humor and even self-mockery in this arrangement.

13. See, for example, Bloom, *Anxiety of Influence*, and Bate, *Burden of the Past*.

14. See, for example, G. Williams, *Change and Decline*, pp. 102–55 and passim, on the inhibiting effect of Greek culture on Roman creativity.

15. See Quintilian 10.1.93, *satura quidem tota nostra est*, and the discussion of the passage by van Rooy, *Studies in Classical Satire*, pp. 117–23; see also n. 16 below.

16. See *Satire* 1.4.1–7. That Horace may have believed in the existence of a dramatic *satura* is irrelevant since he does not derive that hypothetical genre from a Greek source. On the affinities between satire and comedy (which do

not, however, amount to a genealogy), see Coffey, Roman Satire, pp. 54–56, with literature there cited.

17. In "On Shakespeare and Milton," p. 58.

18. See Seidensticker, "Zu Horaz, C. 1.1–9," p. 28 n. 11, who also suggests the possible relevance of nine Muses and of Horace's stylistic ideal, nonum . . . prematur in annum (AP 388).

19. On the relationship between the two poets, see Ferguson, "Catullus and Horace," pp. 1–19; Lee, "Catullus in the Odes of Horace," pp. 33–48; van der Paardt, "Catullus en Horatius," pp. 287–96.

20. See pp. 6–7, with p. 180, n. 19.

21. For an excellent survey of Horace's metrical practice see Wilkinson, Golden Latin Artistry, pp. 102–18, with literature there cited; on the lex Meinekiana see Bohnenkamp, Die horazische Strophe; and on the relationship of content and form see Numberger, Inhalt und Metrum.

22. See Commager, Odes of Horace, p. 158.

23. For the minority view that the Odes were meant to be sung (like, for example, the Carmen Saeculare) see Bonavia-Hunt, Horace the Minstrel, pp. 1–38; Wille, Musica Romana, pp. 234–53.

24. Ovid Tristia 4.10.49–50 (numerosus); Horace C. 3.30.13–14 (princeps Aeolium carmen ad Italos / deduxisse modos), a difficult phrase on which see p. 213, n. 39; Epistle 1.19.32–33 (hunc [Alcaeum] ego, non alio dictum prius ore, Latinus / volgavi fidicen), and the larger discussion of metrical borrowing at lines 23–31. We might just note in passing the inadequacy (to us) of the ancient judgments on Horace: see Quintilian 10.1.96 (at lyricorum idem Horatius fere solus legi dignus; nam et insurgit aliquando et plenus est iucunditatis et gratiae et varius figuris et verbis felicissime audax); and, of course, Petronius's judgment on Horace's lexical curiosa felicitas (118.5), on which see further on p. 213, n. 6.

25. On this aspect of ancient lyric in general and Horace in particular see now the excellent remarks of Johnson, Idea of Lyric; for the addressee as one of the formal characteristics of the Horatian ode, see Heinze, "Die horazische Ode," pp. 153–68, reprinted in his Vom Geist des Römertums, pp. 172–89, with the caveats of Quinn, Latin Explorations, pp. 84–87.

26. See the compendious survey of Horace's sources in Nisbet and Hubbard, Horace: Odes, Book I, pp. xi–xxvi.

27. According to the scholiast to Hephaestion Encheiridion 14.1 who quotes the first strophe of Alcaeus's hymn (fr. 308b L.-P.).

28. See the discussion on pp. 25–26.

29. Said, Beginnings, p. 34 and passim.

30. On programmatic junctures of this sort, see McDermott, "Horatius Callidus," pp. 363–80.

31. See Newman, Concept of Vates. It should be emphasized that the vatic

element is not exclusively Roman, for, though it is absent from Hellenistic poetry, it is a feature of the archaic Greek tradition which Horace wishes to evoke.

32. On the history of the canon see Pfeiffer, *History of Classical Scholarship*, pp. 205–7.

33. T. S. Eliot, "Tradition and the Individual Talent," in *The Sacred Wood*, pp. 49–50.

34. Salat, "La composition du livre I," pp. 554–74.

35. Seidensticker, "Zu Horaz, C. 1.1–9," pp. 26–34.

36. One other scheme is proposed by M. Schmidt, "Die Anordnung der Oden," pp. 207–16; but in its irregularity and neglect of the most obvious connections it is not convincing.

37. Seidensticker, "Zu Horaz, C. 1.1–9," pp. 28–29.

38. The allusions to Vergil in the first book of *Odes* are noted by Cody, *Horace and Callimachean Aesthetics*, pp. 94–97, who does not, however, perceive any progression. Vergil's ascent up the hierarchy of genres is reflected in the suspect lines 1a–1e of *Aeneid* 1 and in his epitaph, *cecini pascua, rura, duces*.

39. The echo may not be specific, however, because it also recalls Jove's prophecy to Venus about her son's future greatness: *sublime feres ad sidera caeli / magnanimum Aenean* (*Aen.* 1.259–60). In any case, regardless of its source, the Vergilian phrasing is apt before C. 1.2, and is not needed to conjure up a pastoral tone for C. 1.1 since the *locus amoenus* and sacred wood in that poem are sufficiently evocative.

40. See Saylor, "Horace, C. 1.2," pp. 20–25.

41. They are the prodigies that followed the assassination of Julius Caesar (Dio 45.17). Porphyrion's view that Horace's storm also refers to that event is discredited by Hirst, "Portents in Horace's *Odes*," pp. 7–9; but see G. Williams, *Figures of Thought*, pp. 9–13. A more likely occasion is the storm that took place on the day in 27 B.C. when Octavian took the name Augustus (Dio 53.20): see MacKay, "Horace, Augustus, and Ode, I,2," pp. 168–77.

42. Elsewhere in Horace the Romans' crime is that of Laomedon (C. 3.3.21–22), Romulus's murder of Remus (*Iamb* 7.17–20), or the civil wars themselves (C. 2.1.5).

43. For this and other points I have drawn on the excellent discussion of the ode by Commager, "Horace, Carmina, I,2," pp. 37–55, and on his *Odes of Horace*, pp. 175–94; see also Womble, "Horace, Carmina, I,2," pp. 1–30; Cairns, "Horace, Odes 1.2," pp. 68–88.

44. For a sensitive discussion of the close of *Georgic* 1 see Putnam, *Virgil's Poem of the Earth*, pp. 73–81.

45. For foreign exploits as an alternative to civil war, see also C. 1.12.53–57, 21.13–16, 35.38–40; *Iamb* 7.5–10. For imperial policy see Seager, "Neu sinas Medos," pp. 103–18, with literature there cited.

46. Nisbet and Hubbard, *Horace: Odes, Book I*, p. 44, characterize the ode as "an accomplished piece of versification, but little more," and assert that "there is not a hint of Virgil's poetry." Most recent critics, however, agree on the ode's Vergilian resonance and possible poetic symbolism: see Commager, *Odes of Horace*, p. 120; Lockyer, "Horace's Propempticon," pp. 42–45; Cody, *Horace and Callimachean Aesthetics*, pp. 73–102; Cairns, *Generic Composition*, pp. 231–35; Kidd, "Virgil's Voyage," pp. 97–103; Basto, "Horace's Propempticon to Vergil," pp. 30–44; see also the literature cited in the notes below.

47. See, for example, Kambylis, *Dichterweihe*; Cody, *Horace and Callimachean Aesthetics*, pp. 82–85, for the ship of poetry motif in Roman poets. See also the discussion of the allegorical ship in C. 1.14 on pp. 46–49 below.

48. On the possible relevance of another Vergilian text, see Hahn, "Horace's Odes to Vergil," pp. xxxii–iii, who suggests that C. 1.3 teases Vergil for attacking seafaring in *Bucolic* 4.38.

49. For further discussion of the *Aetia* prologue and of *recusatio* conventions, see below on C. 1.6, pp. 34–36, 190, n. 71. Other Callimachean echoes in C. 1.3 include the *propempticon* form itself (cf. Call. fr. 400 Pf.) and the phrase, *animae dimidium meae* (8), on which see n. 59 below.

50. Some of these were noted early by Rosenberg, "Über Horatius Carm. I.3," p. 598, and later by Colmant, "Horace, Ode 1.3," pp. 87–90.

51. First noted by Putnam, "Aes Triplex," p. 454.

52. First suggested by Hendrickson, "Horace's Propempticon to Virgil," pp. 100–104. For the form see Jäger, *Das antike Propemptikon*, pp. 4–36; Quinn, *Latin Explorations*, pp. 239–73; Cairns, *Generic Composition*, pp. 231–35; Winniczuk, "Propemptikon," pp. 406–19.

53. Thus, in C. 3.3.9–12 Hercules earned heaven precisely because of his merits (*hac arte*, 9).

54. See Elder, "Horace, C. I,3," pp. 140–58, for the theme of tragic heroism in the ode, and esp. p. 158 for its relevance to the *Aeneid*.

55. See Ball, "Tibullus 2.5 and Vergil's *Aeneid*," pp. 33–50; Buchheit, "Tibulls 2.5 und die *Aeneis*," pp. 104–20.

56. See Tränkle, "Properz über Vergils *Aeneis*," pp. 60–63; for the latent irony, see Commager, *Prolegomenon to Propertius*, pp. 54–55 with n. 39.

57. On the large question of their relationship see Duckworth, "*Animae Dimidium Meae*," pp. 281–316; more recent work is listed in Kissel, "Horaz 1936–1975," p. 1444.

58. See Cody, *Horace and Callimachean Aesthetics*, pp. 97–100, who also finds a literary relevance in *stultitia* as a quality akin to the poet's traditional madness.

59. In addition to being a commonplace (see Festa, "*Animae Dimidium Meae*," pp. 436–41), the phrase translates Callimachus (*Epigr.* 41 Pf. = AP 12.73 = 1057 G.-P.) and Meleager (AP 12.52.2 = 4433 G.-P.); also, as a reference to a coinage reform (see Buttrey, "Halved Coins," pp. 31–48), it fits into the po-

em's financial imagery (e.g. *creditum debes . . . reddas incolumen,* 5–7).

60. For the identity of the Vergil in C. 4.12 see Belmont, "The Vergilius of Horace *Odes* 4.12," pp. 1–20, with literature there cited.

61. See Commager, *Odes of Horace*, pp. 235–306, on "The World of Nature."

62. See Barr, "Horace, Odes 1,4," pp. 5–11, who explains the abrupt appearance of *Pallida Mors* (13) by noting that the urban sacrifice to Faunus was followed closely by a festival of the dead. An April setting for the ode had earlier been proposed by Defourny, "Le printemps," pp. 174–94.

63. Thus Venus, the symbolic equivalent for nature's springtime creativity, functions also as Lucretius's Muse (e.g. *te sociam studeo scribendis versibus esse,* Lucr. 1.24; *quo magis aeternum da dictis, diva, leporem,* Lucr. 1.28). On the goddess' role in the poem see Clay, *Lucretius and Epicurus*, pp. 82–110, 212–34.

64. See Chapter Six, for a discussion of allusions to closure in the winter setting of C. 3.17–19, the farewell forms of C. 3.26 and 27 (retirement dedication and *propempticon*), and the movement from noon to night in C. 3.28.

65. This difference between C. 1.4 and 4.7 is appreciated by Quinn, *Latin Explorations*, pp. 14–28.

66. That the name here is meant to recall Bucolic 7.67 is suggested by Savage, "Art of the Seventh Eclogue," p. 261; his identification of Thyrsis in that poem with Horace is discussed by Nethercut, "Vergil and Bucolic 7," pp. 93–98.

67. See Nisbet and Hubbard, *Horace: Odes, Book I*, pp. 71–72.

68. For Horace's views on love, see Lyne, *Latin Love Poets*, pp. 190–238.

69. For this ambiguity of vocabulary as a function of the elegists' conflation of lover and poet, mistress and muse, see Commager, *Prolegomenon to Propertius*, pp. 5–8. Horace exploits the double meaning of *querellarum* at C. 2.9.18 and of *modus* at C. 1.24.1, 14; both poems, interestingly, are addressed to poets (Valgius and Vergil, respectively) and criticize elegiac postures.

70. See pp. 145–46 below.

71. The standard study is Wimmel, *Kallimachos in Rom*; see also Clausen, "Callimachus and Roman Poetry," pp. 181–96. On the *Aetia* prologue see further Torraca, *Il prologo dei Telchini*; on Hymn 2.105–12, see F. Williams, *Callimachus, Hymn to Apollo*, pp. 85–89; see also the forthcoming study by Alan Cameron, *Callimachus and His Critics*, who argues that the *Aetia* prologue did not itself reject epic but was adapted to that purpose by the Augustan poets.

72. I draw here from the discussion by Commager, *Odes of Horace*, pp. 71–72.

73. See D. West, *Reading Horace*, pp. 112–14.

74. *Aetia* fr. 1.3 Pf.; presumably ἓν here is also translated by Horace's *unum* (5); the phrase, *perpetuum . . . carmen,* occurs in the same sense at Ovid *Metamorphoses* 1.4. It should be noted that Horace has in mind *ktisis* epics and other poems on the foundation and history of cities; for such works and the role of itinerant poets, see now Hardie, *Statius and the Silvae,* passim. Thus, C. 1.6 and

7, taken together, constitute a refusal to undertake not just heroic military epic but also a much wider range of poetry.

75. *Odyssey* 12.208–21, Odysseus's speech to his men reminding them of their past sufferings together. This is also the source for *Aeneid* 1.198–207; for the resemblance between Aeneas's words and Teucer's in the ode, see Highet, *Speeches in Vergil's Aeneid*, p. 195. The sentiment in the ode is also generally consistent with epic: see *Iliad* 24.602–17 where Achilles urges Priam to eat by appealing to the example of the grieving Niobe.

76. See Velleius Paterculus 2.67.3–4.

77. See Kumaniecki, "De Horatii carmine ad Plancum," pp. 5–23, endorsed by D. West, *Reading Horace*, pp. 114–17, who points out that the original audience would have been familiar with the myth from repeat performances of Pacuvius's *Teucer* (cf. Cic. *De Orat.* 2.193). For a slightly different interpretation see G. Williams, *Tradition and Originality*, pp. 83–85, where it is argued that Velleius's story is just a fabrication (derived perhaps from the fictitious orations of Pollio mentioned in Pliny NH Praef. 31), and that the example of Teucer simply consoles Plancus for his brother's death without alluding to rumors of fratricide or cowardice. For other attempts to relate the myth to Plancus, see Elder, "Horace *Carmen* 1.7," pp. 1–8; Bliss, "The Plancus Ode," pp. 30–46; Vaio, "Unity and Historical Occasion," pp. 168–75.

78. This is conveyed even by the metrical form of the poem, the First Archilochian, which alternates epic dactylic hexameters with tetrameters: each couplet opens with epic expansiveness only to contract in the second line to a more private dimension. The same effect is achieved in C. 1.28—see p. 66 below.

79. For the Lydia poems as a sequence see Pavlock, "Horace's Invitation Poems to Maecenas," pp. 84–89; see also pp. 45, 82, and 152–53 below.

80. *Livida* (10), "black and blue," ensures that the *arma* should be distinguished from the discus and javelin (11–12); Nisbet and Hubbard, *Horace: Odes, Book I*, p. 114, suggest chafing by the *lorica*; Alexander, "Horace's Odes and Carmen Saeculare," p. 179, adopts Heinze's suggestion, the broadsword.

81. See Quinn, *Latin Explorations*, pp. 137–40, though his reading of the poem as a pacifist critique of militarism and the myth of manliness is aptly corrected by D. West, *Reading Horace*, pp. 121–24.

82. It is also possible, however, that the Campus has social and athletic associations as well as erotic ones: see Nisbet and Hubbard, *Horace: Odes, Book I*, p. 123.

83. As noted by Seidensticker, "Zu Horaz, C. 1.1–9," and discussed on p. 24 above.

84. The structure of the poem and the function of its nature imagery have been the subjects of intense debate which, fortunately, has little bearing on

our argument: for an attempt to avoid the extremes of both symbolic and literal readings, see Moritz, "Snow and Spring," pp. 169–76; see also the application of various philological and hermeneutic approaches to the poem in Kresic, *Contemporary Literary Hermeneutics*, pp. 275–98.

85. See esp. C. 1.32 and 2.13, discussed on pp. 71–72, 87–90, and 96 below.

86. The collection will, however, continue to define lyric in relation to other genres—e.g., iambic (C. 1.16–17) and elegy (C. 1.33): see pp. 50–52 and 72–73 below.

CHAPTER THREE

1. Kiessling, "Horatius I," pp. 48–75.

2. Apart from the three instances in this poem (lines 1, 6, 18), a delayed caesura is very rare in the Sapphics of the first collection but common in *Odes* 4 and the *Carmen Saeculare*: see Prakken, "Feminine Caesuras," pp. 102–3.

3. For example, the stories told in the third strophe about the theft of Apollo's cattle and quiver are probably from Alcaeus: see Page, *Sappho and Alcaeus*, pp. 252 ff.; on other sources for the ode such as *Homeric Hymn* 4, see Nisbet and Hubbard, *Horace: Odes, Book I*, pp. 126, 132.

4. See Putnam, "*Mercuri, facunde nepos Atlantis*," pp. 215–17, reprinted in his *Essays*, pp. 99–101.

5. For this subtle point see Cairns, "Five 'Religious' Odes," pp. 433–52, esp. pp. 433–40, who also argues that the ode is organized around the three major aspects of the god announced in the second strophe: his roles as *fur* (developed further in strophe 3), *nuntius* (strophe 4), and *lyrae parens* (strophe 5).

6. Commager, *Odes of Horace*, pp. 273–74.

7. C. 1.12 not only opens with a motto from Pindar (O. 2.2) but also displays signs of triadic structure which are at least reminiscent of that poet's practice: see Fraenkel, *Horace*, pp. 291–97.

8. Augustus's inclusion in the list may be analogous to his inclusion among the great men of Rome whose statues adorned his forum: see Drew, "Horace, Odes 1.12," pp. 159–64. In any case, the effect of the ode is to make the praise of the *mos maiorum* cohere with that of Augustus who claimed to have restored it: see G. Williams, *Figures of Thought*, pp. 13–19.

9. For a full description of this technique, see pp. 118–22.

10. This is taken even further by Collinge, *Structure of Horace's Odes*, p. 91 n. 1: "*tu secundo Caesare regnes* is odd. Taken with v. 18 it asks for a revolutionary change in the relation of Jupiter to the universe: now he will have a junior colleague, as never before, if Roman prayers are granted. Moreover, its ambiguity is almost blasphemous, for in the other sense of the adjective (cf. *Iunone*

secunda Virg. Aen. iv.45, secunda Marte ibid x.21 f.; secundis dis Livy vii.26) one piously expects *ille secundo Iove regnet* (cf. v. 57)."

11. See D. West, *Reading Horace*, pp. 65–71.

12. For the Lydia poems as a sequence see Pavlock, "Horace's Invitation Poems to Maecenas," pp. 84–89; see also pp. 38, 82, and 152–53 below.

13. C. 1.13 is a lover's complaint; though the subject of C. 1.14 is very different, it retains erotic language and a plaintive tone. Thus, the ship is personified throughout as an aged woman: it has gender (*filia*, 12), body (*nudum . . . latus*, 4; *saucius*, 5), voice (*gemant*, 6; *voces*, 10; *iactes*, 13), lineage (*nobilis*, 12; *genus et nomen*, 13), clothing (*lintea*, 9), and even cosmetics (*pictis*, 14). After this characterization, the poem ends with language so passionate that it guarantees allegory, since Horace confesses that the ship had previously been a wearisome bother to him (*sollicitum . . . taedium*, 17) but is now an object of loving concern (*desiderium curaque non levis*, 18). In addition to this eroticism, C. 1.14 shares with the preceding poem a querulous tone. As Cairns has interestingly observed, we are inclined to read C. 1.14 only as advice to the ship, but the ancient audience, more attuned to genres than we are, would have recognized the description of the battered ship, threatening wind and sea, and fearful sailor as a propemptic *topos*, the *schetliasmos*, and so "Horace's words would have been regarded as complaints and not as counsel" (*Generic Composition*, p. 255 n. 8; see also pp. 218–21).

14. For a critique of the allegorical interpretation, see Fraenkel, *Horace*, pp. 188–92, including p. 188 n. 2 where the view is traced back to the edition of Cristoforo Landino printed in Florence in 1482; see also Nisbet and Hubbard, *Horace: Odes, Book I*, pp. 189–90.

15. Quintilian's educational purposes may have influenced his choice of an edifying reading, and Alcaeus's ship fragments (frs. 6, 326 L.-P.) offer few parallels that are not conventional; moreover, their allegorical intent rests largely on a fourth-century rhetorician who, as the author of a work on Homeric allegories, clearly had an axe to grind (ps.-Heraclitus Quaest. Hom. 5, ed. Buffière).

16. For the usual form of the *topos* see W. S. Anderson, "Horace *Carm.* 1.14," pp. 84–97; see also the other articles listed in nn. 18, 19, 20 below.

17. See Nisbet and Hubbard, *Horace: Odes, Book I*, p. 187. To this should be added Petronius 139 where *desiderium* is used of a present lover.

18. See Mendell, "Horace I,14," pp. 145–56; Seel, "Zur Ode 1,14 des Horaz," pp. 204–49. The sea of life occurs in Horace at C. 1.34, 2.10, 3.2.29; for examples of metaphorical harbors see the references in Mendell and Seel.

19. See Anderson, "Horace *Carm.* 1.14," pp. 84–97, with further support by Woodman, "The Craft of Horace," pp. 60–67; but see also the skeptical critique of Jocelyn, "Boats, Women, and Horace *Odes* 1.14," pp. 330–35. The best example of the metaphor in Horace is C. 1.5. One advantage of this

theory is that it salvages an Alcaean precedent, as a papyrus commentary published in 1951 (POxy 2307) indicates that Alcaeus compared a woman to a ship in a poem identified plausibly, but not conclusively, with fr. 73 L.-P.

20. See Zumwalt, "Horace's Navis," pp. 249–54, citing the metaphor in Callimachus Hymn to Apollo 2.106; Horace C. 4.15.3–4, 1.3.9–12; Propertius 3.3.15–24, 9.3–4, 35–36. Catullan echoes include not only a great number of nautical terms that occur in Catullus 64 but also several details less likely to result from convention. The thoroughgoing personification of the ship (see n. 13 above), for example, calls to mind the similar treatment of the *phaselus* in Catullus 4, and the phrase *Pontica pinus* (11) even recalls the geographical origin of Catullus's ship (Cat. 4.9). In addition, the descriptions of Horace's ship as a *desiderium curaque non levis* (18) and of the Cyclades as *nitentes* (19) seem to owe something to the phrasing of Catullus 2, *desiderio meo nitenti* (5) and *tristis animi levare curas* (10).

21. Similarly, erotic vocabulary does not ensure erotic content. Thus, the language is harmonized with political allegory by G. Williams, *Figures of Thought*, p. 27: "when the poet purports to reveal his own point of view, he does it in language that is no less figurative than the allegory itself."

22. Commager, *Odes of Horace*, p. 169. Commager, however, does not really address Horace's failure to provide hints. He seems to believe that this is not deliberate because he cites as a parallel phenomenon the diversity of views that are held on the meaning of Dante's Beatrice (e.g. Church, Scholastic Theology, Faith, Divine Reason, Platonic Philosophy). But there is a difference between this multiplicity of interpretations and the indeterminacy of Horace's ode. The various theories about Beatrice are not all equally possible, nor are they mutually compatible. Also, the obscurity of medieval allegory is too far removed from Horace's usual habits of thought to provide a useful parallel to them.

23. This connection had occurred to Anderson, "Horace Carm. 1.14," p. 91. He rejected it, however, since he rejected the ship of poetry allegory. Zumwalt, "Horace's Navis," pp. 249–54, argues for that allegory but sees a different connection, that both poems are about propriety, literary in C. 1.14 and moral and social in C. 1.15. Neither poem, however, openly develops the idea of propriety. For other interpretations of C. 1.15, see Kimber, "Structure of Horace, Odes 1.15," pp. 74–77; O. L. Smith, "A Reading of Horace, Carm. I.15," pp. 67–74.

24. The Stesichorean allusion probably does not go beyond these details: see Nisbet and Hubbard, *Horace: Odes, Book I*, p. 202.

25. This connection among C. 1.15, 16, and 17 is often noted but only as a superficial linkage: see, for example, Collinge, *Structure of Horace's Odes*, pp. 46–47.

26. For the relevance of the central section to the girl, see Nisbet and Hubbard, *Horace: Odes, Book I*, pp. 202–3, and for its relevance to both Horace and the girl, see G. Williams, *Figures of Thought*, pp. 1–5. The failure to recognize this has led to the strange theory that the iambs referred to in the first strophe were written by the girl: see MacKay, "Odes I,16 and 17," pp. 298–300; Dyson, "Horace: *Odes* I.16," pp. 169–79. But the ode's obvious ring composition and its dependence on the situation of Catullus 36 both guarantee that the iambs mentioned at the beginning of the ode are the same as those at the end, namely the poet's.

27. See Sturtevant, "O matre pulchra," pp. 119–22; Hahn, "*Epodes* 5 and 17," pp. 213–30.

28. That C. 1.16 and 17 embody a lyric program was suggested long ago by Hendrickson, "First Publication of Horace's Odes," pp. 1–10. Hendrickson, however, labored under the notion that C. 1.16 was an allegory and also that C. 1.16 and 17 had served as an introduction to a previously published *libellus* (signs of which he also detected in the proemic qualities of C. 1.32 and the epilogue features of C. 2.20).

29. For the literary overtones of the landscape here see Commager, *Odes of Horace*, pp. 348–52; Troxler-Keller, *Dichterlandschaft*, pp. 108–18.

30. Wine certainly functions as a symbol for poetry only a few poems later, in C. 1.20: see pp. 156–57 below.

31. This reading finds support in Horace's practice earlier in the book, where a program ode, C. 1.6, is followed by two odes on *convivia* and *erotica* respectively: see pp. 36–39 above.

32. The first line is a motto from Alcaeus 342 L.-P. (in the same meter). Varus is identified as either the literary figure, Quintilius Varus, whose death is treated a few poems later, in C. 1.24 (see pp. 58–60 below), or the jurist, P. Alfenus Varus (see Nisbet and Hubbard, *Horace: Odes, Book I*, pp. 227–28). In either case, the address does not seem to be integral to the thematic structure of the ode.

33. See Nisbet and Hubbard, *Horace: Odes, Book I*, p. 233, where they cite Nonnus (*Dion.* 48.93 ff.) who tells how Dionysus killed Sithon for falling in love with his own daughter.

34. For another explanation see Silk, "Bacchus and the Horatian *Recusatio*," pp. 193–212, where it is suggested that the three Bacchus odes reproduce the poet's gradual progress from initial skepticism (C. 1.18), to conversion (C. 2.19), to final ecstasy (C. 3.25).

35. On the importance of the midpoint both in the collection and in individual poems see Moritz, "Some 'Central' Thoughts," pp. 116–31.

36. See pp. 156–57 below.

37. This similarity between Chloe and Lalage is reinforced by the latter's

portrayal in C. 2.5, where she is not yet ready for a lover and where the same agricultural imagery (e.g. *inmitis uvae*, 10) and animal metaphors (e.g. 1–4 and *passim*) are applied to her.

38. See pp. 156–57 below.

39. Cairns has shown that C. 1.2 is a paean imagined as being uttered by a chorus ("Horace, *Odes* I,2," pp. 68–88) and that C. 1.21 is a choral-style hymn ("Five 'Religious' Odes," pp. 433–52).

40. Nisbet and Hubbard, *Horace: Odes, Book I*, p. 261.

41. See Fuqua, "Horace *Carm.* I,23–25," pp. 44–46.

42. See Cairns, *Generic Composition*, pp. 88–89.

43. The urban environment is to be inferred from the komastic situation and the reference to sex in alleys (*angiportu*, C. 1.25.10).

44. The threefold division depends on taking *atque* (18) as equivalent to *quam*—see Nisbet and Hubbard, *Horace: Odes, Book I*, p. 298, where it is noted, however, that most editors understand *atque* to join ivy and myrtle. In any case, the point of the imagery is the same.

45. See Lee, *Word, Sound, and Image*, pp. 82–89.

46. Collinge, *Structure of Horace's Odes*, p. 47.

47. For pure springs see Callimachus *Epigr.* 28.3–4 = 1044–45 G.-P., *Hymn to Apollo* 2.110 ff.; see other examples in Nisbet and Hubbard, *Horace: Odes, Book I*, p. 305. For the garland see Sappho 55.2–3 L.-P.; Pindar O. 6.86–87, 9.48–49, N. 7.77 ff.; and other examples in Nisbet and Hubbard, p. 306.

48. See Lee, *Word, Sound, and Image*, pp. 82–89.

49. Lucretius's blossoms are new (*novos*, 1.928) and his garland excellent (*insignem*, 1.929); there is no equivalent to Horace's *apricos*. Similarly, the notion of joy is conveyed by Lucretius's *iuvat* (1.927) which is much weaker than Horace's *gaudes*.

50. See Kilpatrick, "Two Horatian Proems," pp. 312–29. It is not necessary, however, to accept his further suggestion that *sacrare* means "confer upon," and that *hunc* refers to an understood *honorem*, so that lines 9–10 should be translated: "To naught without thee come the honors I have to give; this one with lyre new, this one with Lesbian pick it doth behoove thee and thy sisters to bestow" (p. 223). Consolation need not preclude celebration.

51. The phrase is surprisingly rare in the *Odes*; the only other example is at C. 1.16.22 where it also comes as a surprise: see p. 50 above.

52. For the reconstruction followed here, namely that the ode is a monologue spoken by the shade of a drowned man who first addresses Archytas and then a passing sailor, see Callahan and Musurillo, "A Handful of Dust," pp. 262–69; Nisbet and Hubbard, *Horace: Odes, Book I*, pp. 317–19; G. Williams, *Figures of Thought*, pp. 5–9. A less satisfactory version of the monologue theory —that the poem is a *prosopopoeia* in which Archytas speaks first to himself and then to a passing sailor—goes back to the scholiasts and is supported by

Vessey, "Horace's Archytas Ode," pp. 73–87. Much less convincing are the various versions of the dialogue theory according to which the first part of the ode is spoken by Horace (or by a Ulyssean character modeled on *Odyssey* 11 or Varro's *Sesquiulixes*: see Kilpatrick, "Archytas at the Styx," pp. 201–6), and the second part is spoken by Archytas (or another corpse washed up by Archytas's tomb: see "Patricius," "The Archytas Ode," pp. 51–53).

53. Odes containing substantial speeches are C. 1.7 (Teucer), 15 (Nereus), 3.3 (Juno), 5 (Regulus), 11 (Danaid), 27 (Europa and Venus), 4.4 (Hannibal); see also *Iamb* 2 (Alfenus), 5 (Horace and woman), 12 (young man and Canidia), 13 (Chiron). In all of these there is a narrative frame, and where there is none, as at C. 3.9 (the amoebean exchange between Horace and Lydia) and *Iamb* 17 (two set speeches, Horace's recantation and Canidia's reply), the speaker's identity is clearly signaled by the form of the poem.

54. See p. 206, n. 40.

55. E.g. C. 2.15, 16, 18, as discussed in Chapter Four below.

56. Commager, *Odes of Horace*, p. 55.

57. His royal status can be inferred from *ex aula* (7) and *arcu paterno* (10).

58. For further discussion of this neglected poem, see Goar, "Horace and the Betrayal of Philosophy," pp. 116–18; Wright, "Iccius' Change of Character," pp. 44–52.

59. The context suggests that *Socraticam . . . domum* (14) refers to a specific school rather than to moral philosophy in general (as at C. 3.21.9–10, *Socraticis . . . sermonibus*); a specific reference is possibly intended also at *AP* 310, *Socraticae . . . chartae*, but see Brink, *Horace on Poetry*, p. 131 n. 1.

60. Epistle 1.12.7–8 regarding his vegetarian diet; see McGann, *Studies in Horace's First Book of Epistles*, p. 64, with literature there cited.

61. Nisbet and Hubbard, *Horace: Odes, Book I*, pp. 344, 347.

62. See Babcock, "Horace Carm. I,32," pp. 189–92.

63. For defense of *poscimus* against the well-attested varient *poscimur*, see Nisbet and Hubbard, *Horace: Odes, Book I*, p. 360.

64. See McDermott, "Horatius Callidus," pp. 363–80.

65. For the Meditrinalia see Nisbet and Hubbard, *Horace: Odes, Book I*, p. 350. The same technique of melding public and private celebrations is again exploited at C. 3.8—see p. 129. There is, therefore, no need to dissociate C. 1.31 from the temple dedication as was suggested by Veyne, "Quid dedicatum," pp. 932–48.

66. Though such political poems may be implied in the references to war, arms, and a ship (6–8).

67. Venus and Cupid occur in both odes; the Graces in C. 1.30 are similar to the Muses in C. 1.32 (cf. their association at C. 3.19.13–17), just as the Nymphs in the former poem perhaps correspond to the latter's Bacchus (whom they elsewhere attend: cf. C. 1.1.31, Epist. 1.19.3–4); finally, Lycus in

C. 1.32 is the concrete embodiment of the earlier poem's Youth and Mercury.

68. See Kilpatrick, "Two Horatian Proems," pp. 29–39, on C. 1.33 as the *consolatio* for which Horace prays at C. 1.32.14–15.

69. See Commager, *Odes of Horace*, pp. 240–41; Putnam, "Horace and Tibullus," pp. 81–88, reprinted in his *Essays*, pp. 152–59. This critique of Tibullus's one-sidedness in his life and poetry establishes a further connection with C. 1.32 and its more balanced hero, Alcaeus: see Lyne, *Latin Love Poets*, p. 203.

70. See Lucretius 6.400–403.

71. See Reckford, "Horace, Odes I.34," p. 511 with n. 18.

72. See Nisbet and Hubbard, *Horace: Odes, Book I*, pp. 385–86; G. Williams, *Figures of Thought*, pp. 70–71.

73. See Muth, "Horaz—'parcus deorum cultor,'" pp. 171–206.

74. The other occurrence of the motif, at C. 1.3.38–40, is more general in its application; for further discussion of the analogy between Augustus and Jove and its basis in Greek views of kingship, see pp. 118–22, on the Roman Odes.

75. See Zumwalt, "Horace C. 1.34," p. 435–67; but see also the critique by Fredricksmeyer, "Horace C. 1.34," pp. 155–76.

76. See Jacobson, "Horace and Augustus," pp. 106–13, on which I have drawn in the following discussion.

77. See G. Williams, *Figures of Thought*, pp. 153–61.

78. See Kiessling and Heinze, *Oden und Epoden*, p. 151.

79. See Nisbet and Hubbard, *Horace: Odes, Book I*, p. 401.

80. Many discussions of this complex ode rightly emphasize Cleopatra's nobility: see, for example, Commager, "Horace, *Carmina* 1.37," pp. 47–58, and his *Odes of Horace*, pp. 89–97. This does not, however, detract from Octavian's accomplishment, for it represents Cleopatra as a worthy antagonist.

81. See Toohey, "A Note on Horace, Odes I 38," pp. 171–74, where the ode is compared to the *Abbruchsformel* or breaking-off formula familiar from Greek poetry, especially Pindar and Callimachus; for another view of the relationship between the last two odes see Nussbaum, "A Study of Odes I,37 and 38," pp. 91–97.

82. See Wili, *Horaz und die augusteische Kultur*, p. 154.

83. Fraenkel, *Horace*, pp. 298–99.

84. Nisbet and Hubbard, *Horace: Odes, Book I*, pp. 422–23.

85. See Mette, "Genus tenue und mensa tenuis," pp. 136–39; Cody, *Horace and Callimachean Aesthetics*, pp. 36–38 and passim.

86. See Cody, *Horace and Callimachean Aesthetics*, pp. 39–44.

87. See Nisbet and Hubbard, *Horace: Odes, Book I*, pp. xxviii–xxx; Wilkinson, "The Earliest Odes," pp. 495–99.

88. See Salat, "La composition du livre I," pp. 554–74.

CHAPTER FOUR

1. Books 1 and 3 are metrically richer, containing ten and seven meters respectively. But as these books contain more poems than Book 2, the latter's economy can be more accurately gauged by comparison with Book 4 which contains five fewer poems but employs twice as many meters.

2. Klingner, *Römische Geisteswelt*, pp. 336–37.

3. Verrall, *Studies Literary and Historical*, p. 8; Wili, *Horaz und die augusteische Kultur*, p. 232.

4. Perhaps also in C. 2.20.6, if Plüss is correct in understanding by *quem vocas* that Maecenas is calling Horace back to life from the pyre (*Horazstudien*, pp. 179 ff.); for further discussion of that poem see pp. 107–8 and 159–60.

5. See Nisbet and Hubbard, *Horace: Odes, Book II*, pp. 1, 10.

6. See Verrall, *Studies Literary and Historical*, pp. 11–89, on Murena, with the conclusion on p. 99: "The function of the Second Book is to bring upon the stage with suitable accompaniments the figure of Murena."

7. The publication of the *Odes* is safely assigned to 23 B.C. No datable poem is later, and the prominent placement of C. 1.4 can only be explained as a tribute to its addressee, Sestius, in the year of his consulship, 23 B.C.: see Nisbet and Hubbard, *Horace: Odes, Book I*, pp. xxxv–vii. The fall of Murena must have occurred after publication, or Horace would presumably have deleted not only C. 2.10 but perhaps also C. 2.2.5–8 in praise of Murena's brother, Proculeius. For the vexed dating of Murena's downfall (assigned to 22 B.C. in Dio 54.3 but to 23 B.C. by the Capitoline Fasti), see Nisbet and Hubbard, *Horace: Odes, Book II*, pp. 153–158, with literature abundantly cited.

8. Both men were close to Augustus: Sallustius was second only to Maecenas in the emperor's counsels (Tac. *Ann.* 3.30) and Proculeius was entrusted with the arrest of Cleopatra (Plut. *Ant.* 79, Dio 51.11) and was considered as a possible husband for Julia (Tac. *Ann.* 4.40.8). Thus, irony is unlikely in this poem, *pace* Calder, "Irony in Horace *Carm.* 2.2," pp. 175–78. Also, it is not relevant to the Horatian context that Proculeius later fell out of favor—see Bastomsky, "Proculeius and Augustus," pp. 129–31.

9. See Seneca *Suasoriae* 1.7 (*desultorem bellorum civilium*).

10. On Pollio's neutrality see Velleius Paterculus 2.86; for his political and literary career see Nisbet and Hubbard, *Horace: Odes, Book II*, pp. 7–11, with literature there cited.

11. Seneca, *De clementia* 1.10.

12. If we knew more about the addressees of the other poems we might be able to recognize other political references. Verrall, *Studies Literary and Historical*, p. 11, hazarded the guess that the name Pompeius and his Sicilian property identify the addressee of C. 2.16 as a republican. Similarly, the advice to Valgius in C. 2.9 that he sing of Caesar rather than lament the past may suggest

the need for political conversion. Finally, it would be helpful to know for certain if the Quinctius of C. 2.11 was Pollio's relative, as is suggested in Nisbet and Hubbard, *Horace: Odes, Book II*, p. 168.

13. See section three.

14. For this reason, the arrangement proposed by M. Schmidt, "Die Anordnung der Oden," pp. 207-16, is unconvincing. Although acknowledging metrical alternation and some pairing of poems in the first half of the book, Schmidt attributes to this regularity only a decorative function, and she divides the book instead into two tetrads and a triad punctuated by four "pillars" (C. 2.1, 6-7, 12-13, and 17-20).

15. Port, "Die Anordnung," pp. 299-300.

16. Ludwig, "Zu Horaz, C. 2,1-12," pp. 336-45.

17. For this and other objections to Ludwig, see Collinge, *Structure of Horace's Odes*, pp. 43-46; Eisenberger, "Bilden die horazischen Oden 2.1-12 einen Zyklus?" pp. 262-74. On the *sphragis* see the literature cited in Collinge, p. 44 n. 2, to which should be added Kranz, "Sphragis," pp. 3-46, 97-124; Lloyd-Jones, "The Seal of Posidippus," pp. 75-99.

18. Collinge, *Structure of Horace's Odes*, p. 46 n. 1; see also Nisbet and Hubbard, *Horace: Odes, Book II*, p. 6.

19. For another level on which they are related, see the discussion of C. 2.9 on pp. 91-93 below.

20. C. 2.6 is addressed to a friend, and even the landscape is assimilated to the idea of friendship when Aulon is described as *amicus . . . / fertili Baccho* (18-19). Yet here, as often in Horace, the landscape functions as a token for poetry. Thus, the final strophe (21-24), in which Septimius sheds a tear over the warm ashes of his friend, validates not only their affection but also Horace's artistic talent. The poem ends, after all, not with *amici* but with *vatis amici*, and the two ideas cannot be detached. For further discussion see Segal, "Horace, Odes 2.6," pp. 235-53; see also Troxler-Keller, *Dichterlandschaft*, pp. 14-15, 127, 159 ff.

21. See p. 185, n. 58, above.

22. Collinge, *Structure of Horace's Odes*, p. 54.

23. Fraenkel, *Horace*, pp. 163-65, denies that Mercury has a special personal or poetic significance for Horace in the *Odes*. But see Commager, *Odes of Horace*, p. 171. n. 23; Nisbet and Hubbard, *Horace: Odes, Book I*, pp. 127-28 (on C. 1.10), and Book II, pp. 116 (on C. 2.7.13), 286 (on C. 2.17.29).

24. For the inversion here of the amatory "threat-prophecy" see Cairns, *Generic Composition*, pp. 86, 137.

25. For this reason C. 2.12 has even been read as a marriage song: see G. Williams, "Poetry in the Moral Climate," pp. 35 ff.; G. Williams, *Tradition and Originality*, pp. 301-3. On the use and development of *domina* in a technical

amatory sense see Baker, "Domina at Catullus 68,68," pp. 124-29, with literature there cited.

26. For full discussion and bibliography see Santirocco, "Strategy and Structure," pp. 223-36; see also p. 157 below, for the poem's position in the sequence of Maecenas odes.

27. For this view see Quinn, *Latin Explorations*, pp. 158-62; W. S. Anderson, "Two Odes of Horace's Book Two," pp. 35-45. On the form of the *consolatio* see Volkmann, *Die Rhetorik der Griechen und Römer*, pp. 358 ff.; Kassell, *Untersuchungen zur Konsolationsliteratur*.

28. The phrasing is that of Kiessling and Heinze, *Oden und Epoden*, p. 194.

29. C. 2.9 is delineated by stanzas, whereas C. 2.11 proceeds more loosely; the former consists largely of concrete examples drawn from nature and myth, as opposed to the latter which relies more heavily on generalizations; finally, C. 2.9 operates in the indicative and imperative modes, the world of fact and injunction, whereas C. 2.11 is structured around questions, that posed by Quinctius at the beginning of the ode (*Quid bellicosis Cantaber et Scythes, / . . . cogitet*, 1-2) and the whole series of questions with which Horace replies and in which he couches his recommendations (*quid . . . fatigas? cur non . . . potamus? quis . . . restinguet? quis . . . eliciet?* 11-22).

30. For a brief comparison of C. 2.9 and 11 see Commager, *Odes of Horace*, pp. 242-44.

31. For discussion of the personification see Nisbet and Hubbard, *Horace: Odes, Book II*, pp. 139 ff. and passim.

32. The plane and pine (13-17) may also recall the oaks and ash of C. 2.9.7-8, although the trees are no longer included as an *exemplum* but are incorporated directly into the injunction itself.

33. See Reagan, "Horace Carmen 2.10," pp. 177-85, with examples cited; for other lexical matters see Levin, "Horace, Carm. 2.10," pp. 169-71.

34. For a different view of the poem's structure see Collinge, *Structure of Horace's Odes*, pp. 70-72, with literature there cited.

35. We have previously located the midpoint of Book 2 at C. 2.12 by calculating line totals; if, however, we exclude C. 2.20 as an epilogue, then calculation by the number of poems puts C. 2.10 in the middle. Both poems are close enough to the center that, depending on the poet's purpose, either can be considered the focus.

36. For full discussion of C. 2.12 as a *recusatio* see n. 26 above.

37. See Lee, *Word, Sound, and Image*, p. 118. n. 1: "The ode *Ille et nefasto* (2.13) is an elaborate means of proclaiming the Alcaic the best of all possible meters, better even than the Sapphic (cf. lines 29 ff.)."

38. Perret, *Horace*, p. 82.

39. See Ludwig, "Zu Horaz, C. 2.1-12," p. 345 n. 1: "Im zweiten [Lieder-

zyklus] scheint in der Tat der Tod des Menschen mit seinem Gegensatz, der Unvergänglichkeit der Dichtung, das 'Thema' zu bilden."

40. W. S. Anderson, "Two Odes of Horace's Book Two," p. 59.

41. Ibid.

42. See Commager, "The Function of Wine," pp. 68–80.

43. See Mendell, "Horace, Odes II,18," pp. 279–92, for the moralist tradition; for the social history of such estates see D'Arms, *Romans on the Bay of Naples*.

44. See Campbell, *Horace: Odes and Epodes*, ad loc.

45. See C. 2.18.19–20, 3.24.3–4, 3.1.33–34, and 2.3.17–20 if *exstructis in altum divitiis* means not "riches piled on high" but "riches piled into the deep," as is suggested by A. R. Anderson, "Note on Horace C. 2.3.17–20," p. 456. On this imagery see Commager, *Odes of Horace*, pp. 85–88 (comparing C. 2.15 and 18); Pearcy, "Horace's Architectural Imagery," pp. 772–81; Mendell, "Horace, Odes II,18," pp. 279–92.

46. See Womble, "Horace, Carmina, II,16," pp. 385–409, with literature there cited; I have drawn freely on this interpretation in my discussion of the poem.

47. On the relation between Horace's style of life and his style of writing, see Mette, "*Genus tenue* und *mensa tenuis*," pp. 136–39; Cody, *Horace and Callimachean Aesthetics*, pp. 36–38 and passim.

48. For full discussion of the astrological element see Boll, *Kleine Schriften*, pp. 115 ff.; Franke-Klein, "Horace and the Stars," pp. 154–58; Coutts, "Astrology in Horace," pp. 26–27; Dicks, "Astrology and Astronomy in Horace," pp. 60–73.

49. For other encomiastic techniques here see Cairns, *Generic Composition*, pp. 223–24.

50. See C. 1.17 (*di me tuentur, dis pietas mea / et musa cordi est*, 13–14), 1.20 (the tree), 1.22 (the wolf), 1.26 (*Musis amicus . . . unice securus*, 1–6), 2.7 (Philippi), 2.13 (the tree), 2.17 (the tree), 3.4 (safety as a child in the woods and later escapes from Philippi, the tree, and shipwreck), and 3.8 (the tree). For the significance of the motif see discussion of these passages; also on Mercury see n. 23 above, and on Faunus see Commager, *Odes of Horace*, pp. 348–52; Troxler-Keller, *Dichterlandschaft*, pp. 108–18.

51. Although lines 17–fin. refer to a generalized second person (*tu*, 17), Maecenas is suggested by several details (e.g. the reference to the Sabine farm, 14), and so the poet's portrayal of himself being sought out by the rich man (10–11) hints at a role reversal between poet and patron. For full discussion of this interpretation see pp. 158–59.

52. Onians, *Origins of European Thought*, p. 64, rejects the mining image at C. 2.18.9–10 for an anatomical one, the *vena* as a vessel or pipe containing the liquid of *ingenium*. In interpreting the image in C. 2.18, however, the context is

surely more pertinent than Onians's citations of the anatomical use of *venae* elsewhere in Latin literature (including Hor. AP 409–10).

53. See pp. 159–60.

54. For discussion of parallel passages see Tatum, "Non usitata nec tenui ferar," pp. 4–25; see also Stewart, "The Poet as Bird," pp. 357–61. For full discussion of the evidence concerning the dithyramb, see Pickard-Cambridge, *Dithyramb, Tragedy, and Comedy*, pp. 1–59; the god is called *Dithyrambos* in Euripides *Bacchae* 526—see Dodds, *Euripides' Bacchae*, p. 143.

55. For the comic element in Horace's persona here see Johnson, "The Boastful Bird," pp. 272–75. For another level of irony possibly underlying C. 2.20 see Tatum, "Non usitata nec tenui ferar," p. 20: "Horace follows Aristophanes and many other Greek authors in imagining a fantastic alternative to the unavoidable end of every human life. Yet he also sees to it that such a solution is really no solution at all.... If we change into a swan and surpass the fame of Icarus, our audience will be barbarians, our stage wild and deserted places."

CHAPTER FIVE

1. A. Parry, "Two Voices," pp. 66–80, reprinted in Commager, *Virgil*, pp. 107–23.

2. Anti-Augustanism is readily admitted for Propertius: see Commager, *Prolegomenon to Propertius*, pp. 37–97; Hubbard, *Propertius*, pp. 93–115; Sullivan, *Propertius*, pp. 54–75; Stahl, *Propertius*. It may be overreading for other authors, however: see Solmsen, "Tibullus as an Augustan Poet," pp. 295–325; Galinsky, *Ovid's Metamorphoses*, pp. 210–65; G. Williams, *Change and Decline*, pp. 52–101. For a conservative view even of Vergil see Stahl, "Aeneas—An 'Unheroic' Hero?" pp. 157–77.

3. Highet, *Poets in a Landscape*, p. 131; see also Shackleton Bailey, *Profile of Horace*, pp. 44–45, who notes that "the gap is too wide for comfort" and concludes that "Horace invests in his standard themes as a limited partner." This tension or gap is explored more fully by, for example, Pöschl, *Horaz und die Politik*, and La Penna, *Orazio e l'ideologia del principato*.

4. For C. 1.31 and 32, see pp. 69–72.

5. Plüss, *Horazstudien*, pp. 185 ff.

6. See Duckworth, "*Animae Dimidium Meae*," p. 304; Nethercut, "The Ironic Priest," pp. 385–405.

7. For a brief overview of the group see Fraenkel, *Horace*, pp. 260 ff.; Syndikus, *Die Lyrik des Horaz*, 2:3–6. More detailed discussions of the cycle include Amundsen, "The 'Roman Odes,'" pp. 1–24; André, "Les odes romaines," pp. 31–46; Büchner, *Studien zur römischen Literatur III: Horaz*, pp. 125–38; Heinze,

Vom Geist des Römertums, pp. 190–204; Klingner, "Horazens Römeroden," pp. 118–36; Krokowski, "De Horati odis," pp. 3–13; Oppermann, "Zum Aufbau der Römeroden," pp. 204–17; Trenkel, *Zusammenhänge und Beziehungen*; Reckford, *Horace*, pp. 70–84. For further bibliography see the notes below and also the excellent new study by Witke, *Horace's Roman Odes*, which appeared only after my own study was completed.

8. See Silk, "Horace, II,20," pp. 255–63.

9. Apart from the Roman Odes, the longest metrical run consists of three poems (C. 2.13–15), and the others are all pairs (C. 1.16–17, 26–27, 34–35; 2.19–20; 3.24–25; 4.14–15).

10. Campbell, *Horace: Odes and Epodes*, ad loc., regards C. 2.15 as a proem to C. 3.6; and Fraenkel, *Horace*, p. 259, observes that "poems of the type of the Roman Odes had begun to shape themselves in his mind when he conceived the enthusiastic hymn iii.25." On C. 3.24 see Mancuso, *Orazio poeta civile*, p. 67.

11. See Wili, *Horaz und die augusteische Kultur*, pp. 201–10; Duckworth, "*Animae Dimidium Meae*," pp. 300–302, with literature there cited.

12. See Solmsen, "Horace's First Roman Ode," pp. 337–52; Fenik, "Horace's First and Sixth Roman Odes," pp. 72–96.

13. See Port, "Die Anordnung," pp. 300–301; Klingner, "Horazens Römeroden," p. 128; Duckworth, "*Animae Dimidium Meae*," pp. 300–302.

14. See Perret, *Horace*, 83–84, relying on Maury, *Horace et le secret de Virgile*.

15. For a convenient survey of these architectural views see Rudd, *Lines of Enquiry*, pp. 119–44, to which should now be added Van Sickle, *Design of Virgil's Bucolics*.

16. So Duckworth; but an overlap of only two schemes is not impossible: see my analysis of C. 2.7–13 above.

17. Mommsen, "Reden zur Feier," pp. 23–35, reprinted in his *Reden und Aufsätze*, pp. 168–84.

18. Domaszewski, "Untersuchungen zur römischen Kaisergeschichte VI," pp. 302–10, reprinted in his *Abhandlungen zur römischen Religion*, pp. 111 ff. See also Traut, "Horaz Römeroden und der clupeus aureus," pp. 317–20; Markowski, "De quattuor virtutibus Augusti," pp. 109–20; Charlesworth, "The Virtues of a Roman Emperor," pp. 105–33, esp. pp. 111–14.

19. See the tabulation of the various headings applied by scholars to each of the six odes in Wagenvoort, *De Horatii quae dicuntur Odis Romanis*, p. 15.

20. E.g. references to Parthians (C. 3.2.3, 5.4), resettlement of veterans (C. 3.4.37–40), temple restorations (C. 3.6.2–4), and Antony (though only in mythological guise, at C. 3.3.19–20, 4.42 ff.). Other alleged allusions are not convincing: e.g. that Juno's hostility to a rebuilt Troy in C. 3.3 refers to plans to move the capital east (Suet. *Iul.* 76), or that the just man's constancy in storms in C. 3.3.1–8 recalls Augustus's adventures at sea after Actium (DeWitt, "Horace Odes III.3," pp. 65–66), or, finally, that Horace's unwillingness to

exchange his farm for riches in C. 3.1.47–48 alludes to his refusal of an imperial secretaryship (Kroll, "Horaz' Oden und die Philosophie," pp. 223–38; the same claim, incidentally, was made for C. 3.16 by Frank, "On Augustus' References to Horace," pp. 26–30).

21. Trenkel, Zusammenhänge und Beziehungen, p. 6; Collinge, Structure of Horace's Odes, p. 51; Silk, "Horace Carm. III.1," p. 138.

22. The comparison is made by Silk, "Horace Carm. III.1," p. 137, who speaks of "the plot of the drama" and "the tragic conclusion of the action."

23. The idea of poverty also extends to C. 3.3 in which Juno advises against expeditions for plunder (49 ff.) and C. 3.6 which pictures the good old days of subsistence farming (33–41).

24. Howald, Das Wesen der lateinischen Dichtung, cited and criticized by Collinge, Structure of Horace's Odes, p. 128 n. 1.

25. Collinge, Structure of Horace's Odes, p. 47.

26. See Ross, Backgrounds to Augustan Poetry, p. 142.

27. For brief discussion of these concepts, see G. Williams, Tradition and Originality, pp. 160–70; Nisbet and Hubbard, Horace: Odes, Book I, pp. 164–65. It should be noted that this is one topic on which the Augustan poets are still ill served by some literary critics who mislead by downplaying the element of ruler worship in the texts. For recent and controversial historical research on the subject, see Dvornik, Early Christian and Byzantine Political Philosophy, 1:205–77 (on Hellenistic political philosophy), and 2:453–557 (on the Hellenization of Roman political theory), esp. pp. 486–500 (on ruler worship); den Boer, Le culte des souverains; Liebeschuetz, Continuity and Change in Roman Religion, pp. 65–90; Price, Rituals and Power; Millar, "State and Subject," pp. 37–60.

28. The word rex can apply to Augustus because its connotations are not invariably negative: see Murphy, "Attitude of the Augustan Poets toward rex," pp. 241–46.

29. The list of demigods is traditional, but on the special applicability of the Dioscuri to Augustus see Bellinger, "Immortality of Alexander and Augustus," pp. 91–100; Scott, "The Dioscuri," pp. 379–80; Scott, "Drusus, Nicknamed Castor," pp. 151–61. Most relevant to Augustus, however, was Quirinus, the deified Romulus. The emperor had wished to assume the name Romulus, and the title he eventually chose instead kept that association alive: for full discussion see Taylor, Divinity of the Roman Emperor, pp. 142–81.

30. For full discussion see Commager, Odes of Horace, pp. 194–201, with literature there cited; Hornsby, "Horace on Art and Politics," pp. 97–104; Thornton, "Horace's Ode to Calliope," pp. 96–102; Dunston, "Horace Odes III.4," pp. 9–19.

31. It should be noted that posthumous deification is sometimes connected with Euhemerism: see, for example, Commager, Odes of Horace, p. 210. But Euhemerus discredited the gods as men whose great deeds led to their

being worshipped after their death, whereas the situation in Horace is actually the reverse of this, for he suggests that men can in fact become gods by performing great deeds.

32. See Silk, "Horace *Carm*. III.1," pp. 131–45. It might be added that the identification of the *volgus* (1) with the ambitious rich people in the rest of the ode is facilitated by the treatment of both as impious. Just as the crowd is *profanum*, so too are the wealthy man over whose *impious* neck (*inpia / cervice*, 17–18) anxiety hangs and the contractor whose engineering feats transgress the natural boundary between sea and land and symbolize, only a few poems earlier, a denial of mortality (C. 2.15, 18.17–22, on both of which see pp. 99–101, 105–7).

33. This agreement may be underscored by the description of *virtus* as winged (23–24). If C. 2.20, Horace's metamorphosis into a bird, is read as a prologue to the Roman Odes (see n. 8 above), this reference to wings in C. 3.2 may suggest that Horace and *virtus* share not only a distaste for the crowd but also an airborne position above it!

34. On the possible meanings of Troy, see Commager, *Odes of Horace*, pp. 217 ff.

35. See G. Williams, "Poetry in the Moral Climate," pp. 28–46.

36. Reckford, *Horace*, p. 82.

37. In order to clarify the distinction between the two authors, I have posed it in somewhat stark and simplistic terms. I do not mean to suggest, however, that Vergil is not also interested in societal problems. In fact, the problem of mob emotions and mob violence is a very important theme throughout the *Aeneid*. But Vergil is also interested in how mob violence and the violence of the individual are related both in their causes and in their manifestations. Thus, at the end of the poem, Aeneas fails to control the violence not only in others but also in himself. On the last scene of the *Aeneid*, see now Putnam, "The Hesitation of Aeneas."

38. Klingner, "Gedanken über Horaz," pp. 23–44, reprinted in his *Römische Geisteswelt*, pp. 353–75, esp. p. 374; Mutschler, "Beobachtungen zur Gedichtanordnung," pp. 109–33, esp. p. 124; Mutschler, "Kaufmannsliebe," pp. 111–31, esp. p. 126. See also Pöschl, "Bemerkungen zu den Horazoden III 7–12," pp. 505–9.

39. See pp. 54–55 above.

40. That C. 3.12 is a soliloquy by Neobule rather than an address to her by the poet (*pace* Porphyrion) is suggested by the form of its possible model, Alcaeus fr. 10 L.-P. On a parallel situation in *Corpus Tibullianum* 4.8 see Santirocco, "Sulpicia Reconsidered," pp. 229–39, esp. pp. 231–32.

41. Collinge, *Structure of Horace's Odes*, p. 54. C. 3.13 is at least compatible with its neighbors owing to its small scale and personal tone. It is also possible to

take C. 3.13 and 14 as a pair of poems that are connected to each other and to C. 3.8 through the motif of the votive sacrifice.

42. The amoebean C. 3.8 finds a parallel not only in Catullus 45 but also Sappho fr. 121 L.-P.; for C. 3.12 see above n. 40; the filly comparison in C. 3.10.9–10 derives from Anacreon 147 (cf. C. 2.5); finally, epigrammatic touches include the surprise ending of C. 3.7, the rustic dedication in C. 3.13, and the *paraclausithyron* in C. 3.10, for all of which see G. Williams, *Third Book of Horace's Odes*, pp. 152–59.

43. Only in C. 3.14 does Horace address the people at large (*o plebs*, 1; *o pueri et puellae*, 10), and even here his attention eventually shifts to a slave boy (*puer*, 17). All the other odes in the group are directed to specific addressees, either real, such as Maecenas (C. 3.8) and Bandusia (C. 3.13), or imaginary, such as the women Asterie (C. 3.7), Lydia (9), Lyce (10), Neòbule (12), and Chloris (15). Finally, although C. 3.11 is technically addressed to Mercury (1) and the lyre (3), it is really directed to Lyde, as the hortatory tale indicates.

44. For the specific relevance of the address to Maecenas see the more complete discussion of C. 3.8 on pp. 160–61.

45. For political interpretations of the ode see Doblhofer, "Zum Augustusbild," pp. 325–39; Kienast, "Horaz und die erste Krise des Principats," pp. 239–51; Scholz, "*Herculis ritu*," pp. 123–37; Dyson, "Horace Odes III,14," pp. 169–79.

CHAPTER SIX

1. The original version of this chapter appeared in *Ramus* 13 (1984): 74–91 and is reproduced here by permission of Aureal Publications.

2. See Kiessling and Heinze, *Oden und Epoden*, p. 330.

3. See Verrall, *Studies Literary and Historical*, pp. 108–10, for seasonal links.

4. See Commager, *Odes of Horace*, pp. 259–61.

5. For the family's history see Treggiari, "Cicero, Horace, and Mutual Friends," pp. 245–61.

6. See pp. 57–60, with p. 196, n. 41.

7. See pp. 91–95, with p. 201, n. 30.

8. For a different view, see Gornall, "Horace, Odes III.19," pp. 188–90, with literature there cited.

9. The youth's indifference is conveyed by the final picture of him standing aloof with hair scattered (*sparsum*, 14) in the breeze. This imagery perhaps establishes a slight link with the two preceding odes where the scattering of roses and leaves occurs (*sparge rosas*, C. 3.19.22; *spargit . . . frondes*, C. 3.18.14).

10. Collinge, *Structure of Horace's Odes*, p. 54, observes that, despite their topi-

cal interconnection, each of these odes has a different "mental climate": "The reader is invited to pass from the hearty and heated and naive banqueters and their demens strepitus to the cold, sophisticated scene with Nearchus ... ; and thence to resort to the dusty but more humane air of a scholar's study where a jar is unsealed and a learned parody worked out."

11. Norden, *Agnostos Theos*, p. 163.

12. E.g. by Kroll, *Studien zum Verständnis*, p. 227 n. 6; Commager, *Odes of Horace*, p. 127.

13. This may also refer indirectly to Messalla's speech on wine in Maecenas's *Symposium* (Servius on *Aen*. 8.310). No further philosophical resonance, however, should be detected, *pace* Onians, *Origins of European Thought*, p. 43, where *madet* is said to refer to the ancient concept of wisdom as moisture!

14. Norden, *Agnostos Theos*, pp. 143–63.

15. For this inconsistency see G. Williams, *Tradition and Originality*, pp. 150–51.

16. In answer to those who would argue from line 17 that moral innocence, not simplicity, is at issue, it should be noted that *inmunis* means "giftless" (i.e. "without large gifts"; see G. Williams, *Third Book of Horace's Odes*, p. 121) rather than "guiltless" (*pace* Porphyrion; see also Camps, "Critical and Exegetical Notes," pp. 143–44; Syndikus, *Die Lyrik des Horaz*, 2:205 n. 17). The former sense is consistent with the context here and with Horatian usage elsewhere (*C*. 4.12.23; *Epist*. 1.14.33), and, as Bentley observed (*Q. Horatius Flaccus*, 1:204–5), *inmunis* is unparalleled in the latter sense without a defining word (e.g. *inmunis scelerum*).

17. See G. Williams, "Poetry in the Moral Climate," pp. 28–46.

18. See p. 112, with p. 204, n. 8.

19. See preceding note.

20. For further comparison of the Bacchus odes, see Fraenkel, *Horace*, pp. 257–60; on the god's development in the collection, see Silk, "Bacchus and the Horatian *Recusatio*," pp. 193–212; and for ambiguities in Horace's attitude to political poetry see Connor, "Enthusiasm, Poetry, and Politics," pp. 266–74.

21. See Silk, "Horace, II,20," p. 263: "in Book III,25, the Bacchic enthusiasm is presented as an apologetic or explicatory epilogue to the long poem (III,24)."

22. See Copley, *Exclusus Amator*, pp. 55–58; Henderson, "The Paraclausithyron Motif," pp. 51–67, with p. 66 n. 45 on the text of line 7.

23. Jones, "*Tange Chloen*," pp. 81–83, citing Hellenistic parallels for the *topos* of the disdainful beloved's future misery; other examples are in Cairns, *Generic Composition*, pp. 80–81, though *C*. 3.26 is omitted.

24. Kiessling and Heinze, *Oden und Epoden*, p. 363.

25. See Lieberman, "Horace and le mot juste," pp. 214, 219–20.

26. For Thracian cold as the counterpoint to love see, for example, C. 1.25.9–12; Vergil Bucolic 10.66.

27. Kiessling and Heinze, Oden und Epoden, p. 361.

28. The same technique occurs at C. 1.14–15 where the shared nautical imagery underscores the poems' allegorical intent.

29. See B. Smith, Poetic Closure, p. 172.

30. Ibid., pp. 175–76.

31. For the frame of C. 1.5 and 3.26 see Wili, Horaz und die augusteische Kultur, p. 182; on its programmatic function see Jones, "Tange Chloen," p. 82. This parallelism provides further support for Zielinski's despised deae at C. 1.5.16 —see Nisbet and Hubbard, Horace: Odes, Book I, pp. 79–80. For further discussion see the remarks on C. 1.5 on pp. 33–34 above; see also the remarks on the framing of the entire three books on pp. 150–52.

32. See Quinn, Latin Explorations, pp. 253–66; for the relation of the two parts of the ode see also Friedrich, "Europa und der Stier," pp. 81–100.

33. Kilpatrick, "Remember Us, Galatea," pp. 191–204, citing as a close parallel Epistle 1.20 in which Horace's book is compared to a slave (liber) rashly leaving his master's house and then experiencing the same fear, self-recrimination, and glory as the traveler in C. 3.27.

34. The Vergilian umbra is most naturally understood as dusk. But even if daytime shade is meant, its closural implications are unmistakable because the sentence also contains a programmatic element in the word surgamus, which suggests not just the end of the Bucolics but also Vergil's ascent to a new genre. Such a programmatic aspect is absent from the closural allusion to nox in C. 3.28.

35. The general meaning, "song," assigned to the word here by both Lewis and Short and the new Oxford Latin Dictionary is otherwise unexampled and neglects the force of its primary context. Most commentators, however, recognize some nuance, either of slowness, repetitiveness, or finality: see, for example, Nisbet and Hubbard, Horace: Odes, Book II, pp. 30–31; Kiessling and Heinze, Oden und Epoden, p. 374; G. Williams, Third Book of Horace's Odes, p. 143. The sense of finality suits the context best, and derives easily from the figurative use of nenia in the idiom, neniam dicere + dative = "to put an end to," which Horace adapts here in the passive (dicetur ... Nox ... nenia).

36. For another interpretation of the poem see Pöschl, Horazische Lyrik, pp. 180–96.

37. Kermode, The Sense of an Ending.

CHAPTER SEVEN

1. See pp. 85–87, with p. 200, nn. 15, 16, 17, 18.

2. On the framing of Book 1, see pp. 80–81; and for framing in Book 3 (after the Roman Odes) and in the collection as a whole, see Mutschler, "Beobachtungen zur Gedichtanordnung," pp. 109–33. The way in which the first six poems in Book 1 balance the last six in Book 3 has been noted also by Dettmer, *Horace: A Study in Structure*, pp. 140–67, and had been previously suggested by Santirocco, "Horace's *Odes* and the Ancient Poetry Book," p. 50. Dettmer, however, continues to move in from each end of the collection and to detect ring composition throughout it: see the fold-out diagram at the end of her book. For general methodological and philosophical problems with this approach, see pp. 3–4, and esp. p. 177, n. 7, above. It may be useful to take a specific and representative case. Dettmer (ibid., pp. 177–82) claims that C. 1.17 (*Velox amoenum*) and 3.14 (*Herculis ritu*) balance each other: both are in the seventeenth position from their respective ends of the ensemble, both deal with an epiphany of sorts (Faunus, Augustus), both mention the poet's safety, and both invite a woman to join in the fun (Tyndaris, Neaera). But would a reader be likely to notice a correspondence of poems seventeen places in from the ends of the collection? The correspondence is itself tenuous in any case. The invitational element common to both poems, for example, results from the sympotic convention in which so many of Horace's odes are cast and cannot serve as hard evidence of intentional pairing. Again, the motif of the poet's safety may be common to both poems (as it is to many others: see p. 202, n. 50, above), but in C. 1.17 it is attributed to Horace's status as a poet, whereas in C. 3.14 it results from Augustus's victories. Finally, the tone of both poems is so different that one is led to ask what critical significance could possibly underlie the pairing of Horace's delicate invitation to Tyndaris to visit his farm and the great ode, *Herculis ritu*, which celebrates Augustus's return from Spain. (Dettmer, ibid., pp. 181–82, makes the unlikely suggestion that "through the two parallels Horace is subtly identifying Augustus with Faunus. Here, however, is where the resemblance ends, for the presence of Augustus, unlike that of Faunus, does not inspire poetry." The point of the alleged correspondence, then, is an implicit political critique, "to counterpose the effect the protection of the gods and the presence of Faunus had on Horace, poetic inspiration, to that of Augustus, lack of inspiration.") If C. 3.14 is part of any symmetrical design, it has seemed more useful and critically significant to note how it balances C. 3.8, and then to observe how these two odes attempt to harmonize the public voice of the Roman Odes with the private voice heard in the poems that follow that cycle: see pp. 128–31 above.

3. The only other occurrence of the meter is in the later fourth book of *Odes*, significantly in a programmatic poem, C. 4.8.

4. On the symbolism of C. 1.3, see pp. 27–30 above; on C. 3.27, see pp. 144–46.

5. On C. 1.4 and 5, see pp. 30–34; on C. 3.26 and 28, see pp. 142–47.

6. On C. 2.19 and 20 as the introduction to the Roman Odes, see p. 112, with p. 204, n. 8.

7. See p. 82.

8. This is not to say, however, that they do not reflect a real social background: see Lyne, *Latin Love Poets*, pp. 192–200.

9. On the Lydia and Glycera sequences, see p. 82.

10. On the Bacchus odes, see above, pp. 52–54, 107, 140–43.

11. See Dalzell, "Maecenas and the Poets," pp. 151–62; Reckford, "Horace and Maecenas," pp. 195–208.

12. See Wimmel, *Kallimachos in Rom*; Clausen, "Callimachus and Roman Poetry," pp. 181–96; P. L. Smith, "Poetic Tensions in the Horatian *Recusatio*," pp. 56–65. For a different view of the reality behind *recusationes*, see Griffin, "Augustan Poetry and the Life of Luxury," p. 104 with n. 243. For further discussion of *recusationes*, see pp. 34–36 above.

13. See Zetzel, "Poetics of Patronage," pp. 87–102; Bright, *Haec Mihi Fingebam*, pp. 38–65.

14. See Taylor, "Horace's Equestrian Career," pp. 161–70; Taylor, "Republican and Augustan Writers Enrolled in the Equestrian Census," pp. 469–86; Nicolet, *L'ordre équestre*, 1:441–56.

15. See White, "*Amicitia* and the Profession of Poetry," pp. 74–92; and, more generally, Brunt, "*Amicitia* in the Late Roman Republic," pp. 1–20; Saller, *Personal Patronage*, pp. 7–39, on the language and ideology of patronage.

16. See Santirocco, "Poet and Patron," pp. 56–62.

17. Compare the numerologically significant placement of Maecenas's name in Vergil's *Georgics*: 1.2, 2.41, 3.41, 4.2.

18. The only position closer to the beginning of the book was reserved for a poem marking both a break and a transition from the Roman Odes, C. 3.7: see p. 125.

19. See pp. 54–55.

20. See, for example, Collinge, *Structure of Horace's Odes*, p. 108: "The first and last couplets certainly look to be outside the general scheme; they might be read continuously, were it not for the *quodsi*, which takes account of what intervenes."

21. See the full discussion of C. 1.1 on pp. 15–19.

22. See Cairns, "Catullus I," pp. 153–58; Levine, "Catullus c. 1," pp. 209–16; Singleton, "A Note on Catullus' First Poem," pp. 192–96; Wiseman, *Clio's*

Cosmetics, pp. 167–74. For a different view, however, see Elder, "Catullus I," pp. 143–49.

23. On Maecenas's dubious ancestry, see MacKay, "Notes on Horace," pp. 79–80.

24. See Commager, *Odes of Horace*, pp. 325–26; Putnam, "Horace c. 1.20," pp. 153–57; Race, "Odes 1.20," pp. 179–96.

25. But for the other view, see Race, "Odes 1.20," pp. 153–57.

26. For full discussion of these points, see Santirocco, "Strategy and Structure," pp. 223–36.

27. Connections have been seen, not just between the last two odes (e.g. Silk, "Horace, II,20," pp. 255–63, who views them as a prelude to the Roman Odes; see further p. 112 above), but also among the last four: see Wili, *Horaz und die augusteische Kultur*, pp. 233 ff., on the poet's triumph over death, and Commager, *Odes of Horace*, pp. 311–12, who notes briefly their movement away from Maecenas but does not pursue it beyond these four odes.

28. See Commager, *Odes of Horace*, pp. 348–52; Troxler-Keller, *Dichterlandschaft*, pp. 108–18.

29. E.g. C. 1.19.13–16, where the *hostia* parallels the poem in that both are offered to Venus; C. 4.2.53–60, where the contrast between the two sacrifices recapitulates the earlier contrast between Horatian and Pindaric lyric.

30. For other indirect references to Maecenas in this and other poems, see Nisbet and Hubbard, *Horace: Odes, Book II*, pp. 289–90; for discussion of second person pronouns generally and of the function of addressees as a metaphor for the reader, see Johnson, *Idea of Lyric*, pp. 1–23, and, on Horace, p. 127; see also p. 21 above.

31. In patronage contexts *peto* usually signifies the client's role: to the references in Nisbet and Hubbard, *Horace: Odes, Book II*, p. 299, add Catullus 28.13 (*pete nobiles amicos*); *Laus Pisonis* 218–19 (*dignare tuos aperire Penates, / hoc solum petimus*); Horace C. 3.16.22–23 (*nil cupientium / nudus castra peto*), on which see further below.

32. Reckford, "Horace and Maecenas," pp. 195–208, observes a role reversal in the relationship, but he sees it only in biographical terms and not also as an artistic principle organizing a sequence of poems.

33. See Bradshaw, "Some Stylistic Oddities," pp. 145–50.

34. As often: see Commager, "The Function of Wine," pp. 68–80.

35. Schork, "*Aemulos Reges*," p. 531; I have drawn from the entire article (pp. 515–39) in the preceding discussion.

36. So effectively does Horace decline further aid, that the poem has been read as his refusal of an imperial secretaryship: see Frank, "On Augustus' References to Horace," pp. 26–30.

37. See Mørland, "Wortbrechungen und Hypermetra," pp. 108–14; Commager, "Some Horatian Vagaries," pp. 59–70.

38. The point is unaffected by punctuation, whether *vixi* alone or the entire passage, 43-fin., is enclosed by quotation marks.

39. That is, in the phrase, *princeps Aeolium carmen ad Italos / deduxisse modos* (13–14), we would expect the song to have been called Italian and the meters Aeolic. Collinge, *Structure of Horace's Odes*, p. 32 n. 1, explains that "when he actually penned iii.30 he may well have been 'underwriting' a piece of bravado by means of a stylistic figure." But perhaps the epithets are reversed from what we would expect for some other purpose: *Italos*, for example, can be proleptic, or perhaps Horace has in mind his technical adjustments that Latinized what were originally Greek meters.

40. See, for example, Collinge, *Structure of Horace's Odes*, pp. 69–70: "The ode is basically uncertain and diffident in tone, and in structure is really a three-part run-down." Even G. Williams, who accepts the traditional view that this is a proud document, notes of its ending that "the pleasure he feels in the pride of his humble hometown and the prayer of thanks to the Muse are two successive steps down from the assertion of his own achievement in 1–9" (*Third Book of Horace's Odes*, p. 152).

41. For other points of contact between the epilogue and C. 1.1, see Zetzel, "Poetics of Patronage," pp. 95–97; and, among the many recent studies of the epilogue, see Woodman, "Exegi Monumentum," pp. 115–28; Putnam, "Horace C. 3.30," pp. 1–19, reprinted in his *Essays*, pp. 133–51.

CHAPTER EIGHT

1. See Fraenkel, *Horace*, pp. 26, 208–9, 370 n. 1.
2. See p. 185, n. 58, above.
3. A good example of this is the collocation of C. 1.27 and 28 whose very different themes—drink and death—reproduce the sequence of ideas in individual odes like C. 1.4, where the sympotic invitation to Sestius leads to thoughts of *Pallida Mors*.
4. Harrison, *Complete Works of Poe*, 14:195–96, cited by Rosenthal and Gall, *Modern Poetic Sequence*, p. 6.
5. From Eliot's 1959 *Paris Review* interview cited by Rosenthal and Gall, *Modern Poetic Sequence*, p. 165.
6. Nietzsche, "Was ich den Alten verdanke," in *Götzendämmerung*; Petronius 118.5. In the latter text there is no warrant for emending *felicitas* to *facilitas* (Giardina, "Note a Petronio," pp. 178–87); on the meaning of the phrase see Mantovanelli, "Curiosa felicitas," pp. 59–71, who suggests that it indicates the equilibrium of *ars* and *ingenium*.

BIBLIOGRAPHY

Alexander, W. H. "Horace's Odes and Carmen Saeculare: Observations and Interpretations." *University of California Publications in Classical Philology* 13 (1947): 173–240.
Amundsen, L. "The 'Roman Odes' of Horace." In *Serta Eitremiana*, pp. 1–24. Symbolae Osloenses Supplement, no. 11. Oslo, 1942.
Anderson, A. R. "Note on Horace C. 2.3.17–20." *Classical Philology* 10 (1915): 456.
Anderson, W. S. "Horace Carm. 1.14: What Kind of Ship?" *Classical Philology* 61 (1966): 84–97.
———. "Two Odes of Horace's Book Two." *California Studies in Classical Antiquity* 1 (1968): 35–45.
———. "The Form, Purpose, and Position of Horace, Satire I, 8." *American Journal of Philology* 93 (1972): 6–13.
———. *Essays on Roman Satire*. Princeton: Princeton University Press, 1982.
André, J. M. "Les odes romaines." In *Hommages à Marcel Renard*, pp. 31–46. Collection Latomus, no. 101. Brussels, 1969.
Armstrong, D. "Horace, Satires I, 1–3: A Structural Study." *Arion* 3 (1964): 86–96.
Babcock, C. L. "Horace Carm. I,32 and the Dedication of Palatine Apollo." *Classical Philology* 62 (1967): 189–92.
Baker, R. J. "Domina at Catullus 68,68: Mistress or Chatelaine?" *Rheinisches Museum* n.s. 118 (1975): 124–29.
Ball, R. J. "Tibullus 2.5 and Vergil's Aeneid." *Vergilius* 21 (1975): 33–50.
———. *Tibullus the Elegist: A Critical Survey*. Hypomnemata, no. 77. Göttingen: Vandenhoeck & Ruprecht, 1983.
Balogh, J. "Voces Paginarum." *Philologus* 82 (1927): 84–109, 202–40.
Barr, W. "Horace, Odes 1,4." *Classical Review* 12 (1962): 5–11.
Barsby, J. A. "The Composition and Publication of the First Three Books of Propertius." *Greece and Rome* 21 (1974): 128–37.
Barwick, K. "Zyklen bei Martial und in den kleinen Gedichten des Catull." *Philologus* 102 (1958): 284–318.

Basto, R. "Horace's Propempticon to Vergil: A Re-examination." *Vergilius* 28 (1982): 30–44.
Bastomsky, S. J. "Proculeius and Augustus: A Note on a Friendship Turned Sour." *Latomus* 36 (1977): 129–31.
Bate, W. J. *The Burden of the Past and the English Poet.* Cambridge: Harvard University Press, 1970.
Belling, H. *Studien über die Liederbücher des Horaz.* Berlin: Gaertners, 1903.
Bellinger, A. R. "The Immortality of Alexander and Augustus." *Yale Classical Studies* 15 (1957): 91–100.
Belmont, D. E. "The Vergilius of Horace Odes 4.12." *Transactions of the American Philological Association* 110 (1980): 1–20.
Bentley, R., ed. *Q. Horatius Flaccus.* 2d ed. 2 vols. Berlin: Weidmann, 1869. Reprint. New York: Garland, 1978.
Bliss, F. P. "The Plancus Ode." *Transactions of the American Philological Association* 91 (1960): 30–46.
Bloom, H. *The Anxiety of Influence: A Theory of Poetry.* Oxford: Oxford University Press, 1973.
Boer, W. den, ed. *Le culte des souverains dans l'empire romaine.* Fondation Hardt Entretiens, no. 19. Geneva, 1973.
Bohnenkamp, K. E. *Die horazische Strophe: Studien zur 'Lex Meinekiana.'* Spudasmata, no. 30. Hildesheim: Olms, 1972.
Boll, F. *Kleine Schriften zur Sternkunde des Altertums.* Leipzig: Koehler & Amelang, 1950.
Bonavia-Hunt, N. A. *Horace the Minstrel: A Practical and Aesthetic Study of His Aeolic Verse.* Kineton: Roundwood, 1969.
Bowra, C. M. *Greek Lyric Poetry: From Alcman to Simonides.* 2d ed. Oxford: Oxford University Press, 1961.
Bradshaw, A. "Some Stylistic Oddities in Horace, Odes III,8." *Philologus* 114 (1970): 145–50.
Bright, D. F. *Haec Mihi Fingebam: Tibullus in His World.* Cincinnati Classical Studies, no. 3. Leiden: Brill, 1978.
Brink, C. O. *Horace on Poetry: Prolegomena to the Literary Epistles.* Cambridge: Cambridge University Press, 1963.
Brunt, P. A. "Amicitia in the Late Roman Republic." *Proceedings of the Cambridge Philological Society* 11 (1965): 1–20.
Buchheit, V. *Studien zur Corpus Priapeorum.* Munich: Beck, 1962.
———. "Tibulls 2.5 und die *Aeneis.*" *Philologus* 109 (1965): 104–20.
Büchner, K. *Studien zur römischen Literatur III: Horaz.* Wiesbaden: Steiner, 1962.
Buffière, F., ed. *Héraclite: Allégories d'Homère.* Paris: Belles Lettres, 1962.
Butrica, J. L. "The Propertian Corpus in Antiquity." *Abstracts of the American Philological Association Meeting* (1982): 6.
Buttrey, T. V. "Halved Coins, the Augustan Reforms, and Horace, *Odes* I,3." *American Journal of Archaeology* 76 (1972): 31–48.

Cairns, F. "Catullus I." *Mnemosyne* 22 (1969): 153–58.
———. "Five 'Religious' Odes of Horace." *American Journal of Philology* 92 (1971): 433–52.
———. "Horace, Odes I.2." *Eranos* 69 (1971): 68–88.
———. *Generic Composition in Greek and Roman Poetry.* Edinburgh: Edinburgh University Press, 1972.
Calder, W. M., III. "Irony in Horace Carm. 2.2: *Nullus argento color est avaris.*" *Classical Philology* 56 (1961): 175–78.
Callahan, P. V., and Musurillo, H. "A Handful of Dust: The Archytas Ode (Hor. Carm. I,28)." *Classical Philology* 59 (1964): 262–69.
Cameron, A. D. E. "The First Edition of Ovid's Amores." *Classical Quarterly* n.s. 18 (1968): 320–33.
———. "The Garlands of Meleager and Philip." *Greek, Roman, and Byzantine Studies* 9 (1968): 323–49.
———. *The Greek Anthology: From Meleager to Planudes.* Oxford: Oxford University Press. Forthcoming.
Campbell, A. Y. *Horace: A New Interpretation.* London: Methuen, 1924.
———, ed. *Horace: Odes and Epodes.* 2d ed. Liverpool: University Press of Liverpool, 1953.
Camps, W. A. "Critical and Exegetical Notes." *American Journal of Philology* 94 (1973): 131–46.
———, ed. *Propertius: Elegies, Book I.* Cambridge: Cambridge University Press, 1961.
Carrubba, R. W. *The Epodes of Horace.* Studies in Classical Literature, no. 9. The Hague: Mouton, 1969.
Charlesworth, M. P. "The Virtues of a Roman Emperor: Propaganda and the Creation of Belief." *Proceedings of the British Academy* 23 (1937): 105–33.
Christ, W. von. "Über die Verskunst des Horaz im Lichte der alten Überlieferung." *Sitzungsberichte der Königlichen bayerischen Akademie der Wissenschaften zu München.* Jahrgang 1868, Band 1, pp. 1–44.
Clausen, W. V. "Callimachus and Roman Poetry." *Greek, Roman, and Byzantine Studies* 5 (1964): 181–96.
———. "Catulli Veronensis Liber." *Classical Philology* 71 (1976): 37–43.
Clay, D. *Lucretius and Epicurus.* Ithaca, N.Y.: Cornell University Press, 1983.
Clayman, D. L. "Callimachus' Thirteenth Iamb: The Last Word." *Hermes* 104 (1976): 29–35.
———. *Callimachus' Iambi.* Mnemosyne Supplement, no. 59. Leiden: Brill, 1980.
Cody, J. V. *Horace and Callimachean Aesthetics.* Collection Latomus, no. 147. Brussels, 1976.
Coffey, M. *Roman Satire.* London: Methuen, 1976.
Collinge, N. E. *The Structure of Horace's Odes.* London: Oxford University Press, 1961.

Colmant, P. "Horace, Ode 1.3." *Les Études Classiques* 8 (1939): 87–90.
Commager, S. "The Function of Wine in Horace's Odes." *Transactions of the American Philological Association* 88 (1957): 68–80.
―――. "Horace, Carmina 1.37." *Phoenix* 12 (1958): 47–58.
―――. "Horace, Carmina, I,2." *American Journal of Philology* 80 (1959): 37–55.
―――. *The Odes of Horace: A Critical Study.* New Haven: Yale University Press, 1962.
―――. *A Prolegomenon to Propertius.* Lectures in Memory of Louise Taft Semple, The University of Cincinnati. Norman: University of Oklahoma Press, 1974.
―――. "Some Horatian Vagaries." *Symbolae Osloenses* 55 (1980): 59–70.
―――, ed. *Virgil: A Collection of Critical Essays.* Englewood Cliffs, N.J.: Prentice-Hall, 1966.
Connor, P. J. "Enthusiasm, Poetry, and Politics: A Consideration of Horace, Odes, III,25." *American Journal of Philology* 92 (1971): 266–74.
Copley, F. O. *Exclusus Amator: A Study in Latin Love Poetry.* American Philological Association Monographs, no. 17. Baltimore, 1956.
Coutts, R. L. "Astrology in Horace, Odes II, 17." *Proceedings of the Classical Association* 61 (1964): 26–27.
Cuartero, F. J. "Estudios sobre el escolio ático." *Boletín del Instituto de Estudios helénicos* 1 (1967): 5–38.
Cunningham, I. C. "Herodas 6 and 7." *Classical Quarterly* n.s. 14 (1964): 32–35.
―――. *Herodas: Mimiamboi.* Oxford: Oxford University Press, 1971.
Daly, L. W. *Contributions to a History of Alphabetization in Antiquity and the Middle Ages.* Collection Latomus, no. 90. Brussels, 1967.
Dalzell, A. "Maecenas and the Poets." *Phoenix* 10 (1956): 151–62.
―――. Review of *Structural Patterns and Proportions in the Aeneid,* by G. Duckworth. *Phoenix* 17 (1963): 314–16.
D'Arms, J. W. *Romans on the Bay of Naples.* Cambridge: Harvard University Press, 1970.
Davison, J. A. *From Archilochus to Pindar: Papers on Greek Literature of the Archaic Period.* London: Macmillan, 1968.
Dawson, C. M. "The Iambi of Callimachus." *Yale Classical Studies* 11 (1950): 1–168.
Defourny, P. "Le printemps dans l'ode à Sestius (I.4)." *Les Études Classiques* 14 (1946): 174–94.
Dettmer, H. *Horace: A Study in Structure.* Altertumswissenschaftliche Texte und Studien, no. 12. Hildesheim: Olms-Weidmann, 1983.
Deubner, L. "Ein Stilprinzip hellenistischer Dichtkunst." *Neue Jahrbücher für klassischen Altertums* 47 (1921): 361–78.
DeWitt, N. W. "An Interpretation of Horace Odes III.3." *Classical Review* 34 (1920): 65–66.

Dicks, D. R. "Astrology and Astronomy in Horace." *Hermes* 91 (1963): 60–73.
Doblhofer, E. "Zum Augustusbild des Horaz." *Rheinisches Museum* 107 (1964): 325–39.
Dodds, E. R., ed. *Euripides' Bacchae.* Oxford: Oxford University Press, 1944.
Domaszewski, A. von. "Untersuchungen zur römischen Kaisergeschichte VI: Der Festgesang des Horaz auf die Begründung des Principates." *Rheinisches Museum* 59 (1904): 302–10.
———. *Abhandlungen zur römischen Religion.* Leipzig: Teubner, 1909. Reprint. New York: Arno, 1975.
Draheim, H. "Die Anordnung der Gedichte im 1. Buche der Oden des Horaz." *Wochenschrift für klassische Philologie* 17 (1900): 1268–70.
Drew, D. L. "Horace, Odes 1.12 and the Forum Augustum." *Classical Quarterly* 19 (1925): 159–64.
Duckworth, G. E. "*Animae Dimidium Meae*: Two Poets of Rome." *Transactions of the American Philological Association* 87 (1956): 281–316.
———. *Structural Patterns and Proportions in the Aeneid.* Ann Arbor: University of Michigan Press, 1962.
Dunston, A. J. "Horace Odes III.4 and the Virtues of Augustus." *AUMLA: Journal of the Australasian Universities Language and Literature Association* 31 (1969): 9–19.
Dvornik, F. *Early Christian and Byzantine Political Philosophy: Origins and Background.* 2 vols. Dumbarton Oaks Studies, no. 9. Washington, D.C., 1966.
Dyson, M. "Horace: Odes I.16." *AUMLA: Journal of the Australasian Universities Language and Literature Association* 30 (1968): 169–79.
———. "Horace Odes III,14." *Greece and Rome* 20 (1973): 169–79.
Eichgrün, E. *Kallimachos und Apollonios Rhodios.* Dissertation, University of Berlin, 1961.
Eisenberger, H. "Bilden die horazischen Oden 2.1–12 einen Zyklus?" *Gymnasium* 87 (1980): 262–74.
Elder, J. P. "Horace, C. I,3." *American Journal of Philology* 73 (1952): 140–58.
———. "Horace Carmen 1.7." *Classical Philology* 48 (1953): 1–8.
———. "Catullus I, His Poetic Creed, and Nepos." *Harvard Studies in Classical Philology* 71 (1966): 143–49.
Eliot, T. S. *The Sacred Wood.* London: Methuen, 1920.
Ellis, R. *A Commentary on Catullus.* 2d ed. Oxford: Oxford University Press, 1889. Reprint. New York: Garland, 1979.
Evans, H. B. *Publica Carmina: Ovid's Books from Exile.* Lincoln: University of Nebraska Press, 1983.
Fenik, B. "Horace's First and Sixth Roman Odes and the Second Georgic." *Hermes* 90 (1962): 72–96.
Ferguson, J. "Catullus and Horace." *American Journal of Philology* 77 (1956): 1–19.
Ferrero, L. *Interpretazione di Catullo.* Turin: Rosenberg & Sellier, 1955.

Festa, N. "*Animae Dimidium Meae.*" Sophia 1 (1933): 436–41.
Fontaine, F. Enchaînement et groupement des poèmes dans l'oeuvre lyrique d'Horace. Mémoire de licence, Liège, 1941–42.
Fraenkel, E. Horace. Oxford: Oxford University Press, 1957.
Frank, T. "On Augustus' References to Horace." Classical Philology 20 (1925): 26–30.
Franke-Klein, F. "Horace and the Stars." In Commentationes ad antiquitatem classicam pertinentes in memoriam B. Katz, edited by M. Roselaar and B. Shimron, pp. 154–58. Tel Aviv: Tel Aviv University Press, 1970.
Fraser, P. M. Ptolemaic Alexandria. 3 vols. Oxford: Oxford University Press, 1972.
Fredricksmeyer, E. A. "Horace C. 1.34: The Conversion." Transactions of the American Philological Association 106 (1976): 155–76.
Friedrich, W.-H. "Europa und der Stier: Angewandte Mythologie bei Horaz und Properz." Nachrichten von der Gesellschaft der Wissenschaften zu Göttingen. Phil.-hist. Kl. 5 (1959): 81–100.
Fuqua, C. "Horace Carm. I,23–25." Classical Philology 63 (1968): 44–46.
Galinsky, G. K. Ovid's Metamorphoses: An Introduction to the Basic Aspects. Berkeley: University of California Press, 1975.
Ghiselli, A. "Lettura dell'Ode 1,1 di Orazio." Lingua e Stile 7 (1972): 103–46.
Giangrande, G. Review of Theocritus' Coan Pastorals, by Gilbert Lawall. Journal of Hellenic Studies 88 (1968): 170–73.
Giardina, G. "Sulla struttura delle odi di Orazio." Lingua e Stile 5 (1970): 45–55.
———. "Note a Petronio." Museum Criticum 5–7 (1970–72): 187–88.
Glare, P. G. W., ed. Oxford Latin Dictionary. Oxford: Oxford University Press, 1982.
Goar, R. J. "Horace and the Betrayal of Philosophy: Odes 1.29." Classical Journal 68 (1972): 116–18.
Gold, B. K., ed. Literary and Artistic Patronage in Ancient Rome. Austin: University of Texas Press, 1982.
Gornall, J. F. C. "Horace, Odes III.19: Does It Contain a Gap in Time?" Greece and Rome 18 (1971): 188–90.
Gow, A. S. F. Theocritus. 2 vols. Cambridge: Cambridge University Press, 1952.
———, and Page, D. L. The Greek Anthology: Hellenistic Epigrams. 2 vols. Cambridge: Cambridge University Press, 1965.
Griffin, J. "Augustan Poetry and the Life of Luxury." Journal of Roman Studies 66 (1976): 87–105.
Hahn, E. A. "Epodes 5 and 17, Carmina 1.16 and 1.17." Transactions of the American Philological Association 70 (1939): 213–30.
———. "Horace's Odes to Vergil." Transactions of the American Philological Association 76 (1945): xxxii–iii.
Halperin, D. M. Before Pastoral: Theocritus and the Ancient Tradition of Bucolic Poetry.

New Haven: Yale University Press, 1983.
Hardie, A. *Statius and the Silvae: Poets, Patrons and Epideixis in the Graeco-Roman World*. Classical and Medieval Texts, Papers and Monographs, no. 9. Liverpool: Francis Cairns, 1983.
Harrauer, H. *A Bibliography to Tibullus*. Bibliography to the Augustan Poetry, no. 1. Hildesheim: Gerstenberg, 1971.
———. *A Bibliography to Propertius*. Bibliography to the Augustan Poetry, no. 2. Hildesheim: Gerstenberg, 1973.
Harrison, J. A., ed. *The Complete Works of Edgar Allan Poe*. 17 vols. New York: De Fau, 1902. Reprint. New York: AMS Press, 1965.
Harvey, A. E. "The Classification of Greek Lyric Poetry." *Classical Quarterly* n.s. 5 (1955): 157–75.
Häusser, J. Review of "Die Frage nach der Anordnung der horazischen Oden: Eine kritische Übersicht," by A. Raiz, and *Zur Anordnung der Oden des Horaz*, by J. A. Simon. *Berliner Philologische Wochenschrift* 17 (1897): 362–66.
Havelock, E. A. *The Literate Revolution in Greece and Its Cultural Consequences*. Princeton: Princeton University Press, 1982.
Hazlitt, W. *Lectures on the English Poets*. Introduced by C. M. MacLean. Everyman's Library, no. 459. London: Dent, 1960.
Heinze, R. "Die horazische Ode." *Neue Jahrbücher für das klassische Altertum* 51 (1923): 153–68.
———. *Vom Geist des Römertums*. 3d ed. Leipzig: Teubner, 1938.
Henderson, W. J. "The Paraclausithyron Motif in Horace's Odes." *Acta Classica* 16 (1973): 51–67.
Hendrickson, G. L. "Horace's Propempticon to Virgil." *Classical Journal* 3 (1907–8): 100–104.
———. "Ancient Reading." *Classical Journal* 25 (1929): 182–96.
———. "The First Publication of Horace's Odes." *Classical Philology* 26 (1931): 1–10.
Highet, G. *Poets in a Landscape*. New York: Knopf, 1957.
———. *The Speeches in Vergil's Aeneid*. Princeton: Princeton University Press, 1972.
Hirst, M. E. "The Portents in Horace's Odes I,2,1–30." *Classical Quarterly* 32 (1938): 7–9.
Hornsby, R. J. "Horace on Art and Politics (Ode III,4)." *Classical Journal* 58 (1962): 97–102.
Howald, E. *Das Wesen der lateinischen Dichtung*. Zürich: Rentsch, 1948.
Hubbard, M. *Propertius*. New York: Scribner's, 1975.
Huber, G. *Wortwiederholungen in den Oden des Horaz*. Zürich: Juris-Verlag, 1970.
Hutchinson, G. O. "Propertius and the Unity of the Book." *Journal of Roman Studies* 74 (1984): 99–106.
Jacobson, H. "Horace and Augustus: An Interpretation of Carm. 1,35." *Classical*

Philology 63 (1968): 106–13.

———. *Ovid's Heroides.* Princeton: Princeton University Press, 1974.

Jäger, F. *Das antike Propemptikon und das 17. Gedicht von Paulinus von Nola.* Rosenheim: Niedermayr, 1913.

Jensen, J. J. "The Secret Art of Horace." *Classica et Mediaevalia* 27 (1968): 208–15.

Jocelyn, H. D. "Boats, Women, and Horace Odes 1.14." *Classical Philology* 77 (1982): 330–35.

Johnson, W. R. "The Boastful Bird: Notes on Horatian Modesty." *Classical Journal* 61 (1966): 272–75.

———. *The Idea of Lyric: Lyric Modes in Ancient and Modern Poetry.* Berkeley: University of California Press, 1982.

Jones, C. P. "*Tange Chloen semel arrogantem.*" *Harvard Studies in Classical Philology* 75 (1971): 81–83.

Kambylis, A. *Die Dichterweihe und ihre Symbolik.* Heidelberg: Winter, 1965.

Kassell, R. *Untersuchungen zur griechischen und römischen Konsolationsliteratur.* Zetemata, no. 18. Munich: Beck, 1958.

Kermode, F. *The Sense of an Ending: Studies in the Theory of Fiction.* New York: Oxford University Press, 1967.

Kidd, D. A. "Virgil's Voyage." *Prudentia* 9.2 (1977): 97–103.

Kienast, D. "Horaz und die erste Krise des Principats: Die Ode Herculis ritu." *Chiron* 1 (1971): 239–51.

Kiessling, A. "Horatius I: Zur Chronologie und Anordnung der Oden." *Philologische Untersuchungen* 2 (1881): 48–75.

———, and Heinze, R., eds. *Q. Horatius Flaccus: Oden und Epoden.* 8th ed. Berlin: Weidmann, 1955.

Kilpatrick, R. S. "Archytas at the Styx (Horace, Carm. I,28)." *Classical Philology* 63 (1968): 201–6.

———. "Two Horatian Proems: Carm. 1.26 and 1.32." *Yale Classical Studies* 21 (1969): 312–19.

———. "Remember Us, Galatea: Horace, Carm. 3.27." *Grazer Beiträge* 3 (1975): 191–204.

Kimber, R. B. "The Structure of Horace, Odes 1.15." *Classical Journal* 53 (1957–58): 74–77.

King, J. K. "Propertius' Programmatic Poetry and the Unity of the Monobiblos." *Classical Journal* 71 (1975–76): 108–24.

Kinsey, T. E. "Catullus 11." *Latomus* 24 (1965): 537–44.

Kissel, W. "Horaz 1936–1975: Eine Gesamtbibliographie." *Aufstieg und Niedergang der römischen Welt* II.31.3 (1981).

Klingner, F. "Gedanken über Horaz." *Die Antike* 5 (1929): 23–44.

———. "Horazens Römeroden." In *Varia Variorum: Festgabe für Karl Reinhardt,* pp. 118–36. Cologne: Böhlau, 1952.

———. *Römische Geisteswelt*. Munich: Ellermann, 1961.
Knox, B. M. W. "Silent Reading in Antiquity." *Greek, Roman, and Byzantine Studies* 9 (1968): 421–35.
Kranz, W. "Sphragis." *Rheinisches Museum* 104 (1961): 3–46, 97–124.
Kresic, S., ed. *Contemporary Literary Hermeneutics and Interpretation of Classical Texts*. Ottawa: Ottawa University Press, 1981.
Krokowski, J. "De Horati odis quae dicuntur Romanis." *Meander* 22 (1967): 3–13.
Kroll, W. "Horaz' Oden und die Philosophie." *Wiener Studien* 37 (1915): 223–38.
———. *Studien zum Verständnis der römischen Literatur*. Stuttgart: Metzler, 1924. Reprint. New York: Garland, 1978.
———, ed. *C. Valerius Catullus*. 3d ed. Stuttgart: Teubner, 1959.
Kumaniecki, C. F. "De Horatii carmine ad Plancum (Carm. I,7)." *Eos* 42.1 (1947): 5–23.
La Penna, A. *Orazio e l'ideologia del principato*. Turin: Einaudi, 1963.
———. "A proposito della struttura della prima ode di Orazio e di struttura letterarie in generale." *Maia* 25 (1973): 326–30.
Lasserre, F. "Aux origines de l'Anthologie, I: Le Papyrus P. Brit. Mus. Inv. 589 (Pack 1121)." *Rheinisches Museum* 102 (1959): 222–47.
Lawall, G. *Theocritus' Coan Pastorals: A Poetry Book*. Publications of the Center for Hellenic Studies. Cambridge: Harvard University Press, 1967.
Leach, E. W. "Vergil, Horace, Tibullus: Three Collections of Ten." *Ramus* 7 (1978): 79–105.
———. "Poetics and Poetic Design in Tibullus' First Elegiac Book." *Arethusa* 13 (1980): 79–96.
Lee, M. Owen. *Word, Sound, and Image in the Odes of Horace*. Ann Arbor: University of Michigan Press, 1969.
———. "Catullus in the Odes of Horace." *Ramus* 4 (1975): 33–48.
Levin, D. N. "Horace, Carm. 2.10: Stylistic Observations." *Classical Journal* 54 (1958–59): 169–71.
Levine, P. "Catullus c. 1: A Prayerful Dedication." *California Studies in Classical Antiquity* 2 (1969): 209–16.
Lewis, C. T., and Short, C. *A Latin Dictionary*. Oxford: Oxford University Press, 1879.
Lieberman, S. "Horace and le mot juste." *Classical World* 62 (1969): 214, 219–20.
Liebeschuetz, J. H. W. G. *Continuity and Change in Roman Religion*. Oxford: Oxford University Press, 1979.
Lloyd-Jones, H. "The Seal of Posidippus." *Journal of Hellenic Studies* 83 (1963): 75–99.
Lobel, E. Σαπφοῦς Μέλη: *The Fragments of the Lyrical Poems of Sappho*. Oxford:

Oxford University Press, 1925.

Lockyer, C. W., Jr. "Horace's Propempticon and Vergil's Voyage." *Classical World* 61 (1967): 42–45.

Loercher, G. *Der Aufbau der drei Bücher von Ovids Amores.* Heuremata, no. 3. Amsterdam: Grüner, 1975.

Ludwig, W. "Zu Horaz, C. 2,1–12." *Hermes* 85 (1957): 336–45.

———. "Die Anordnung des vierten Horazischen Odenbuches." *Museum Helveticum* 18 (1961): 1–10.

———. Review of *The Structure of Horace's Odes*, by N. E. Collinge. *Gnomon* 35 (1963): 171–77.

———. *Struktur und Einheit der Metamorphosen Ovids.* Berlin: de Gruyter, 1965.

———. "Die Komposition der beiden Satirenbücher des Horaz." *Poetica* 2 (1968): 304–25.

Lyne, R. O. A. M. *The Latin Love Poets: From Catullus to Horace.* Oxford: Oxford University Press, 1980.

McDermott, E. A. "Horatius Callidus." *American Journal of Philology* 98 (1977): 363–80.

McGann, M. J. *Studies in Horace's First Book of Epistles.* Collection Latomus, no. 100. Brussels, 1969.

MacKay, L. A. "Notes on Horace." *Classical Philology* 37 (1942): 79–81.

———. "Horace, Augustus, and Ode, I,2." *American Journal of Philology* 83 (1962): 168–77.

———. "Odes I,16 and 17: *matre pulchra . . . velox amoenum.*" *American Journal of Philology* 83 (1962): 298–300.

Macleod, C. W. "Catullus 116." *Classical Quarterly* n.s. 23 (1973): 304–9.

———. *Collected Essays.* Oxford: Oxford University Press, 1983.

Mancuso, U. *Orazio poeta civile: Dalle odi romani alle odi cesaree.* Rome: Ateneo, 1953.

Mantovanelli, P. "Curiosa felicitas." *Quaderni dell' Istituto di Filologia Latina* 2 (1972): 59–71.

Markowski, H. "De quattuor virtutibus Augusti in clupeo aureo ei dato inscriptis." *Eos* 37 (1936): 109–20.

Maury, P. *Horace et le secret de Virgile.* Paris: author's imprint, 1945.

Mendell, C. W. "Horace I,14." *Classical Philology* 33 (1938): 145–56.

———. "Horace, Odes II,18." *Yale Classical Studies* 11 (1950): 279–92.

Mette, H. J. "Genus tenue und mensa tenuis bei Horaz." *Museum Helveticum* 18 (1961): 136–39.

Michelfeit, J. "Das augusteische Gedichtbuch." *Rheinisches Museum* 112 (1969): 347–70.

Millar, F. "State and Subject: The Impact of Monarchy." In *Caesar Augustus: Seven Aspects*, edited by F. Millar and E. Segal, pp. 37–60. Oxford: Oxford University Press, 1984.

Mommsen, T. "Reden zur Feier der Geburtstage König Friedrichs II. und Kaiser Wilhelms II." *Sitzungsberichte der Preussischen Akademie* (1889): 23–35.

———. *Reden und Aufsätze*. Berlin: Weidmann, 1905.

Morel, W., ed. *Fragmenta Poetarum Latinorum Epicorum et Lyricorum*. 2d ed. Stuttgart: Teubner, 1927.

Moritz, L. A. "Some 'Central' Thoughts on Horace's Odes." *Classical Quarterly* n.s. 18 (1968): 116–31.

———. "Snow and Spring: Horace's Soracte Ode Again." *Greece and Rome* n.s. 23.2 (1976): 169–76.

Mørland, H. "Wortbrechungen und Hypermetra in den Oden des Horaz." *Symbolae Osloenses* 41 (1966): 108–14.

Most, G. W. "On the Arrangement of Catullus' Carmina Maiora." *Philologus* 125 (1981): 109–25.

Murphy, R. J. "The Attitude of the Augustan Poets toward *rex* and Related Words." *Classical Journal* 60 (1965): 241–46.

Musurillo, H. "The Poet's Apotheosis: Horace, Odes 1.1." *Transactions of the American Philological Association* 93 (1962): 230–39.

Muth, R. "Horaz—'parcus deorum cultor et infrequens': zu C. 1,34." *Grazer Beiträge* 4 (1975): 171–206.

Mutschler, F.-H. "Beobachtungen zur Gedichtanordnung in der ersten Odensammlung des Horaz." *Rheinisches Museum* n.s. 117 (1974): 109–33.

———. "Kaufmannsliebe: Eine Interpretation der Horazode 'Quid Fles Asterie' (C. 3.7)." *Symbolae Osloenses* 53 (1978): 111–31.

———. *Die poetische Kunst Tibulls*. Studien zur klassischen Philologie, no. 18. Frankfurt: Lang, 1985.

Nethercut, W. R. "Vergil and Bucolic 7." *Classical World* 62 (1968): 93–98.

———. "The Ironic Priest. Propertius' 'Roman Elegies,' III, 1–5: Imitations of Horace and Vergil." *American Journal of Philology* 91 (1970): 285–405.

Newman, J. K. *The Concept of Vates in Augustan Poetry*. Collection Latomus, no. 89. Brussels, 1967.

Newmyer, S. T. *The Silvae of Statius: Structure and Theme*. Mnemosyne Supplement, no. 53. Leiden: Brill, 1979.

Nicolet, C. *L'Ordre équestre à l'époque républicaine*. 2 vols. Paris: de Boccard, 1966.

Nisbet, R. G. M., and Hubbard, M., eds. *A Commentary on Horace: Odes, Book I*. Oxford: Oxford University Press, 1970.

———. *A Commentary on Horace: Odes, Book II*. Oxford: Oxford University Press, 1978.

Norden, E. *Agnostos Theos*. Berlin: Teubner, 1913.

Numberger, K. *Inhalt und Metrum in der Lyrik des Horaz*. Dissertation, Ludwig-Maximilians-Universität. Munich, 1959.

Nussbaum, G. B. "A Study of Odes I,37 and 38: The Psychology of Conflict and Horace's Humanitas." *Arethusa* 4 (1971): 91–97.

———. "Cras donaberis haedo (Horace Carm. III,13)." *Phoenix* 25 (1971): 151–59.
Onians, R. B. *The Origins of European Thought.* Cambridge: Cambridge University Press, 1954.
Oppermann, H. "Zum Aufbau der Römeroden." *Gymnasium* 66 (1959): 204–17.
Otis, B. "Propertius' Single Book." *Harvard Studies in Classical Philology* 70 (1965): 1–44.
———. *Ovid as an Epic Poet.* Cambridge: Cambridge University Press, 1966.
———. Review of *Tradition and Originality in Roman Poetry,* by G. Williams. *American Journal of Philology* 92 (1971): 316–30.
Paardt, R. T. van der. "Catullus en Horatius." *Hermeneus* 40 (1969): 287–96.
Pack, R. A. *The Greek and Latin Literary Texts from Greco-Roman Egypt.* 2d ed. Ann Arbor: University of Michigan Press, 1965.
Page, D. L. *Sappho and Alcaeus: An Introduction to the Study of Ancient Lesbian Poetry.* Oxford: Oxford University Press, 1955.
Parry, A. "The Two Voices of Virgil's Aeneid." *Arion* 2 (1963): 66–80.
Parry, H. *The Lyric Poems of Greek Tragedy.* Toronto: Samuel Stevens, 1978.
Parsons, P. "Callimachus: Victoria Berenices." *Zeitschrift für Papyrologie und Epigraphik* 25 (1977): 1–50.
Pasoli, E. "Per una rilettura del proemio di Orazio lirico." In *Studi filologici e storici in onore di V. de Falco,* pp. 409–33. Naples: Libreria scientifica editrice, 1971.
Pasquali, G. *Orazio lirico: Studi.* Florence: Le Monnier, 1920. Reprinted with additions by A. La Penna. Florence: Le Monnier, 1964.
"Patricius." "The Archytas Ode." *Greece and Rome* 12 (1965): 51–53.
Pavlock, B. "Horace's Invitation Poems to Maecenas: Gifts to a Patron." *Ramus* 11 (1982): 84–89.
Pearcy, L. T., Jr. "Horace's Architectural Imagery." *Latomus* 36 (1977): 772–81.
Perret, J. *Horace.* English translation by B. Humez. New York: New York University Press, 1964.
Pfeiffer, R. "Ein neues Altersgedicht des Kallimachos." *Hermes* 63 (1928): 302–41.
———. *Callimachus.* 2 vols. Oxford: Oxford University Press, 1949–53.
———. *History of Classical Scholarship: From the Beginnings to the End of the Hellenistic Age.* Oxford: Oxford University Press, 1968.
Pickard-Cambridge, A. *Dithyramb, Tragedy, and Comedy.* 2d ed. Revised by T. B. L. Webster. Oxford: Oxford University Press, 1962.
Plüss, H. T. *Horazstudien.* Leipzig: Teubner, 1882.
Pomeroy, A. J. "A Man at a Spring: Horace, Odes 1.1." *Ramus* 7 (1978): 34–50.
Port, W. "Die Anordnung in den Gedichtbüchern der augusteische Zeit." *Philologus* 81 (1926): 280–308, 427–68.
Pöschl, V. *Horaz und die Politik.* Sitzungsberichte der Heidelberger Akademie

der Wissenschaften, Phil.-hist. Kl. Jahrgang 1956. 4. Abhandlung. Heidelberg: Winter, 1956.
———. *Horazische Lyrik: Interpretationen.* Heidelberg: Winter, 1970.
———. "Bemerkungen zu den Horazoden III 7–12." In *Letterature Comparate, Problemi e Metodo: Studi in Onore di Ettore Paratore,* vol. 2, pp. 505–9. Bologna: Pàtron, 1981.
Powell, B. B. "The Ordering of Tibullus Book I." *Classical Philology* 69 (1974): 107–12.
Prakken, D. W. "Feminine Caesuras in Horatian Sapphic Stanzas." *Classical Philology* 49 (1954): 102–3.
Price, S. *Rituals and Power: The Roman Imperial Cult in Asia Minor.* Cambridge: Cambridge University Press, 1984.
Puelma-Piwonka, M. *Lucilius und Kallimachos.* Frankfurt am Main: Klostermann, 1949.
Putnam, M. C. J. "Horace c. 1.20." *Classical Journal* 64 (1969): 153–57.
———. "Aes Triplex (Horace, Ode 1.3.9)." *Classical Quarterly* 21 (1971): 454.
———. "Horace and Tibullus." *Classical Philology* 67 (1972): 81–88.
———. "Horace C. 3.30: The Lyricist as Hero." *Ramus* 2 (1973): 1–19.
———. "Mercuri, facunde nepos Atlantis." *Classical Philology* 69 (1974): 215–17.
———. *Virgil's Poem of the Earth: Studies in the Georgics.* Princeton: Princeton University Press, 1979.
———. "Propertius' Third Book: Patterns of Cohesion." *Arethusa* 13 (1980): 97–113.
———. "The Hesitation of Aeneas." *Atti del Convegno mondiale scientifico di studi su Virgilio,* vol. 2, pp. 233–52. Milan: Mondadori, 1984.
———. *Essays on Latin Lyric, Elegy, and Epic.* Princeton: Princeton University Press, 1982.
———. *Artifices of Eternity: Horace's Fourth Book of Odes.* Ithaca, N.Y.: Cornell University Press, 1986.
Quinn, K. *Latin Explorations: Critical Studies in Roman Literature.* London: Routledge and Kegan Paul, 1963.
———. *Catullus: An Interpretation.* New York: Barnes and Noble, 1973.
Race, W. H. "Odes 1.20: An Horatian Recusatio." *California Studies in Classical Antiquity* 11 (1978): 179–96.
———. *The Classical Priamel from Homer to Boethius.* Mnemosyne Supplement, no. 74. Leiden: Brill, 1982.
———. "POxy 2438 and the Order of Pindar's Works." *Abstracts of the American Philological Association Meeting* (1984): 106.
Radinger, C. *Meleagros von Gadara.* Innsbruck: Wagner, 1895.
Raiz, A. "Die Frage nach der Anordnung der horazischen Oden: Eine kritische Übersicht." *Festschrift des deutschen Akademische Philologenvereins in Graz* (1896): 43–56.

Rambaux, C. "La composition d'ensemble du livre I des satires d'Horace." *Revue des Études Latines* 49 (1971): 179–204.

Reagan, C. J. "Horace Carmen 2.10: The Use of Oxymoron as a Thematic Statement." *Rivista di Studi Classici* 18 (1970): 177–85.

Reckford, K. J. "Horace and Maecenas." *Transactions of the American Philological Association* 90 (1959): 195–208.

⸻. "Horace, Odes I.34: An Interpretation." *University of North Carolina Studies in Philology* 63 (1966): 499–532.

⸻. *Horace*. Twayne World Author Series, no. 73. New York: Twayne, 1969.

Reitzenstein, R. *Epigramm und Skolion: Ein Beitrag zur Geschichte der alexandrinischen Dichtung*. Giessen: Ricker'sche Buchhandlung, 1893.

Rooy, C. A. van. *Studies in Classical Satire and Related Literary Theory*. Leiden: Brill, 1965.

⸻. "Arrangement and Structure of Satires in Horace, Sermones, Book I, with More Special Reference to Satires 1–4." *Acta Classica* 11 (1968): 38–72.

⸻. "Arrangement and Structure of Satires in Horace, Sermones, Book I: Satires 4 and 10." *Acta Classica* 13 (1970): 7–27.

⸻. "Arrangement and Structure of Satires in Horace, Sermones, Book I: Satires 5 and 6." *Acta Classica* 13 (1970): 45–59.

⸻. "Arrangement and Structure of Satires in Horace, Sermones, Book I: Satire 7 as Related to Satires 10 and 8." *Acta Classica* 14 (1971): 67–90.

⸻. "Arrangement and Structure of Satires in Horace, Sermones, Book I: Satires 9 and 10." *Acta Classica* 15 (1972): 37–52.

⸻. "'Imitatio' of Vergil, *Eclogues* in Horace, *Satires*, Book I." *Acta Classica* 16 (1973): 69–88.

Rosenberg, E. "Über Horatius Carm. I.3." *Zeitschrift für die Gymnasial-Wesen* (1881): 598.

Rosenthal, M. L., and Gall, S. *The Modern Poetic Sequence: The Genius of Modern Poetry*. Oxford: Oxford University Press, 1983.

Ross, D. O. *Style and Tradition in Catullus*. Cambridge: Harvard University Press, 1969.

⸻. *Backgrounds to Augustan Poetry: Gallus, Elegy, and Rome*. Cambridge: Cambridge University Press, 1975.

Rudd, N. *Lines of Enquiry: Studies in Latin Poetry*. Cambridge: Cambridge University Press, 1976.

Ruoff, A. LaV. "Walter Savage Landor's Criticism of Horace: The Odes and Epodes." *Arion* 9 (1970): 189–204.

Said, E. W. *Beginnings: Intention and Method*. New York: Basic Books, 1975.

Salat, P. "La composition du livre I des odes d'Horace." *Latomus* 28 (1969): 554–74.

Saller, R. P. *Personal Patronage under the Early Empire*. Cambridge: Cambridge University Press, 1981.

Santirocco, M. S. *The Order of Horace's Odes, Books II and III.* Ph.D. dissertation, Columbia University, 1979.

———. "Sulpicia Reconsidered." *Classical Journal* 74 (1979): 229–39.

———. "Horace's Odes and the Ancient Poetry Book." *Arethusa* 13 (1980): 43–57.

———. "Strategy and Structure in Horace, C. 2.12." In *Studies in Latin Literature and Roman History*, vol. 2, edited by C. Deroux, pp. 223–36. Collection Latomus, no. 168. Brussels, 1980.

———. "Poet and Patron in Ancient Rome." *Book Forum* 6 (1982): 56–62.

———. "The Maecenas Odes." *Transactions of the American Philological Association* 114 (1984): 241–53.

———. "The Poetics of Closure: Horace, Odes 3.17–28." *Ramus* 13 (1984): 74–91.

———. "The Two Voices of Horace: Odes 3.1–15." In *The Augustan Age: The Rise of Imperial Ideology*, edited by R. Winkes, pp. 9–28. Archaeologia Transatlantica 5. Providence and Louvain, 1986.

Savage, J. J. H. "The Art of the Seventh Eclogue of Vergil." *Transactions of the American Philological Association* 94 (1963): 248–67.

Saylor, C. F. "Horace, C. 1.2 and Vergil's Storm (Aen. 1.81 ff.)." *Vergilius* 25 (1979): 20–25.

Schanz, M. von, and Hosius, C. *Geschichte der römischen Literatur*. 4 vols. Munich: Beck, 1927–59.

Schmidt, E. A. "Catulls Anordnung seiner Gedichte." *Philologus* 117 (1973): 215–42.

Schmidt, M. "Die Anordnung der Oden des Horaz." *Wissenschaftliche Zeitschrift der Karl-Marx-Universität Leipzig* 4 (1954–55): 207–16.

Schoenberger, O. "Horatius, Carm. I,1." *Gymnasium* 73 (1966): 388–412.

Scholz, U. W. "Herculis ritu, Augustus, consule Planco." *Wiener Studien* n.s. 5 (1971): 123–37.

Schork, R. J. "*Aemulos Reges*: Allusion and Theme in Horace 3.16." *Transactions of the American Philological Association* 102 (1971): 515–39.

Schulze, K. P. "Über das Princip der Variatio bei römischen Dichtern." *Neue Jahrbücher für Philologie* 131 (1885): 857–78.

Scott, K. "The Dioscuri and the Imperial Cult." *Classical Philology* 25 (1930): 379–80.

———. "Drusus, Nicknamed Castor." *Classical Philology* 25 (1930): 155–56.

Seager, R. "Neu sinas Medos equitare inultos: Horace, the Parthians, and Augustan Foreign Policy." *Athenaeum* 58 (1980): 103–18.

Seel, O. "Zur Ode 1,14 des Horaz: Zweifel an einer communis opinio." In *Festschrift Karl Vretska*, edited by D. von Ableitinger and H. Gügel, pp. 204–49. Heidelberg: Winter, 1970.

Segal, C. P. "Ancient Texts and Modern Literary Criticism." *Arethusa* 1 (1968): 1–25.

———. "The Order of Catullus, Poems 2–11." *Latomus* 27 (1968): 305–21.
———. "Horace, Odes 2.6 (*Septimi Gadis aditure mecum*): Poetic Landscape and Poetic Imagination." *Classical Philology* 113 (1969): 235–53.
———. "Thematic Coherence and Levels of Style in Theocritus' Bucolic Idylls." *Wiener Studien* n.s. 11 (1977): 35–68.
———. *Poetry and Myth in Ancient Pastoral: Essays on Theocritus and Virgil*. Princeton: Princeton University Press, 1981.
Seidensticker, B. "Zu Horaz, C. 1.1–9." *Gymnasium* 83 (1976): 26–34.
Setaioli, A. "Il proemio dei Carmina oraziani." *Atti e Memorie dell' Accademia Toscana La Colombaria* 38 (1973): 1–59.
Shackleton Bailey, D. R. *Cicero's Letters to Atticus*. 7 vols. Cambridge: Cambridge University Press, 1965–70.
———. *Cicero: Epistulae ad Familiares*. 2 vols. Cambridge: Cambridge University Press, 1977.
———. *Profile of Horace*. Cambridge: Harvard University Press, 1982.
Sherwin-White, A. N. *The Letters of Pliny*. Oxford: Oxford University Press, 1966.
Shey, H. J. "The Poet's Progress: Horace Odes I.1." *Arethusa* 4 (1971): 185–96.
Silk, E. T. "Notes on Cicero and the Odes of Horace." *Yale Classical Studies* 13 (1952): 149–57.
———. "A Fresh Approach to Horace, II,20." *American Journal of Philology* 77 (1956): 255–63.
———. "On Theme and Design in the Poetry of Horace." *Ventures* 7 (1967): 47–54.
———. "Bacchus and the Horatian Recusatio." *Yale Classical Studies* 21 (1969): 193–212.
———. "Towards a Fresh Interpretation of Horace Carm. III.1." *Yale Classical Studies* 23 (1973): 131–45.
Simon, J. A. *Zur Anordnung der Oden des Horaz*. Progr. des Marzellen-Gymnasiums in Köln. Cologne, 1896.
Singleton, D. "A Note on Catullus' First Poem." *Classical Philology* 67 (1972): 192–96.
Skinner, M. B. *Catullus' Passer: The Arrangement of the Book of Polymetric Poems*. New York: Arno, 1981.
Smith, B. Herrnstein. *Poetic Closure: A Study of How Poems End*. Chicago: University of Chicago Press, 1968.
Smith, O. L. "A Reading of Horace, Carm. I.15." *Classica et Mediaevalia* 29 (1972): 67–74.
Smith, P. L. "Poetic Tensions in the Horatian Recusatio." *American Journal of Philology* 89 (1968): 56–65.
Solmsen, F. "Horace's First Roman Ode." *American Journal of Philology* 68 (1947): 337–52.

———. "Tibullus as an Augustan Poet." *Hermes* 90 (1962): 295–325.
Stahl, H.-P. "Aeneas—An 'Unheroic' Hero?" *Arethusa* 14 (1981): 157–77.
———. *Propertius: "Love and War": Individual and State under Augustus.* Berkeley: University of California Press, 1985.
Stemplinger, E. "Horatius." In *Paulys Realencyclopädie der classischen Altertumswissenschaft,* edited by G. Wissowa and W. Kroll, vol. 8.2, cols. 2336–99. Stuttgart: Druckenmüller, 1913.
Stewart, D. "The Poet as Bird in Aristophanes and Horace." *Classical Journal* 62 (1967): 357–61.
Sturtevant, E. H. "O matre pulchra filia pulchrior." *Classical Review* 26 (1912): 119–22.
Sullivan, J. P. *Propertius: A Critical Introduction.* Cambridge: Cambridge University Press, 1976.
Syndikus, H.-P. *Die Lyrik des Horaz: Eine Interpretation der Oden.* 2 vols. Impulse der Forschung, no. 7. Darmstadt: Wissenschaftliche Buchgesellschaft, 1972–73.
———. Review of *Horace: A Study in Structure,* by H. Dettmer. *Gnomon* 57.1 (1985): 11–15.
Tatum, J. "*Non usitata nec tenui ferar.*" *American Journal of Philology* 94 (1973): 4–25.
Taylor, L. R. "Horace's Equestrian Career." *American Journal of Philology* 46 (1925): 161–70.
———. *The Divinity of the Roman Emperor.* American Philological Monograph, no. 1. Middletown, 1931.
———. "Republican and Augustan Writers Enrolled in the Equestrian Census." *Transactions of the American Philological Association* 90 (1968): 469–86.
Thornton, A. H. F. "Horace's Ode to Calliope (III,4)." *AUMLA: Journal of the Australasian Universities Language and Literature Association* 23 (1965): 96–102.
Toohey, P. G. "A Note on Horace, Odes I 38." *Maia* 32 (1980): 171–74.
Torraca, L. *Il prologo dei Telchini e l'inizio degli Aitia di Callimaco.* Collana di studi greci, no. 48. Naples: Libreria scientifica, 1969.
Tränkel, H. "Properz über Vergils *Aeneis.*" *Museum Helveticum* 28 (1971): 60–63.
Traut, H. "Horaz Römeroden und der clupeus aureus 6.13 ff. des Monumentum Ancyranum." *Philologus* 70 (1911): 317–20.
Treggiari, S. "Cicero, Horace, and Mutual Friends: Lamiae and Varrones Murenae." *Phoenix* 27 (1973): 245–61.
Trenkel, P. *Zusammenhänge und Beziehungen in Horaz' Römeroden.* Wissenschaftliche Beilage zum Jahresbericht des staatlichen Karls-Gymnasiums in Bernburg. Gotha: Perthes, 1926.
Troxler-Keller, I. *Die Dichterlandschaft des Horaz.* Heidelberg: Winter, 1964.
Ullman, B. L. "The Book Division of Propertius." *Classical Philology* 4 (1909): 45–52.
Vaio, J. "The Unity and Historical Occasion of Horace *Carm.* 1.7." *Classical Philology* 61 (1966): 168–75.

Van Sickle, J. "Theocritus and the Development of the Conception of Bucolic Genre." *Ramus* 5 (1976): 18–44.
———. *The Design of Virgil's Bucolics*. Rome: Ateneo e Bizzarri, 1978.
———. "The Book Roll and Some Conventions of the Poetic Book." *Arethusa* 13 (1980): 5–42.
———. "Poetics of Opening and Closure in Meleager, Catullus, and Gallus." *Classical World* 75 (1981): 65–75.
Vendler, H. *The Odes of John Keats*. Cambridge: Harvard University Press, 1983.
Verrall, A. W. *Studies Literary and Historical in the Odes of Horace*. London: Macmillan, 1884. Reprint. Port Washington, N.Y.: Kennikat Press, 1969.
Vessey, D. W. T. "Horace's Archytas Ode: A Reconsideration." *Ziva Antika* 26 (1976): 73–87.
Veyne, P. "Quid dedicatum poscit Apollinem." *Latomus* 24 (1965): 932–48.
Volkmann, R. *Die Rhetorik der Griechen und Römer*. Leipzig: Teubner, 1885.
Vretska, K. "Horatius, carm. I,1." *Hermes* 99 (1971): 323–35.
Wagenvoort, H. *De Horatii quae dicuntur Odis Romanis*. Groningen: Wolters, 1911.
Webster, T. B. L. *Hellenistic Poetry and Art*. London: Methuen, 1964.
Weisshäupl, R. "Zur den Quellen der Anthologia Palatina." In *Serta Harteliana*, pp. 184–88. Vienna: Tempsky, 1896.
West, D. *Reading Horace*. Edinburgh: Edinburgh University Press, 1967.
West, M. L. *Studies in Greek Elegy and Iambos*. Berlin: de Gruyter, 1974.
White, P. "*Amicitia* and the Profession of Poetry in Early Imperial Rome." *Journal of Roman Studies* 68 (1978): 74–92.
Wickham, E. C., ed. *Quinti Horatii Flacci Opera Omnia: The Works of Horace*. 2 vols. Oxford: Oxford University Press, 1896.
Wilamowitz-Moellendorff, U. von. *Aristoteles und Athen*. 2 vols. Berlin: Weidmann, 1893.
———. *Die Textgeschichte der griechischen Lyriker*. Berlin: Weidmann, 1900.
———. *Sappho und Simonides: Untersuchungen über griechische Lyrik*. Berlin: Weidmann, 1913.
Wili, W. *Horaz und die augusteische Kultur*. Basel: Schwabe, 1948.
Wilkinson, L. P. *Horace and His Lyric Poetry*. 2d ed. Cambridge: Cambridge University Press, 1951.
———. "The Earliest Odes of Horace." *Hermes* 84 (1956): 495–99.
———. *Golden Latin Artistry*. Cambridge: Cambridge University Press, 1963.
———. *The Georgics of Virgil: A Critical Survey*. Cambridge: Cambridge University Press, 1969.
———. "Ancient Literature and Modern Literary Criticism." *Proceedings of the Classical Association* 69 (1972): 13–26.
Wille, G. *Musica Romana: Die Bedeutung der Musik im Leben der Römer*. Amsterdam: Schippers, 1967.
Williams, F. *Callimachus, Hymn to Apollo: A Commentary*. Oxford: Oxford University Press, 1978.

Williams, G. "Poetry in the Moral Climate of Augustan Rome." *Journal of Roman Studies* 52 (1962): 28–46.
———. *Tradition and Originality in Roman Poetry*. Oxford: Oxford University Press, 1968.
———. *The Third Book of Horace's Odes*. Oxford: Oxford University Press, 1969.
———. *Horace*. Greece and Rome New Surveys in the Classics, no. 6. Oxford: Oxford University Press, 1972.
———. *Change and Decline: Roman Literature in the Early Empire*. Berkeley: University of California Press, 1978.
———. *Figures of Thought in Roman Poetry*. New Haven: Yale University Press, 1980.
Wimmel, W. *Kallimachos in Rom: Die Nachfolge seines apologetischen Dichtens in der Augusteerzeit*. Hermes Einzelschrift, no. 16. Wiesbaden: Steiner, 1960.
Winniczuk, L. "Propemptikon." *Meander* 13 (1958): 406–19.
Wiseman, T. P. *Catullan Questions*. Leicester: Leicester University Press, 1969.
———. *Clio's Cosmetics: Three Studies in Greco-Roman Literature*. Leicester: Leicester University Press, 1979.
———. *Catullus and His World: A Reappraisal*. Cambridge: Cambridge University Press, 1985.
Witke, C. *Horace's Roman Odes: A Critical Examination*. Mnemosyne Supplement, no. 77. Leiden: Brill, 1983.
Womble, H. "Horace, Carmina, II,16." *American Journal of Philology* 88 (1967): 385–409.
———. "Horace, Carmina, I,2." *American Journal of Philology* 91 (1970): 1–30.
Woodman, A. J. "Exegi Monumentum: Hor., Odes 3,30." In *Quality and Pleasure in Latin Poetry*, edited by T. Woodman and D. West, pp. 115–28. Cambridge: Cambridge University Press, 1974.
———. "The Craft of Horace in Odes 1.14." *Classical Philology* 75 (1980): 60–67.
Wright, J. R. G. "Iccius' Change of Character: Horace, Odes I 29." *Mnemosyne* 27 (1974): 44–52.
Zetzel, J. E. G. "The Poetics of Patronage in the Late First Century B.C." In *Literary and Artistic Patronage in Ancient Rome*, edited by B. K. Gold, pp. 87–102. Austin: University of Texas Press, 1982.
Zumwalt, N. K. "Horace C. 1.34: Poetic Change and Political Equivocation." *Transactions of the American Philological Association* 104 (1974): 435–67.
———. "Horace's Navis of Love Poetry (C. 1.14)." *Classical World* 71 (1977): 249–54.

I. INDEX OF WORKS CITED FROM HORACE

Ars Poetica: 187 (n. 18), 197 (n. 59), 202 (n. 52)
Carmen Saeculare: 137, 187 (n. 23), 192 (n. 2)
Carmina (Odes):
  1.1, 4, 15–19, 22–23, 24, 25, 30, 32, 55–56, 61, 80, 81, 82, 107, 151, 152, 154, 155–57, 158, 159, 166, 168, 172, 185 (n. 58), 186 (n. 8), 188 (n. 39), 197 (n. 67)
  1.2, 21–22, 23, 24–26, 31, 42–43, 44–46, 56, 75, 78, 80, 81, 82, 89, 118, 151, 180 (n. 19), 186 (n. 10), 188 (n. 39), 196 (n. 39)
  1.3, 25, 27–30, 31, 35, 46, 51, 56, 58, 75, 80, 81, 82, 151, 189 (nn. 48, 49, 54, 59), 194 (n. 20), 198 (n. 74)
  1.4, 19, 24, 30–32, 34, 39, 40–41, 44, 45, 56, 57, 63, 133, 151, 190 (nn. 62, 65), 199 (n. 7)
  1.5, 19, 24, 32–34, 38, 46, 90, 145, 148, 151, 174, 193 (n. 19), 209 (n. 31)
  1.6, 19, 23, 24, 34–36, 39, 41, 75, 82, 151, 157, 190 (n. 74)
  1.7, 19, 23, 36–38, 39, 41, 151, 190 (n. 74), 191 (nn. 75, 77, 78), 197 (n. 53), 210 (n. 2)
  1.8, 19, 24, 36, 38–39, 41, 45, 46, 82, 153, 191 (nn. 80, 81)
  1.9, 24, 39–41, 44, 45, 133
  1.10, 21, 23, 42, 43, 45, 69, 81, 89, 186 (n. 10), 192 (nn. 3, 5), 200 (n. 23)
  1.11, 19, 42, 43, 44, 45
  1.12, 42, 43, 44–45, 46, 75, 78, 118, 186 (n. 10), 188 (n. 45), 192 (nn. 7, 8, 10)
  1.13, 33, 38, 43, 45, 46, 82, 153, 193 (n. 13)
  1.14, 46–49, 75, 81, 193 (n. 13), 194 (nn. 20, 23), 197 (n. 53)
  1.15, 46–47, 48–50, 81, 193 (n. 15), 194 (n. 23), 197 (n. 53)
  1.16, 49–51, 52, 70, 73, 74, 82, 192 (n. 86), 194 (n. 23), 195 (nn. 26, 28), 196 (n. 51), 204 (n. 9)
  1.17, 50–53, 54, 60, 70, 73, 74, 82, 192 (n. 86), 195 (n. 28), 202 (n. 50), 204 (n. 9), 210 (n. 2)
  1.18, 19, 52–54, 153, 195 (n. 34)
  1.19, 17, 33, 53–54, 82, 153, 212 (n. 29)
  1.20, 54–56, 126, 154, 156–57, 158, 160, 161, 163, 165, 202 (n. 50)
  1.21, 55, 56, 69, 75, 78, 81, 137, 188 (n. 45), 196 (n. 39)

1.22, 55, 56, 60–61, 202 (n. 50)
1.23, 33, 55, 56–57, 58, 91, 135
1.24, 56, 57, 58–60, 62, 136, 190 (n. 69), 195 (n. 32)
1.25, 33, 47, 57, 58, 60, 82, 91, 135, 153, 196 (nn. 43, 44), 209 (n. 26)
1.26, 60–62, 70, 72, 74, 81, 82, 196 (n. 50), 202 (n. 50), 204 (n. 9)
1.27, 60, 62–65, 66, 74, 171, 173, 204 (n. 9)
1.28, 19, 62–67, 68, 81, 171, 173, 191 (n. 78), 196 (n. 52)
1.29, 65–68
1.30, 68–69, 72, 82, 153, 197 (n. 67)
1.31, 68, 69–71, 81, 111, 129, 185 (n. 58), 197 (n. 65)
1.32, 68–73, 76, 78, 82, 111, 185 (n. 58), 192 (n. 85), 195 (n. 28), 197 (n. 67), 198 (nn. 68, 69)
1.33, 69, 72–73, 74, 76, 82, 153, 192 (n. 86), 198 (n. 68)
1.34, 73–76, 77, 78, 193 (n. 18), 204 (n. 9)
1.35, 74, 76–78, 79, 81, 188 (n. 45), 204 (n. 9)
1.36, 78–79, 80, 133
1.37, 76, 78, 79, 80, 82, 133
1.38, 79–80, 81, 82, 108, 133, 173, 175, 198 (n. 81)
2.1, 55, 84–85, 95, 108, 110, 142, 147, 157, 177 (n. 1), 188 (n. 42), 200 (n. 14)
2.2, 84–85, 86, 199 (n. 7)
2.3, 83, 84–85, 86, 202 (n. 45)
2.4, 33, 85
2.5, 33, 85, 195 (n. 37)
2.6, 83, 85, 86, 200 (nn. 14, 20)
2.7, 85, 86, 87–90, 200 (nn. 14, 23), 202 (n. 50)
2.8, 85, 86, 87, 90–91
2.9, 83, 84, 85, 86, 87, 91–93, 136, 190 (n. 69), 199 (n. 12), 201 (nn. 29, 32)
2.10, 83, 84, 85, 87, 93–95, 136, 170, 193 (n. 18), 199 (n. 7), 201 (n. 35)
2.11, 83, 84, 85, 86, 87, 91–93, 136, 199 (n. 12), 201 (n. 29)
2.12, 84, 85, 87, 90–91, 95–96, 103, 126, 157, 200 (n. 14), 201 (n. 35)
2.13, 83, 87–90, 96, 97–99, 108, 109, 158, 192 (n. 85), 200 (nn. 14, 37), 202 (n. 50), 204 (n. 9)
2.14, 83, 96, 97–99, 108, 204 (n. 9)
2.15, 84, 96, 99–101, 105, 108, 113, 202 (n. 45), 204 (nn. 9, 10), 206 (n. 32)
2.16, 80, 96, 101–3, 105, 106, 107, 108, 199 (n. 12)
2.17, 83, 88, 89, 96, 103–5, 106, 107, 109, 155, 157–58, 159, 160, 200 (nn. 14, 23), 202 (n. 50)
2.18, 19, 84, 96, 100, 105–7, 109, 158, 159, 160, 165, 200 (n. 14), 202 (nn. 45, 51, 52), 206 (n. 32)
2.19, 53, 96, 107–8, 112, 113, 139, 141, 152, 153, 159, 195 (n. 34), 200 (n. 14), 204 (n. 9)
2.20, 80, 87, 96, 107–8, 112, 113, 139, 140, 147, 152, 154, 159, 160, 167, 195 (n. 28), 199 (n. 4), 200 (n. 14), 201 (n. 35), 203 (n. 55), 204 (n. 9), 206 (n. 33)
3.1, 107, 112, 113–15, 116, 119, 121–24, 130, 139, 140, 172, 202 (n. 45), 204 (n. 20), 205 (n. 20), 206 (n. 32)
3.2, 113–15, 116, 119, 121–24, 193 (n. 18), 204 (n. 20), 206 (n. 33)
3.3, 108, 113–15, 116, 117, 120–21, 123, 130, 140, 142, 188 (n. 42), 189 (n. 53), 197 (n. 53), 202

Index of Works Cited from Horace

(n. 50), 204 (n. 20), 205 (n. 23)
3.4, 88, 113–15, 117, 120–21, 123, 172, 202 (n. 50), 204 (n. 20)
3.5, 113–15, 117–18, 121, 123–24, 140, 171, 197 (n. 53), 204 (n. 20)
3.6, 112, 113–15, 118, 124–25, 139, 171, 172, 204 (n. 10, 20), 205 (n. 23)
3.7, 33, 125–28, 171, 207 (nn. 42, 43), 211 (n. 18)
3.8, 55, 88, 92, 125–31, 155, 157, 160, 161, 163, 164, 170, 197 (n. 65), 202 (n. 50), 206 (n. 41), 207 (nn. 42, 43)
3.9, 125–28, 144, 153, 197 (n. 53), 207 (n. 43)
3.10, 125–28, 207 (nn. 42, 43)
3.11, 33, 69, 89, 125–28, 197 (n. 53), 207 (n. 43)
3.12, 19, 33, 65, 125–28, 206 (n. 40), 207 (nn. 42–43)
3.13, 126–27, 138, 173, 206 (n. 41), 207 (nn. 42, 43)
3.14, 118, 126–31, 170, 177 (n. 1), 206 (n. 41), 207 (n. 43), 210 (n. 2)
3.15, 33, 126–28
3.16, 55, 110, 126, 128, 132, 154, 157, 161–63, 164, 165, 204 (n. 20), 212 (nn. 31, 36)
3.17, 128, 132–36, 145, 148, 171, 190 (n. 64)
3.18, 133, 136, 145, 148, 171, 190 (n. 64), 207 (n. 9)
3.19, 133, 135–36, 145, 148, 171, 190 (n. 64), 197 (n. 67), 207 (nn. 9, 10)
3.20, 33, 136, 148, 207 (nn. 9, 10)
3.21, 74, 128, 136–38, 148, 171, 197 (n. 59), 207 (n. 10), 208 (n. 13)
3.22, 136–38, 171
3.23, 128, 136, 138–39, 208 (n. 51)
3.24, 113, 139–40, 142, 148, 151, 202 (n. 45), 204 (n. 9)
3.25, 53, 107, 113, 140–45, 148, 151, 153, 174, 195 (n. 34), 204 (n. 9)
3.26, 33, 34, 128, 142–45, 148, 151, 174, 190 (n. 64), 208 (n. 23), 209 (n. 31)
3.27, 144–46, 148, 151, 190 (n. 64), 197 (n. 53), 209 (n. 33)
3.28, 144–47, 148, 151, 190 (n. 64), 209 (n. 35)
3.29, 92, 128, 132, 147, 149, 151, 154, 157, 158, 163–66, 168, 213 (n. 38)
3.30, 4, 19, 80, 110, 147, 149, 151, 152, 156, 167, 168, 172, 185 (n. 58), 187 (n. 24), 213 (n. 39)
4, 131, 147, 179 (n. 15), 186 (n. 10), 199 (n. 1)
4.1, 17, 33
4.2, 212 (n. 29)
4.4, 197 (n. 53)
4.7, 32, 190 (n. 65)
4.8, 211 (n. 3)
4.12, 31, 190 (n. 60)
4.14, 204 (n. 9)
4.15, 27, 80, 194 (n. 20), 204 (n. 9)
Epistles: 179 (n. 15)
1.1, 17, 145, 154, 159
1.12, 68, 197 (n. 60)
1.13, 179 (n. 12)
1.19, 156, 187 (n. 24), 197 (n. 67)
1.20, 209 (n. 33)
Iambi (Epodes): 51, 179 (n. 14), 183 (n. 46)
2, 65, 186 (n. 4), 197 (n. 53)
5, 51, 195 (n. 27), 197 (n. 53)
7, 188 (nn. 42, 45)
12, 197 (n. 53)
13, 197 (n. 53)
17, 51, 195 (n. 27), 197 (n. 53)

Sermones (*Satires*): 5, 9, 16, 17, 20, 24, 155, 179 (n. 14), 183 (n. 46), 186 (n. 4)
    1.1, 16, 159
    1.4, 186 (n. 16)
    1.8, 51
    2.6, 154

II. INDEX OF OTHER ANCIENT AUTHORS AND WORKS

ps.-Acro, 69
Alcaeus, 14, 18, 21, 22, 39, 43, 47, 52, 70, 71, 72, 76, 79, 89, 96, 111, 180 (n. 19), 192 (n. 3), 198 (n. 69); fr. 6, 193 (n. 15); 10, 206 (n. 40); 73, 193 (n. 19); 308, 43; 308b, 187 (n. 27); 326, 193 (n. 15); 332, 79; 342, 195 (n. 32)
Anacreon, 52, 58; fr. 147, 207 (n. 42)
Anthologia Palatina. See Asclepiades; Callimachus; Hedylus; Meleager; Mnasalkes; Posidippus; *Soros*; *Symmeikta Epigrammata*; Tullius Laurea
Antimachus: *Lyde*, 181 (n. 26)
Archilochus, 14
Asclepiades, 8, 185 (n. 1)
Athenaeus, 181 (n. 26)

Bacchylides, 6–7, 47

Callimachus, 7, 8, 11, 14, 27, 28, 34, 36, 61, 75, 80, 186 (n. 9), 189 (n. 49), 190 (n. 71), 198 (n. 81); *Aetia*, 8, 181 (n. 29), 182 (nn. 30, 31); fr. 1, 8, 27, 75, 80, 81, 82, 103, 104, 158, 189 (n. 49), 190 (nn. 71, 74); fr. 112, 8; fr. 226–29, 185 (n. 1); fr. 400, 189 (n. 49); *Epigr.* 28, 28, 114, 196 (n. 47); *Epigr.* 41, 189 (n. 59); *H.* 2, 34, 103, 190 (n. 71), 194 (n. 20), 196 (n. 47); *Iambs*, 7, 182 (n. 31); Milan Diegesis, 182 (n. 31)
Catullus, 9, 10, 11, 14, 20, 33, 34, 45, 48, 153, 155, 171, 178 (n. 7), 183 (n. 47); *Passer*, 10; *Poem* 1, 155, 156, 211 (n. 22); 2, 194 (n. 20); 4, 194 (n. 20); 5/7, 184 (n. 54); 9–11, 184 (n. 55); 21/23, 184 (n. 54); 24/26, 184 (n. 54); 28, 212 (n. 31); 34, 137; 36, 195 (n. 26); 37/39, 184 (n. 54); 45, 207 (n. 42); 50–54, 184 (n. 55); 51, 45; 55, 45; 64, 194 (n. 20); 68, 201 (n. 25); 70/72, 184 (n. 54); 88–91, 184 (n. 55); 95, 34; 116, 184 (n. 50)
Cercidas, 14; *Meliambi*, 185 (n. 1)
Cicero, 75, 99, 100, 183 (n. 44); *De Leg.*, 75; *De Orat.*, 80, 191 (n. 77); *Pro Flacco*, 100; *Letters*, 183 (n. 44); *Pro Murena*, 100
Corinna, 23
Cornelius. See Nepos

Dio Cassius, 188 (n. 41), 199 (n. 8)

Euripides: *Bacchae*, 203 (n. 54)

Gallus, 180 (n. 16)
Greek Anthology. See Anthologia Palatina

Hedylus, 8
Hephaestion: *Encheiridion*, 187 (n. 27)
ps.-Heraclitus: *Quaest. Hom.*, 193 (n. 15)
Herodas: *Mimiamboi*, 8, 11, 182 (nn. 32, 34)
Hesiod: *Theogony*, 8
Hipponax, 14
Homer: *Hom. Hymn* 4, 192 (n. 3); *Iliad*, 8, 35, 191 (n. 75); *Odyssey*, 134, 138, 191 (n. 75), 197 (n. 52); Scholia to Iliad, 8

Laevius, 9, 11, 14, 185 (n. 1)
Laus Pisonis, 212 (n. 31)
Livy, 75, 193 (n. 10)
Lucian: *Gallus*, 181 (n. 24)
Lucilius, 9, 14, 20, 183 (n. 43)
Lucretius, 31, 61, 190 (n. 63), 196 (n. 49), 198 (n. 70)

Martial, 10
Meleager, 8–9, 189 (n. 59)
Menander Rhetor, 29
Mimnermus: *Nanno*, 181 (n. 26)
Mnasalkes, 182 (n. 35)

Nepos, Cornelius, 155
Nonnus: *Dionysiaca*, 195 (n. 33)

Ovid, 21, 33, 110, 179 (n. 15); *Am.* 1.11–12, 185 (n. 58); *Met.* 1.4, 190 (n. 74); *Tr.* 4.10, 187 (n. 24)

Pacuvius: *Teucer*, 191 (n. 77)
Papyrus Köln (PKöln) 204, 182 (n. 35)
Papyrus Oxyrhynchus (POxy.) 1011, 182 (n. 31); 1231, 180 (n. 20); 2307, 194 (n. 19); 2438, 180 (n. 19)
Petronius, 175; *Satyrica*, 187 (n. 26), 193 (n. 17), 213 (n. 6)
Pindar, 6–7, 18, 24–25, 128, 171, 180 (n. 19), 186 (n. 9), 198 (n. 81); N. 7, 196 (n. 47); O. 1, 181 (n. 24); 2, 192 (n. 7); 6, 196 (n. 47), 9, 196 (n. 47); Scholia to, 181 (n. 25)
Plato: *Laws*, 181 (n. 25)
Pliny the Elder: *NH*, 191 (n. 77)
Pliny the Younger: *Epistles*, 10, 183 (nn. 44, 47)
Plutarch: *Antony*, 199 (n. 8)
Porphyrion, 47, 51, 91, 112, 116, 188 (n. 41)
Posidippus, 8, 137, 182 (n. 39); *sphragis* of, 8
Priapea, 179 (n. 15)
Propertius, 5, 29–30, 83, 110, 112, 154, 179 (n. 13), 180 (n. 16), 203 (n. 10); *Elegy* 2.1, 33; 2.34, 30; 3.3, 194 (n. 20); 3.4–5, 185 (n. 58); 3.9, 194 (n. 20)

Quintilian, 46, 47, 186 (n. 15), 187 (n. 24), 193 (n. 15)

Sallust, 99
Sappho, 6, 14, 18, 33, 45, 52, 89, 96, 180 (n. 20); *Epithalamia*, 6, 180 (n. 21); fr. 31, 45; 55, 196 (n. 47); 121, 207 (n. 42)
Scolia, Attic, 181 (n. 26)
Seneca the Elder: *Suasoriae*, 199 (n. 9)
Seneca the Younger, 85; *De Clem.*, 199 (n. 11)
Servius: *ad Aen.* 8.310, 208 (n. 13)

Simonides, 7
Soros, 8-9, 182 (nn. 38, 39)
Statius, 179 (n. 15)
Stesichorus, 49
Suetonius: *Iulius*, 204 (n. 20)
Sulpicia. *See* Tibullus: *Corp. Tib.* 4.8
Symmeikta Epigrammata, 183 (n. 39)

Tacitus: *Annales*, 199 (n. 8)
Theocritus, 8, 11, 14, 182 (nn. 32, 33); *Idylls* 1–7, 8; 7, 182 (n. 38); 28–30, 185 (n. 1)
Theognis, 181 (n. 26)
Tibullus, 5, 9, 29, 72, 73, 82, 110, 153, 154, 179 (n. 13), 183 (n. 46), 185 (n. 3), 198 (n. 69); *Corp. Tib.* 4.8, 206 (n. 40); *Elegy* 2.5, 29, 189 (n. 55)
Tullius Laurea, 6

Varro: *Sesquiulixes*, 197 (n. 52)
Velleius Paterculus, 191 (n. 76), 199 (n. 10)

Vergil, 5, 9, 19, 24, 25, 26, 27, 29, 30, 31, 32, 35, 51, 56, 57, 58, 59, 62, 80, 110, 112, 113, 115, 120, 125, 131, 134, 136, 147, 151, 169, 190 (n. 6), 203 (n. 2), 206 (n. 37); *Aeneid*, 3–4, 28, 29, 30, 32, 51, 59, 110, 111, 120, 125, 131, 151, 169, 170, 188 (nn. 38, 39), 189 (n. 54); *Aeneid* 1.1a-1e, 188 (n. 38); 1.81 ff., 28; 1.198–207, 191 (n. 75); 1.259–60, 188 (n. 39); 4.45, 192 (n. 10); 6.14–41, 28; 8.184–279, 28; 8.628–70, 115; 10.21–22, 192 (n. 10); 10.784, 28; *Bucolics*, 9, 115, 147, 179 (n. 13), 183 (n. 46), 185 (n. 58); *Bucolic* 4.38, 189 (n. 48); 7, 32; 7.67, 190 (n. 66); 9, 32; 9.29, 25; 10.66, 209 (n. 26); 10.75, 147, 209 (n. 34); epitaph of, 188 (n. 38); *Georgics*, 30, 32; *Georgic* 1, 188 (n. 44); 1.2, 211 (n. 17); 2.41, 211 (n. 17); 2.458–542, 113; 3.41, 211 (n. 17); 4.2, 211 (n. 17); 4.453–527, 59

III. GENERAL INDEX

This index, which contains proper names and general topics, is not meant to be exhaustive. In particular, for modern scholars cited in the text, selectivity seemed in order; since all are listed in the Bibliography, only those whose works bear directly on the argument of this book have been included. For citations from Horace and other ancient writers, see Indexes I and II.

Achilles, 35, 38–39. *See also* Homer (Index II)
Actium, battle of, 26, 70, 76, 121, 204 (n. 20)
Addressee: as metaphor for reader, 21, 187 (n. 25)
Aeolic poetry, 20, 21–22, 61, 213 (n. 39). *See also* Alcaeus; Sappho (Index II)
Aeolus, 28
Agrippa, 19, 34–36
Ajax, Telamonian, 37
Alcaic meter, 19, 41, 69, 74, 83, 85, 88, 95, 96, 97, 99, 107, 112, 125, 128, 139, 170, 201 (n. 37)
Alexandrianism. *See* Callimachean aesthetics
Alfenus. *See* Varus, Alfenus
Amicitia. *See* Maecenas

Amphiaraus, 161
Anderson, W. S., 97, 193 (nn. 16, 19), 194 (n. 23), 202 (nn. 40, 41)
Antony, 46, 75, 77, 79, 80, 84, 120, 204 (n. 20). *See also* Actium; Augustus
Aphrodite, 69, 144. *See also* Venus
Apollo, 26, 28, 34, 43, 55, 56, 69–70, 75, 94, 111, 120, 136, 137
Arabia, 65, 68, 139
Archilochian meter, 191 (n. 78)
Archytas, 62–68, 196 (n. 52)
Arrangement of Odes: numerological, 3–4, 24, 54–55, 96, 113–15, 172, 177 (nn. 5, 7), 195 (n. 35), 201 (n. 35), 211 (n. 17); schematic, 3–4, 23–25, 42–43, 54–57, 80, 85–87, 95–97, 113–15, 126–27, 135–36, 147–48, 150–52, 154–55, 172–73, 177 (n. 7), 210 (n. 2)
Asclepiadean meters, 48, 95, 96, 125, 151, 185 (n. 1)
Asterie, 33, 125, 207 (n. 43)
Athena, 45
Attalus, 158
Augustus, 19, 24–26, 31, 44–46, 56, 70, 74–80, 82, 85, 87–89, 111, 114–16, 118–25, 127, 128–31, 132, 139, 140–43, 151, 152, 162, 168, 192 (nn. 8, 10), 198 (n. 74), 199 (nn. 8, 12), 203 (n. 2), 204 (n. 20),

205 (n. 29), 210 (n. 2). See also Actium; Ruler cult
Aurea mediocritas. See Golden Mean

Bacchus, 52–54, 72, 88, 107–8, 129, 136, 140–44, 148, 151, 153, 159, 197 (n. 67); revelry of, 53, 60–62, 114, 141. See also Dionysus
Bandusia, 126, 173, 207 (n. 43)
Barine, 86, 87, 90–91
Bate, W. J., 186 (n. 13)
Berenice, 182 (n. 30)
Bird: poet as, 107–8, 159–60, 203 (nn. 54, 55), 206 (n. 33)
Bloom, H., 186 (n. 13)
Borges, J., 71
Britain, 56, 78, 123

Cacus, 28
Caesar, Augustus. See Augustus
Caesar, Julius, 26, 188 (n. 41)
Cairns, F., 189 (nn. 46, 52), 192 (n. 5), 193 (n. 13), 196 (nn. 39, 42), 200 (n. 24), 202 (n. 49), 208 (n. 23), 211 (n. 22)
Callimachean aesthetics, 10, 18, 27–28, 34–36, 73, 80–82, 103–5, 113–14, 117, 154, 155, 158, 189 (nn. 49, 58), 190 (n. 71). See also Callimachus (Index II)
Calliope, 117. See also Muses
Camena, 103. See also Muses
Cameron, Alan, 9, 181 (n. 29), 182 (n. 35), 183 (n. 40), 190 (n. 71)
Canidia, 51
Canon, lyric, 14, 20, 23, 156, 188 (n. 32)
Cantabrians. See Spain
Carrhae, battle of, 123
Caucasus, 56
Centaurs, 53
Cerberus, 107
Chloe, 33, 55, 57–58, 91, 135, 143–44, 195 (n. 37)
Chloris, 127, 207 (n. 43)
Christ, W. von, 3, 177 (n. 2), 185 (n. 2)
Civil Wars. See Actium, battle of; Antony; Augustus; Cleopatra; Philippi, battle of
Cleopatra, 46, 75, 77, 79, 80, 120, 198 (n. 80)
Closure, poetic, 39–40, 80, 145–49, 151, 170, 190 (n. 64), 209 (n. 34)
Cnidos, 68
Cody, J. V., 188 (n. 38), 189 (nn. 46, 47, 58), 198 (n. 86), 202 (n. 47)
Collinge, N. E., 60, 86, 87, 126, 173, 178 (n. 8), 186 (n. 8), 192 (n. 10), 194 (n. 25), 196 (n. 46), 200 (nn. 17, 18, 22), 201 (n. 34), 205 (nn. 21, 24, 25), 206 (n. 41), 207 (n. 10), 211 (n. 20), 213 (nn. 39, 40)
Commager, S., 44, 48, 178 (n. 8), 186 (n. 7), 187 (n. 22), 188 (n. 43), 189 (nn. 46, 56), 190 (nn. 61, 69, 71), 192 (n. 6), 194 (n. 22), 195 (n. 29), 197 (n. 56), 198 (nn. 69, 80), 200 (n. 23), 201 (n. 30), 202 (nn. 42, 45, 50), 203 (nn. 1, 2), 205 (nn. 30, 31), 206 (n. 34), 207 (n. 4), 208 (n. 12), 212 (nn. 24, 27, 28, 34, 37)
Consolatio, 58, 72, 91–93, 198 (n. 68), 201 (n. 27). See also Death
Convivia: and erotica, 32–41, 52–54, 55, 57, 58, 60–62, 63–64, 66, 71–72, 78–81, 130, 136, 169, 195 (n. 31). See also Drinking songs; Love
Cupid, 26, 29, 69, 72, 197 (n. 67)
Curia, Julian, 115
Cybele, 54
Cyprus, 143–44
Cyrus, 53

Dacians, 76, 129
Daedalus, 29
Damalis, 79
Danae, 161
Danaids, 97, 126, 127, 197 (n. 53)
Dante, 194 (n. 22)
Death, 32, 58–60, 62, 63–69, 72–73, 82, 83–84, 85, 96, 97–99, 103, 105–7, 108–9, 136, 139–42, 170, 213 (n. 3); escape from, 87–88, 96, 98, 103–5, 108–9, 114, 128–31, 158, 161, 199 (n. 4), 202 (n. 50), 213 (n. 3). See also *Consolatio*; Immortality; *Pallida Mors*
Dedications, votive, 69, 126, 137, 143–45, 151, 190 (n. 64), 206 (n. 41), 207 (n. 42); temple, 71, 197 (n. 65)
Degeneracy, Roman, 114, 116, 118, 122–25, 139, 170, 172, 206 (n. 32)
Dellius, 83, 84, 85, 136
Demeter, 34
Dettmer, H., 177 (n. 7), 178 (n. 8), 179 (nn. 13, 14), 201 (n. 1)
Diana, 55, 56, 75, 137, 138
Dido, 59. See also Vergil (Index II)
Diespiter, 74. See also Jupiter; Zeus
Dionysus, 69, 195 (n. 33). See also Bacchus
Dithyramb, 108, 143
Domaszewski, A. von, 115, 204 (n. 18)
Drinking songs, 54, 55, 62, 78–80, 89, 136, 137, 160–61, 213 (n. 3). See also *Convivia*
Duckworth, G. E., 3, 177 (n. 5), 189 (n. 57), 203 (n. 6), 204 (nn. 11, 13, 16)

Elegy: lyric defined in relation to, 33, 72–73, 82, 190 (n. 69), 192 (n. 86). See also Propertius; Tibullus (Index II)

Eleusinian mysteries, 123
Eliot, T. S., 23, 175, 188 (n. 33), 213 (n. 5)
Encomium, 61, 62, 78, 82, 111. See also Ruler cult
Enipeus, 125
Epic: lyric defined in relation to, 24–25, 28–30, 34–41, 47, 52, 73, 75, 82, 169, 190 (nn. 71, 74), 191 (nn. 75, 78). See also Homer (Index II); Vergil (Index II)
Epicureanism, 61, 86, 111
Epigram, 8, 10, 128, 171, 182 (n. 35), 185 (n. 1). See also *Anthologia Palatina* (Index II); Dedications, votive
Epitaphs, 7, 64
Equites, 134, 154, 156–57, 162
Erotica. See *Convivia*; Love
Euhemerism, 205 (n. 31)
Euphorbus, 66–67. See also Neo-Pythagoreanism
Europa, 144, 146

Faith, personified, 76
Fates, 105
Faunalia, 133, 151. See also Faunus
Faunus, 31, 32, 50–52, 60, 88, 104, 157, 190 (n. 62), 210 (n. 2). See also Faunalia; Lupercalia; Pan
Flute. See *Tibia*
Fortuna, 73–79
Fraenkel, E., 80, 173, 178 (n. 8), 192 (n. 7), 193 (n. 14), 198 (n. 83), 200 (n. 23), 203 (n. 7), 204 (n. 10), 208 (n. 20), 213 (n. 1)

Galatea, 144, 146
Gall, S. See Rosenthal, M. L.
Garland: metaphorical for poetry, 60–61, 81, 178 (n. 10), 196 (nn. 47, 49)
Genethliacon, 7
Gigantomachy, 114, 117, 119, 120,

123, 124
Glycera, 33, 53, 54, 68, 69, 72, 82, 136, 153
Golden Mean, 9, 12, 83, 87, 93–95, 136, 170. See also Moderation; Simplicity
Graces, 69, 136, 197 (n. 67)
Greed, 18, 65, 66, 68, 102, 106, 113, 122–23, 206 (n. 32)
Grosphus. See Pompeius

Hazlitt, W., 20, 187 (n. 17)
Hedonist: Horace as, 17–19, 25, 56, 80, 86, 111
Heinze, R., 144, 187 (n. 25), 191 (n. 80), 203 (n. 7). See also Kiessling, A.: and R. Heinze
Helen, 46, 49–50, 51
Helicon, Mt., 8
Hellenistic aesthetics. See Callimachean aesthetics
Hendecasyllable, Phalaecian, 20
Hendrickson, G. L., 180 (n. 17), 189 (n. 52), 195 (n. 28)
Hercules, 28, 29, 118, 130, 145, 189 (n. 53)
Hermes, 21, 22, 43, 69, 180 (n. 19). See also Mercury
Hipponactean meter, 96
Hirpinus. See Quinctius
Hope, personifed, 76
Hubbard, M., 203 (n. 12). See also Nisbet, R. G. M.
Hymns, 7, 53–54, 55, 56, 68–70, 74, 81, 82, 136–39, 142–44, 153, 196 (n. 39)

Iambics, 14, 50–54, 73, 82, 192 (n. 86), 195 (n. 26)
Iccius, 65–68
Ilia, 25
Immortality, poetic, 25, 30, 80, 89, 98–99, 108–9, 151, 152, 156, 160, 167–68, 170
India, 139
Irony, 66–68, 108, 121, 199 (n. 8)
Isis, 144

Johnson, W. R., 186 (n. 10), 187 (n. 25), 203 (n. 55), 212 (n. 30)
Journey, metaphorical. See Nautical imagery
Jove. See Diespiter; Jupiter; Zeus
Juno, 114, 117, 123, 142, 205 (n. 20)
Jupiter, 25, 45, 46, 75, 78, 94, 104, 117–22, 123, 157, 188 (n. 39). See also Diespiter; Zeus

Keats, J., 12
Kermode, F., 149, 209 (n. 37)
Kiessling, A., 3, 42, 177 (n. 2), 192 (n. 1); and R. Heinze, 144, 178 (n. 8), 198 (n. 78), 201 (n. 28), 207 (n. 2), 208 (n. 24), 209 (nn. 27, 35)
Kilpatrick, R. S., 146, 196 (nn. 50, 52), 198 (n. 68), 209 (n. 33)
Kingship theory. See Ruler cult
Kletic hymn. See Hymns
Klingner, F., 83, 125, 199 (n. 2), 203 (n. 7), 204 (n. 13), 206 (n. 38)
Knights. See Equites
Kroll, W., 6, 7, 180 (n. 17), 184 (n. 55), 204 (n. 20), 208 (n. 12)

Laestrygonians, 132
Lalage, 55, 56, 195 (n. 37)
Lamia, 60, 61, 62, 79, 133–37
Landor, W. S., 15, 185 (n. 3)
Laomedon, 25
Lapiths, 53
Leda, 49
Lee, M. O., 183 (n. 45), 187 (n. 19), 196 (nn. 45, 48), 201 (n. 37)
Lesbia, 10, 184 (n. 54)

Leuconoe, 44
Licinius. See Murena, Licinius
Licymnia, 87, 90–91, 157
Love, 32–34, 39–41, 44–49, 57, 72, 73, 82, 85, 86, 87, 90–91, 93, 125–28, 136, 142–47, 169, 193 (n. 13), 194 (n. 21). See also Convivia
Lucretilis, Mt., 51
Ludwig, W., 85, 86, 87, 150, 178 (n. 8), 179 (nn. 14, 15), 200 (nn. 16, 17), 201 (n. 39)
Lupercalia, 31, 190 (n. 62). See also Faunus
Luxury. See Wealth
Lycaeus, Mt., 51
Lyce, 127, 207 (n. 43)
Lycidas, 32, 57
Lycus, 72, 136, 197 (n. 67)
Lyde, 93, 144, 146, 207 (n. 43)
Lydia, 33, 38–39, 45, 47, 59, 60, 82, 91, 135, 153, 191 (n. 79), 193 (n. 12), 207 (n. 43)
Lyne, R. O. A. M., 190 (n. 68), 198 (n. 69), 211 (n. 8)
Lyre, 18, 22, 43, 61, 62, 69–72, 196 (n. 50), 207 (n. 43)
Lyric, Greek, 20–23, 24, 70–72, 82, 168, 169. See also Alcaeus; Anacreon; Bacchylides; Corinna; Pindar; Sappho; Simonides; Stesichorus (Index II)

Maecenas, 15, 19, 22, 24, 27, 54–56, 81, 83, 85, 91, 95–96, 103–4, 107, 109, 110, 126, 127, 128–29, 132, 134, 147, 148, 150, 151, 153–68, 170, 174, 199 (n. 7), 201 (n. 26), 202 (n. 51), 207 (n. 43), 208 (n. 13)
Mars, 26, 53
Marsian Wars, 130
Matronalia, 129, 161
Medes. See Persians

Meditrinalia, 71, 111, 197 (n. 65)
Megilla, 63–64
Meinekiana lex, 187 (n. 21)
Melpomene, 58, 168. See also Muses
Memmius, 184 (n. 55)
Mempsimoiria, 17
Menas, 161
Mercury, 21, 23, 25, 26, 43, 44–45, 46, 56, 69, 75, 88, 89, 118, 180 (n. 19), 192 (nn. 3, 5), 197 (n. 67), 207 (n. 43). See also Hermes
Messalla, 84, 137, 185 (n. 3)
Meter, 19, 20–21. See also Alcaic meter; Archilochian meter; Asclepiadean meters; Hendecasyllable, Phalaecian; Hipponactean meter; Iambics; Sapphic meter
Mette, H. J., 186 (n. 7), 198 (n. 85), 202 (n. 47)
Military imagery, 35–36, 38, 54, 143, 191 (n. 80), 197 (n. 66)
Mime, 128
Minos, 66
Mirth, personified, 26
Moderation, 53, 58, 59–60, 63, 70, 80, 83, 85, 87, 93–95, 102–3, 106–7. See also Golden Mean; Simplicity
Mommsen, T., 115, 204 (n. 17)
Monologue, dramatic, 63–65, 171, 173, 196 (n. 52), 197 (n. 53). See also Soliloquy
Murena, Licinius, 83, 84, 87, 133, 199 (nn. 6, 7)
Muses, 8, 18, 34, 59, 60–61, 62, 72, 80, 84, 88, 94, 103, 114, 117, 120, 135, 140, 142, 156, 168, 187 (n. 18), 190 (nn. 63, 69), 197 (n. 67). See also Calliope; Melpomene
Mutschler, F.-H., 125, 179 (n. 13), 206 (n. 38)
Myrtale, 73
Mystes, 91, 93

Nature, 18, 25, 30–32, 39, 44, 56–57, 58, 60, 86, 92–93, 94, 99–101, 106–8, 132–33, 136, 171, 191 (n. 84), 195 (n. 29), 200 (n. 20), 201 (nn. 29, 32)

Nautical imagery, 27–28, 30–31, 46–49, 52, 62–63, 68, 73, 75, 94, 144, 146–47, 151, 166, 189 (n. 47), 193 (nn. 13, 15, 18, 19), 194 (nn. 20, 23), 209 (n. 28)

Neaera, 127, 130, 210 (n. 2)

Nearchus, 136

Necessity, personified, 76

Neobule, 65, 127, 206 (n. 40), 207 (n. 43)

Neo-Pythagoreanism, 65, 68. See also Pythagoras

Neoterics, 10, 34, 157, 183 (n. 49). See also Catullus (Index II)

Neptunalia, 144, 146, 151

Nereus, 46, 47

Nietzsche, F., 175, 213 (n. 6)

Night, personified, 146, 209 (n. 35)

Nisbet, R. G. M.: and M. Hubbard, 4, 69, 80, 158, 178 (n. 10), 186 (n. 9), 187 (n. 26), 189 (n. 46), 190 (n. 67), 191 (nn. 80, 82), 192 (n. 3), 193 (nn. 14, 17), 194 (n. 24), 195 (nn. 26, 32, 33), 196 (nn. 40, 44, 47, 52), 197 (nn. 61, 63, 65), 198 (nn. 72, 79, 84, 87), 199 (nn. 5, 7, 10, 12), 200 (nn. 18, 23), 201 (n. 31), 205 (n. 27), 209 (nn. 31, 35), 212 (nn. 30, 31). See also Hubbard, M.

Norden, E., 136, 137, 208 (nn. 11, 14)

Numerology. See Arrangement of Odes: numerological

Numida, 78–79, 80

Nymphs, 18, 69, 107, 197 (n. 67)

Octavian. See Augustus

Odysseus, 35, 37, 39. See also Homer (Index II)

Old Comedy, 20, 186 (n. 16)

Orcus, 84

Orion, 97

Orpheus, 59, 69

Orphic genealogy, 69

Otium, 18, 101, 103, 106, 109, 184 (n. 55)

Paeans, 7, 196 (n. 39)

Palinode, 49

Pallas. See Athena

Pallida Mors, 52, 57, 63, 190 (n. 62), 213 (n. 3)

Pan, 51. See also Faunus

Panaetius, 68

Paphos, 69

Paraclausithyron, 126, 128, 207 (n. 42), 208 (n. 22)

Parade Odes, 4, 11, 14–41, 42–46, 73, 81, 82, 133, 152, 154, 169, 186 (n. 10)

Paris, 46, 49–50

Parthians, 54, 56, 74, 88, 113, 123, 129, 204 (n. 20)

Pathos, 66–68, 138

Patronage. See Maecenas

Peitho, 69

Perret, J., 96, 178 (n. 8), 201 (n. 38), 204 (n. 14)

Persians, 56, 68

Phidyle, 138, 139

Philip, 161

Philippi, battle of, 26, 87, 88, 89, 130

Philosophy: inadequacy of, 65–68

Phoebus. See Apollo

Phraates, 74

Pindaric style, 44, 56, 112, 113, 186 (n. 9), 212 (n. 29). See also Pindar (Index II)

Plancus, 19, 36–37, 130, 191 (n. 77)
Platonism. See Socratics
Plüss, H. T., 112, 199 (n. 4), 203 (n. 5)
Poetry books, 3–13, 169, 177 (n. 7); 178 (n. 8); 179 (n. 12); 180 (nn. 16, 19); 181 (n. 26); 182 (n. 32); 183 (nn. 44, 46); 184 (nn. 53, 55) 185 (n. 58); 186 (n. 10)
Poikilia, 7, 9, 181 (n. 27). See also *Variatio*
Political themes, 21, 25, 31, 46–47, 52, 56, 70–71, 73, 74–80, 82, 84–85, 86, 87, 89–90, 93, 107, 110–31, 140–43, 145, 148, 151–52, 169, 171, 210 (n. 2). See also Augustus; Civil Wars; Maecenas; Marsian Wars; Punic Wars; Ruler cult; Spartacus; Trojan War
Pollio, Asinius, 55, 84–85, 95, 157, 191 (n. 77), 199 (nn. 10, 12)
Pompeius, Grosphus, 199 (n. 12)
Pompeius, Sextus, 161–62
Pompeius, friend of Pliny, 183 (n. 47)
Pompeius, unidentified, 85, 87–89
Port, W., 85, 87, 178 (n. 8), 200 (n. 15), 204 (n. 13)
Pöschl, V., 178 (n. 8), 203 (n. 3), 206 (n. 38), 209 (n. 36)
Postumus, 83, 98, 108
Poverty: as metaphor, 107, 109, 116, 205 (n. 23). See also Golden Mean; Moderation; Simplicity
Priamel, 17, 18, 70, 156
Princeps, poet as, 168. See also Augustus
Proculeius, 84, 199 (nn. 7, 8)
Prometheus, 29, 97
Propempticon, 27, 29, 35, 56, 80, 144, 151, 189 (n. 49), 190 (n. 64), 193 (n. 13)
Prosphoneticon, 80

Punic Wars, 114
Punishment, personified, 116
Putnam, M. C. J., 179 (nn. 13, 15), 188 (n. 44), 189 (n. 51), 192 (n. 4), 198 (n. 69), 206 (n. 37), 212 (n. 24), 213 (n. 41)
Pyrrha, 19, 90, 145
Pythagoras, 67. See also Neo-Pythagoreanism

Quinctius, 83, 87, 91–93, 136, 199 (n. 12), 200 (n. 12), 201 (n. 29)
Quinn, K., 183 (n. 48), 184 (nn. 50, 53), 187 (n. 25), 189 (n. 52), 190 (n. 65), 191 (n. 81), 201 (n. 27), 209 (n. 32)
Quintilius. See Varus, Quintilius

Reckford, K. J., 198 (n. 71), 203 (n. 7), 206 (n. 36), 211 (n. 11), 212 (n. 32)
Recusatio, 28, 34, 36, 54, 80, 90, 96, 114, 142, 151, 154, 157, 189 (n. 49), 195 (n. 34), 201 (n. 36), 211 (n. 12)
Regulus, 114, 118, 123–24
Religion, 73, 75, 97–98, 123, 136–39, 157, 207 (n. 41), 212 (n. 29). See also Dedications, votive; Hymns; Ruler cult
Rhode, 136
Roma, personified, 118
Roman Odes, 4, 12, 107, 110–25, 126–31, 139, 140, 152, 154, 170, 171, 172, 174, 185 (n. 58), 198 (n. 74), 210 (n. 2)
Rosenthal, M. L.: and S. Gall, 12, 185 (n. 59), 213 (nn. 4, 5)
Ross, D. O., 180 (n. 16), 183 (n. 49), 205 (n. 26)
Ruler cult, 118–22, 198 (n. 74), 205 (n. 27). See also Augustus

Sabine farm, 106, 114, 116, 156, 159, 202 (n. 51), 210 (n. 2)
Said, E. W., 22, 187 (n. 29)
Salat, P., 23–24, 81, 188 (n. 34), 198 (n. 88)
Salii, 79
Sallustius, 84–85, 199 (n. 8)
Sapphic meter, 19, 23, 42, 69, 83, 85, 95, 96, 170, 186 (n. 10), 192 (n. 2), 201 (n. 37)
Satire: lyric defined in relation to, 18–19, 20–21, 52, 73, 82, 155, 169
Satyrs, 18, 52, 107
Schetliasmos, 29, 193 (n. 13)
Schmidt, M., 178 (n. 8), 188 (n. 36), 200 (n. 14)
Scythians, 54, 76, 93, 129
Sea. *See* Nautical imagery
Seasons. *See* Nature
Segal, C. P., 4, 10, 177 (n. 6), 182 (n. 33), 185 (n. 56), 200 (n. 20)
Seidensticker, B., 24, 187 (n. 18), 188 (nn. 35, 37), 191 (n. 83)
Septimius, 83, 200 (n. 20)
Sepulchral epigram. *See* Epitaphs
Sestius, 19, 31, 32, 57, 63, 199 (n. 7), 213 (n. 3)
Shackleton Bailey, D. R., 183 (n. 44), 203 (n. 3)
Ship: metaphorical. *See* Nautical imagery
Sileni, 52
Silk, E. T., 116, 153, 178 (n. 8), 195 (n. 34), 204 (n. 8), 205 (nn. 21, 22), 206 (n. 32), 208 (nn. 20, 21), 212 (n. 27)
Simplicity, 18, 70, 107, 116, 122–25, 138, 139–40, 159, 162–66, 208 (n. 16). *See also* Golden Mean; Moderation
Sin, 25, 29, 97, 116. *See also* Religion
Sisyphus, 97

Sithonians. *See* Thracians
Smith, B. Herrnstein, 145, 209 (nn. 29, 30)
Socratics, 68, 197 (n. 59)
Soliloquy, 128, 206 (n. 40). *See also* Monologue, dramatic
Soracte, Mt., 39, 41, 133
Soros, 8–9, 182 (nn. 38, 39)
Spain, 68, 78–79, 93, 127, 128–29
Spartacus, 130
Sphragis, 86, 200 (n. 17)
Stoicism, 65, 68, 86
Sybaris, 38–39
Symposium. See *Convivia*; Drinking songs
Syndikus, H.-P., 177 (n. 7), 203 (n. 7), 208 (n. 16)
Syrtes, 56

Tanaquil, 75
Tantalus, 66, 97
Tarquinius Priscus, 75
Telephus, 45, 135–37
Terentia. *See* Licymnia
Teucer, 36–37, 191 (n. 77)
Thracians, 26, 53, 144
Tibia, 18, 186 (n. 9)
Time, 57–60, 86, 87, 92–93, 127, 135–36, 146–47
Tiridates, 74
Titans, 123
Tithonus, 66
Tityos, 97
Trojan War, 114, 123, 124. *See also* Homer (Index II)
Troxler-Keller, I., 186 (n. 7), 195 (n. 29), 200 (n. 20), 202 (n. 50), 212 (n. 28)
Tyndareus, 49
Tyndaris, 50–54, 210 (n. 2)

Valgius, 83, 86, 87, 91–93, 136, 190 (n. 69), 199 (n. 12)
Van Sickle, J., 179 (n. 13), 182 (nn. 31, 33), 184 (nn. 50, 51), 204 (n. 15)
Variatio, 7, 10, 11, 14, 42, 74, 99, 111, 140, 169, 172, 174, 181 (n. 27), 183 (nn. 43, 44). See also *Poikilia*
Varius, 34
Varus, Alfenus, 25, 52, 195 (n. 32)
Varus, Quintilius, 57, 58–59, 195 (n. 32)
Vates, 22, 71, 75, 111, 112, 128, 130, 140, 187 (n. 31), 200 (n. 20). See also Ruler cult
Vendler, H., 12, 185 (n. 59)
Venus, 26, 28, 33, 53–54, 68–69, 72, 73, 136, 143–44, 146, 188 (n. 39), 190 (n. 63), 197 (n. 67). See also Aphrodite
Verrall, A. W., 83, 84, 177 (n. 3), 199 (nn. 3, 6, 12), 207 (n. 3)
Virtus, personified, 119–20, 123, 206 (n. 33)

War. See Civil Wars; Marsian Wars; Punic Wars; Spartacus; Trojan War

Wealth, 96, 97, 99–103, 105–7, 108–9, 113, 116, 122, 132, 139–42, 159, 162–66, 170. *See also* Golden Mean; Moderation; Poverty; Simplicity
West, D., 186 (n. 9), 190 (n. 73), 191 (nn. 77, 81), 193 (n. 11)
Wili, W., 83, 178 (n. 8), 198 (n. 82), 199 (n. 3), 204 (n. 11), 209 (n. 31), 212 (n. 27)
Wilkinson, L. P., 177 (nn. 5, 6), 178 (n. 9), 187 (n. 21), 198 (n. 87)
Williams, G., 4, 179 (n. 11), 180 (n. 16), 186 (n. 14), 188 (n. 41), 191 (n. 77), 192 (n. 8), 194 (n. 21), 195 (n. 26), 196 (n. 52), 198 (n. 77), 200 (n. 25), 203 (n. 2), 205 (n. 27), 206 (n. 35), 207 (n. 42), 208 (nn. 15, 16, 17), 209 (n. 35), 213 (n. 40)
Wine, metaphorical, 52, 54–56, 98, 99, 130, 132, 135, 136, 137, 156, 161, 195 (n. 30)

Youth, personified, 69, 197 (n. 67)

Zeus, 34, 118. *See also* Diespiter; Jupiter